AESCHYLUS EURIPIDES

Three Other Theban Plays

AESCHYLUS EURIPIDES

Three Other Theban Plays

Aeschylus' *Seven Against Thebes*
Euripides' *Suppliants*
Euripides' *Phoenician Women*

Translated, with Introduction and Notes, by

Cecelia Eaton Luschnig

Hackett Publishing Company, Inc.
Indianapolis/Cambridge

Printed in the United States of America

19 18 17 16   1 2 3 4 5 6 7

For further information, please address
Hackett Publishing Company, Inc.
P.O. Box 44937
Indianapolis, Indiana 46244-0937

www.hackettpublishing.com

For information regarding performance rights, please email us at
Permissions@hackettpublishing.com

Cover design by Brian Rak
Composition by William Hartman

Library of Congress Cataloging-in-Publication Data

Three other Theban plays / Aeschylus & Euripides ;
translated, with introduction and notes, by Cecelia Eaton Luschnig.
pages cm
Includes bibliographical references.
ISBN 978-1-62466-471-7 (pbk.) —
ISBN 978-1-62466-472-4 (cloth)
1. Greek drama. 2. Greek drama—History and criticism.
I. Luschnig, C. A. E. II. Aeschylus. Seven against Thebes.
English. 2016. III. Euripides. Supplices. English. 2016.
IV. Euripides. Phoenician women. English. 2016.
PA3627.T54 2016
882'.0108—dc23   2015036146

The paper used in this publication meets the minimum requirements of American National Standard for Information Sciences—Permanence of Paper for Printed Library Materials, ANSI Z39.48–1984.

Contents

For my friends,
Michael, Tim, Tom, Edie, Ari, Joan, Josh, Abby,
Dona, Vicki, D.E., Jenn, Lida, Lumin, Kyla, Kelly,
Elizabeth (Liz), Elizabeth (Beth), Jill, Debby,
Thomas, Lori, Cece, Stephanie, Ivan, Chaucey,
David, Betsy, Susan Ruth, Jamie, James, Katie, Erin,
Cristina Irene, Sandi, Sandra, Rebecca, Rebekah,
Forrest, Raven, Robert, and Remington:
with affection.

And in memory of Sammy,
my precious cat, who liked to
take a nap on my translation:
Requiescat in Nepeta.

Introduction

I. Greek Tragedy in Performance

The three tragedies in this selection were written between 467 and 410 BCE. All have been performed on stage in commercial, academic, and community theaters in the twenty-first century in translation as well as in adaptations.[1] It is as if something written today were to be read or performed in the forty-fifth century, if humanity survives that long.

1. Dionysus and the Dramatic Festivals

These plays were not produced in the hope that they would enjoy a long run or even so much as a second night, let alone be revived in theaters all over the populated world for millennia to come. It was not every day that residents of Athens could go to the theater for an afternoon's or evening's entertainment. All the ancient Greek plays we have, whether tragedies or comedies, were written in Athens, by Athenians, originally for single performances at dramatic festivals

---

1. Information on productions is available at http://www.apgrd.ox.ac.uk/. One of the adaptations, by the Scottish poet and playwright, Liz Lochhead, is called *Thebans* (2003), in two parts: "Oedipus" and "Jokasta/Antigone," which is a "conflation and reduction" of six Theban plays into one play. "Oedipus" is closely based on Sophocles' *Oedipus the King*, though Jokasta remains "unhanged" for the second part. The first part of "Jokasta/Antigone" follows Euripides' *Phoenician Women* fairly closely, though it is significantly reduced in length and numbers of characters. The second part blends into Sophocles' *Antigone*, with the entrance of Haemon as the messenger and one of the defenders of Thebes. The unifying core of this trilogy is the chorus, the "eponymous Thebans, all of whom would get great solo arias as principals in the drama too, but would always then return to being part of the team, the choir, the chorus, the ordinary joes" (Lochhead 2003, in "A note from the Playmaker," unnumbered). Needless to say the Greek plays lose their individual characters in this egalitarian adaptation. The American playwright Sam Shepard recently (2013 Londonderry, 2014 New York) produced his version of the Oedipus legend, *A Particle of Dread (Oedipus Variations)*.

held only on specific days of the calendar—though many of them were in fact revived after their authors' deaths. The festivals were held annually and dedicated to the god Dionysus. The most important festival for tragedy was the Greater Dionysia, held in the spring of the year. The Athenians of classical times were a competitive people, and the dramas were put on as a contest. Each playwright would submit his work to the *archons* of the year ("rulers," the chief administrative officers, elected annually by lot) in a group of three tragedies (not necessarily, or even usually, connected in subject or theme) with a satyr play at the end.[2] The work of only three playwrights would be chosen for the year's competition. Each festival, then, included the three tragedies of three playwrights plus a satyr play by each, making twelve plays in all, four on each of the days devoted to drama. About the middle of the fifth century BCE comedies were added to the celebration (although there continued to be other festivals primarily for comedies), bringing the total up to fifteen plays, all to be performed in three days.

Not only was a trip to the theater an emotionally intense experience in fifth-century Athens, it was a physical trial: a lot of seat time was spent on the hard, cold stone. The plays were performed outdoors in the daytime, probably starting quite early in the morning. The festivals also included religious and civic ceremonies. On each of the three days devoted to drama the audience had to sit through four or five plays with only short intervals for the chorus to change costumes. This may seem like a Heraclean labor for the audience, but individual Greek plays, with their four or five short episodes, are in the main much shorter than modern ones with their two or three acts (or even five in the early modern period)—Euripides' *Phoenician Women*, one of the longest, is over 1700 lines, Aeschylus' *Seven against Thebes* is less than 1100, and Euripides' *Suppliants* is just a little longer at 1234—and it has been estimated that the five plays of a festival day could have been performed in about six hours (or less).[3] There were special seats

2. Satyr plays use tragic diction but have a chorus of men dressed as satyrs (comical and randy figures with horse tails and goat feet who are associated with Dionysus) and, perhaps, provided relief from the intensity of tragedy. Of these, only one survives complete, the *Cyclops* of Euripides.

3. A Chicago-based theater group called the Hypocrites (*hypokritēs* is the Greek word for "actor") under the direction of Sean Graney put on an "epic" (abridged) version of all thirty-two Greek tragedies called *All*

with arms and backs for priests and dignitaries in the front row; everyone else sat on the tiered seats that formed the cavea that gives the Greek theater its characteristic shape. The audience was made up of the citizen body as well as resident aliens and visitors. There is some dispute about whether women were allowed to attend theatrical performances. The preponderance of evidence indicates that they were.

The god for whom these plays were put on is Dionysus, also called Bacchus. We know him most familiarly as the god of wine, but that is not all he was nor probably his most important religious aspect. He was the god of drama and dance (dithyrambs, in particular, choral hymns with dance, which were also part of the competition at Dionysiac festivals), the god of the symposium (or drinking party) and wine, and the god of mysteries that promised a better afterlife to those who were initiated into them. The rites of Dionysus are called *orgia*, which becomes "orgies" in English, but the term "orgy" with its connotation of decadence, overindulgence, and promiscuity does not really translate the Greek term, which meant acts of devotion and communion with the god (and is related to the Greek word *erga*, "works"). Of course, the association of music, wine, and women with the rites of Dionysus contributes to the modern, degraded sense of the word, rather like sex, drugs, and rock-and-roll, in the minds of curmudgeons of a certain age. The pejorative meaning was already present in the mind of King Pentheus, a tragic figure in Euripides' last tragedy, *Bacchae*.

The picture we get of Dionysus from literary and artistic sources is ambiguous and many-sided: he is powerful and masculine, but also pretty and effeminate; he is both the hunter and the hunted; the smiling god and a god of primitive violence; he is the liberating god, but also a god who can take such control of a man or woman that he robs that person of dignity and even identity. One of the most beautiful, wondrous, awesome Greek plays to have survived is the *Bacchae* of Euripides (another play set in Thebes in which Cadmus, the city's founder, is a character), which is about Dionysus and his worship. In that tragedy all the ambiguities of the god are present: his liberating force has compelled the women of Thebes to worship

---

Our Tragic, in twelve hours (including three hours of breaks: http://www.the-hypocrites.com/plays-events/) in 2014 (revived in 2015). For a review, see http://www.chicagotribune.com/entertainment/theater/reviews/ct-all-our-tragic-review-column.html#page=1.

him. When its protagonist, Pentheus, the young king of Thebes, is ripped into shreds (by his own mother and her sisters), we see what refusal to worship Dionysus can do to a man, if he rejects this elemental, vital, animal force in nature, and especially if he takes a superior attitude to it and tries to arrest it by brute force. No man is up to the task. As E. R. Dodds writes in the introduction to his edition of the *Bacchae* (1960: xii):

> [Dionysus'] domain is . . . the whole of *hugra phusis* [the principle of moisture or, one might say, of "precious bodily fluids"], not only the liquid fire of the grape, but the sap thrusting in a young tree, the blood pounding in the veins of a young animal, all the mysterious and uncontrollable tides that ebb and flow in the life of nature.

Dionysus' worshipers are liberated from the bondage of reason and social custom; they gain a new vitality as they merge their consciousness with that of the god and the group. The frightening part of this (which, up to a point, seems beautiful and peaceful) is that just below the surface violence is always barely hidden. The same can also be said of the orderly, civilized city-state, so prone to the organized violence of war.

The *Bacchae* is the only surviving ancient play that is about Dionysus and his worship, and it is our primary literary source for that worship. What exactly does drama have to do with Dionysus? This is a good question and one that was asked by the ancients as well. What do the several aspects of Dionysus, Mystery, Drama, and Wine (or inebriation), have in common? One feature they share is *ecstasy*, the standing outside oneself, the giving up of individual identity. Because Dionysus was born in Thebes, his presence is strongly felt in some Theban plays (though not in Aeschylus' *Seven against Thebes* nor Euripides' *Suppliants*, which concerns the Theban Wars but is set in Eleusis). He is one of the gods most frequently called upon and referred to in *Phoenician Women*. In Sophocles' *Antigone*, the earliest of his Theban plays, Dionysus is invoked at crucial times, first in celebration of the victory over the invaders. As the tragedy develops, the references become darker, ending with the chorus singing—as Antigone is being led away to be immured in a cave—of the imprisonment of Dryas, king of the Edonians, who, like Pentheus, tried to stop the women worshipers of Bacchus.

2. The Three Tragedians

When we speak of Greek tragedy we usually refer to the plays of only three men who lived and worked in Athens in the fifth century BCE: Aeschylus, Sophocles, and Euripides. Tragedies were added to the festival of the Greater Dionysia around 500 BCE, so that the oldest of the three Athenian playwrights was in at the beginning, or very close to it. Of course there were more than just three artists writing tragedies (the comedies were written by different authors), but the plays of only three have survived in playable, more or less complete form—or to a pessimist, less or more lacunose. The very first named writer of tragedy was the semi-legendary Thespis (from his name comes the word *thespian*, which means "actor"). He is called the inventor of tragedy, and as the word *thespian* implies he also acted in his plays. The traditional account is that the genre originated in dance, accompanied by choral song, on a mythological theme, and that Thespis "invented" the art of acting by stepping out of the chorus as a character of myth or as a messenger to hold dialogue with the chorus, who would have represented either the followers of a hero or the citizens hearing the hero's story. Some critics would make Aeschylus himself the real father of tragedy, because he is credited with "inventing" the second actor. The presence of two actors with the chorus allows for the development of drama as we know it, with dialogue, several points of view, and the possibility of dramatic conflict. Dialogue takes place between actors and chorus and between actors in the presence of the chorus, which can act as an audience of interested participants. Sophocles added a third actor and that, according to Aristotle, was the end of that: each play thereafter was written so that it needed no more than three actors with speaking roles in addition to a chorus. Though Aeschylus was able to take advantage of the third actor in his *Oresteia*, the earlier *Seven against Thebes* is a two-actor play. How can you tell a two-actor play from a three-actor? No more than two actors are needed for any scene.[4] The cast of characters of *Seven* is short: Eteocles, the

4. Extras such as servants, attendants, or crowds of citizens were also available to the playwright-producer and do not count as actors. In *Seven against Thebes* Eteocles addresses the assembled citizens in the opening scene; the six other Theban champions may be present in the central scene; at the end the bodies of the dead brothers are carried on by extras. In *Phoenician Women* Eteocles is accompanied offstage by servants

Messenger (Eteocles' spy), Antigone, Ismene, and the Herald. Most editors believe that the Herald is a later addition, and many believe that Antigone and Ismene were also added later, the parts assigned to them in manuscripts being sung by the chorus. If that is so, then *Seven against Thebes* is a two-actor play with only two characters. The number of characters played by the three actors proliferates in the later Euripidean plays, with ten speaking parts in *Orestes* and eleven in *Phoenician Women*, two of his latest plays.

(1) Aeschylus

Aeschylus, the oldest of the three tragedians, was born about 525 BCE and died in 456 in Sicily. He was born at Eleusis in Attica, the site of the most famous of the mystery cults, the Eleusinian mysteries, where people were initiated in order to gain a better life both in this world and the next. The setting of Euripides' *Suppliants* is the temple compound of Demeter and Persephone at Eleusis. Aeschylus fought in the battles of Marathon (490 BCE) and Salamis (480 BCE), major actions in the Persian Wars. His first victory in tragedy was in 484 BCE. In all, he wrote eighty-two plays, but only seven have survived (or six, if, as many scholars suspect, *Prometheus* is not his work), of which the trilogy *Oresteia* counts as three. His extant plays are *Persians* (472 BCE), *Seven against Thebes* (467 BCE, which is sometimes referred to as *Septem*, the first word of the title in Latin), *Suppliant Women* (or *Suppliants*, produced in competition with Sophocles and sharing a name with a much later play of Euripides, though the plays are about different groups of suppliants),[5] *Oresteia* (*Agamemnon*, *Libation Bearers*, and *Eumenides* or *Furies*, a connected trilogy, or three plays from the same legend, first staged in 458), and *Prometheus* (date unknown and thought by many not to be the work of Aeschylus; therefore, if the deniers of Aeschylean authorship are right, we would have a complete tragic work by a fourth playwright).

---

carrying his armor; Tiresias comes on with his daughter and Creon's son, Menoeceus, one of whom must be a non-speaking extra (it turns out to be the seer's daughter); in the exodos (last scene) Antigone comes on with attendants carrying the bodies of the dead.

5. You may see *Suppliants*, both Aeschylus' and Euripides', referred to as *Supplices* (the title in Latin; in Greek the plays are called *Hiketides*) or *Suppliant Women*.

All the playwrights wrote a series of three tragedies for the competitions, but only Aeschylus is known to have written connected trilogies; that is, his three plays often presented the development of a single story. Although *Oresteia* is the only trilogy to have survived intact, there is evidence, from titles and fragments of lost plays, and from references within the plays themselves, that *Suppliants* and *Prometheus* were the first parts of connected trilogies, and that *Seven against Thebes* was the last play in such a series, since it is the culmination of the legend of Oedipus. The other two plays in that trilogy were *Laios* and *Oedipus*, of which scant fragments survive. Without these other plays, interpretation must remain tentative (not that any interpretation can be definitive). Aeschylus' earliest play, *Persians*, is not part of a connected trilogy. *Persians* is the only surviving play about a recent historical event: the battle of Salamis and the retreat of the Persian invaders led by Xerxes, which had taken place only eight years before the play was produced. All the other extant plays take their plots from myth and legend, but we must not forget that they always, though indirectly, address contemporary issues (whether artistic, moral, intellectual, social, political, or religious). All have to do with living in the city of Athens, whatever the setting of the dramatic events. We should also bear in mind that the legends were considered history by the ancient Greeks, though much more distant history than the Persian Wars. The end of the *Oresteia*, for example, celebrates the institution of trial by jury in Athens, which Aeschylus endows with mythical, even cosmic, meaning.

Aeschylus' grand vision makes his plays very impressive on the stage. He was apparently fond of the spectacular, an aspect of his art that is often underplayed, in part because only the texts survive without the music, choreography, sets, costumes, or other aspects of production. For those we must rely on two-dimensional vase paintings of theatrical scenes, notes in the ancient commentaries, and a few scant fragments of music. Aristotle, moreover, turned up his nose at *opsis* ("spectacle"), saying that it belongs to the producer's art rather than to the art of writing plays, as if it had slipped his mind that in the earliest days the dramatists themselves were the producers, directors, and chief actors in their plays. After all, theater (Greek, *theatron*) means viewing place, not listening place (the meaning of *auditorium*). How a play looks is a large part of how it affects its audience, which is the subject of the scholarly approach called performance criticism. If we could only *see* the shield scene, the central episode, in the *Seven against Thebes*, for example, it would add another dimension to our understanding of the play. In that scene we hear the names of the seven attackers of the city. In a series of speeches, Eteocles, the king of Thebes, announces one by one which of his men he will station to defend each of the city's seven towers to hold back the attacker leading the assault against it. We do not even know if six silent actors were actually there in front of the audience ready to make their exits, with the king himself to be the seventh. The shield of each of the attackers is described in detail. Perhaps only at the original performance was it known what (if anything) was on the shields of the defenders (with one exception: Hyperbius, defending the fourth gate, is said to display Zeus on his shield, 512–14). One by one the first six men are sent to their posts. We know that one of the attackers is Eteocles' own brother. As each defender departs for his post we feel his inevitable doom closing in on Eteocles. Finally only he is left and there is only one choice left. But it is the choice he wanted: the "fate" to meet and fight his brother, to kill and be killed by him. He accepts it and recognizes it is right:

> Relying on this I will go and I will stand to face him
> myself: What other man has a better right than I?
> Ruler against ruler and brother against brother,
> hater against hater, I will face him. . . . (672–75)

How effectively this scene could be presented to the eye as well as the ear. *Seven against Thebes* is part of the background to Euripides' *Phoenician Women*, in which we are twice introduced to the attackers but know the names of only two of the defenders (Periclymenos and Eteocles himself). Throughout the later play Euripides refers to the earlier Theban plays by both Aeschylus and Sophocles and works surprising changes on them.

Aeschylus worked on a grand scale. A characteristic of Aeschylus' writing is the visualization or reification of images. In *Agamemnon*, for example, you will find Furies mentioned many times somewhat vaguely; the images of the hunt and the net are prominent as well: in the last play of the trilogy we see the image in horrible fullness—the Furies are there, they are the hunters, and their prey is the blood of a man, Orestes. The equality of the two warring brothers is a theme in *Seven against Thebes*, culminating in the measured singing of their two bereaved sisters, each standing beside one of the corpses laid out in the orchestra.[6]

(2) Sophocles

The second of the great Athenian playwrights was Sophocles. He was born at Colonus (then a suburb of Athens and the setting of his last play) in 496 BCE, and he died at the age of ninety in or around 406. The three playwrights were connected in the ancient tradition by a relationship to the battle of Salamis (in 480 BCE): though the story is apocryphal, it is a good device for remembering their relative ages. Aeschylus, who was in the prime of his life, fought in the battle; Sophocles would have been a boy of about sixteen, and he is said to have led the choral hymn of victory after the battle; and Euripides was, according to this tradition, born on the very day of the battle, and his family had estates on the island of Salamis. Sophocles won his first victory as a tragic poet in 468 BCE when he defeated the well-established Aeschylus. Like his predecessors he sang and acted in his own plays, but early in his career his voice faded and he introduced the use of a professional protagonist (or lead actor).

Sophocles was a prominent citizen, actively involved in civic life. He was elected to the board of generals and in that office was a colleague of Pericles, the greatest Athenian statesman of the day (441 BCE). After the Sicilian disaster (when the Athenians escalated the Peloponnesian war by sending their fleet to Sicily where they were catastrophically defeated), Sophocles was appointed to the committee in charge of dealing with the aftermath of the disaster (413 BCE). He was also a priest in the healing cults. He is said to have written a monograph, *On the Chorus*.

Sophocles wrote over 120 plays and won first prize 24 times (that is, 96 of his plays came in first). Otherwise he was second and never came in third. It is interesting that his most famous play, *Oedipus the King* (also known as *Oedipus Tyrannus* and *Oedipus Rex*, the titles in Greek and Latin respectively), was one of the few to place second. The plays that beat it have not survived and we cannot imagine what criteria were used to judge the tragedies of that year. Seven plays of Sophocles survive: *Ajax*, *Electra*, *Trachinian Women*,

6. Or, if the sisters are a later addition as many editors believe, each brother is mourned in turn by the chorus divided into two halves.

and *Philoctetes*, and the three Theban plays (*Antigone*, *Oedipus the King*, and *Oedipus at Colonus*), which were written years apart and are not a trilogy. Of these, *Antigone* (produced around 442 BCE) and *Oedipus the King* (often dated to around 429 BCE because of its depiction of a city suffering from plague and blight that might refer to the deadly plague that Athens suffered in 430 BCE) were produced before Euripides' *Suppliants* and *Phoenician Women* (two plays that, like *Antigone*, cover the war of *Seven against Thebes* and/or its aftermath), and *Oedipus at Colonus* after them.[7]

Sophocles' treatment of the legendary material differs from Aeschylus' in concentrating more on the characters acting within their tragic plots than on the mythical grandeur of the stories. His protagonists are on the lofty side, endowed with grand passions or deeds. Aristotle quotes Sophocles as saying that he made his characters as people ought to be, while Euripides made his as people are (*Poetics* 25.6, 1460b35). Sophocles is also the master of the perfectly made play (*Oedipus the King* has been used since Aristotle's time as the Greek tragedy par excellence) and of tragic irony. We sometimes think of Sophocles and Euripides as having been rivals, and they often competed against one another at the Greater Dionysia, but clearly they admired and responded to one another's work. When news came to Athens that Euripides had died in 406 BCE, Sophocles is said to have dressed his chorus in mourning for his colleague's death.

(3) Euripides

Euripides, the youngest of the three, was born at Phlya, a town east of Mount Hymettus, in 480 BCE, according to tradition, on the day of the great battle of Salamis. Other evidence dates his birth to 485 BCE. He was an innovator in music and dramaturgy and not as popular (or not as favored by the people who counted) in his own time as the other two. After his death, however, his plays became the ones most frequently revived and represented in paintings on vases. He is said to have been a recluse and to have composed his plays in a cave on Salamis: this may simply reflect the fact that he was not as active in Athenian politics as Sophocles, nor

7. The date of Euripides' *Suppliants* is much disputed: "It has been dated as early as 425 and as late as 416" (Storey 2008: 25), though a date of 424 or 423 BCE is most favored; *Phoenician Women* is dated around 410 BCE.

a soldier like Aeschylus. Although he was not politically prominent he did go on an embassy to Syracuse in Sicily. Evidence points to his having belonged to a middle-class family, although the comic poet Aristophanes mocks him for being the son of a greengrocer and represents his mother as selling watercress in the public market.

Euripides, in fact, figures prominently as a character in several plays of Aristophanes, and was a favorite butt of the comedian's jokes. He was accused, for example, of being a misogynist because of the treatment of women in some of his tragedies. Most modern critics find him sympathetic both to women and to what we would call women's issues. It is true he frequently shows us unhappy women (tragedies are usually about people in extreme circumstances), but he does not deny them intelligence nor potency. Because of his depiction of women, his biography includes the information that he was married twice and was miserable with both wives. In the comedy *Thesmophoriazusae* (*Women at the Festival of the Thesmophoria*), Aristophanes presents Euripides trying to get the younger poet Agathon to dress in feminine attire to attend a festival for women in order to defend the elder poet. The women, he says, "plan to kill me today during the Thesmophoria, because I have dared to speak ill of them." Aristophanes manages to make fun of both playwrights at once. Euripides is mocked for his portrayal of women and for his manner of argumentation. The actor playing Agathon enters dressed as a woman because he is at that moment writing a female part for one of his plays, and so is made to appear effeminate. Female characters in both *Suppliants* and *Phoenician Women* (or *Phoenissae*) give the lie to Euripides' alleged misogyny. In *Suppliants*, Aethra says that women must rely on their men, but it is, in fact, her argument that persuades Theseus to take up the suppliants' cause and lead an expedition against Thebes. In *Phoenician Women*, Jocasta is given an opportunity to be someone more than the tragic wife and mother of Oedipus.

Euripides is said to have been prosecuted for impiety (a serious offense: it was the crime for which Socrates was tried and sentenced to death). The charge was brought against the playwright because the character Hippolytus says in Euripides' eponymous play: "my tongue swore, but my heart remains unsworn" (*Hippolytus* 612). This was taken as a subtle way of telling people that it was all right to break an oath. It was a frivolous accusation: in the play, the character is, in fact, ready to die rather than break his oath, which was taken from him unawares, before he knew what he was swearing to. Euripides was acquitted. According to a prevalent story, he left Athens around 408 BCE and moved to Macedonia, to the court of King Archelaus, where he died. The story began to circulate that he died in a most bizarre way, being torn to shreds by the royal hounds. Probably this story came about because such an incident, the myth of Actaeon, was mentioned in *Bacchae*, a play by Euripides that was posthumously produced.

Nineteen of Euripides' plays have survived: ten preserved as school texts and nine in an alphabetical group that was probably part of a complete set of his works. The latter survived by chance, so we have a more random sample of his plays than of either Aeschylus or Sophocles, whose extant plays were consciously selected for reading in school, that is, chosen to be the canon. Euripides won first prize only four times during his lifetime and once after his death with his last plays, which may have been produced by his son. His best known plays now are *Alcestis*, *Medea*, *Hippolytus*, and *Bacchae*. In antiquity the most popular were *Hecuba*, *Orestes*, and *Phoenician Women* (known as the Byzantine triad), possibly because these treated aspects of the legendary material not covered by the other two tragedians. The *Phoenician Women* is Euripides' version of the end of the story of Oedipus and his children. Earlier he had written the *Suppliants*, which is about the bereaved mothers of the seven generals who perished in the attack against Thebes. He is known for his portrayal of strong and intelligent women, and especially for his unheroic heroes. He tends to make his characters speak and act like his contemporaries and this may be one of the reasons that they seem more modern to us. He was interested in the philosophical movements of his day and often put the arguments used and the questions asked by the philosophers into the mouths of his characters. We can see this tendency in the political debates that form the *agonēs* (dispute scenes, in which actors deliver formal speeches) in both *Phoenician Women* and *Suppliants*.

3. The Myths of Tragedy, with Special Emphasis on the Theban Legend

The most common legendary material of tragedy is that concerned with the Trojan War, especially its aftermath. The plays about Troy include Aeschylus' *Oresteia*, the *Electra* plays of Sophocles and Euripides, Euripides' *Orestes*, *Cyclops*, *Rhesus*, *Helen*, *Trojan Women*, *Hecuba*, *Andromache*, both *Iphigenias*, and Sophocles'

Philoctetes and *Ajax*. Although it is rare that a play deals with an incident that actually takes place in the *Iliad* or *Odyssey*, this does not mean that the tragedians avoided going over Homeric ground, for we know that Aeschylus wrote a play about Achilles called *Myrmidons* (no longer extant) and that Sophocles wrote *Nausikaa* (now lost) complete with ball game (using an incident from the *Odyssey*). *Rhesus* (which survives in some manuscripts of Euripides' plays but is thought by many scholars not to be his work)[8] takes its plot from an incident in the *Iliad* (book 10), and the satyr play *Cyclops* is about the blinding of Polyphemus in the *Odyssey* (not a very light episode, even though the play has a chorus of satyrs). It is more likely that one of the criteria for selecting the plays for the school editions was that the subject matter filled in rather than repeated myths and legends that were well known from Homer.

The second most popular subject matter is the Theban cycle. Legends about Thebes, its founding and royal families, were also treated in epic poems, now mostly lost. Sophocles' two *Oedipus* plays and *Antigone*, Aeschylus' *Seven against Thebes*, and Euripides' *Phoenician Women* and *Suppliants* deal with the house of Laios, his son Oedipus, and his grandchildren. *Bacchae* takes place in Thebes during the lifetime of Cadmus, the legendary founder of the city.

The part of the story of the Theban royal family that is most often treated in tragedy relates that Laios (son of Labdacus), king of Thebes, was warned by Apollo's oracle at Delphi not to have any children, for if he did, his son would murder him (for more details on that oracle see the second part of this introduction). Not only that, but it was also predicted (in some versions) that the son of Laios would become the husband of his own mother. Laios was careless, and his wife Jocasta conceived and bore a son. It was too late to avoid the consequences. A common feature of stories that center around oracles is that human beings try to cheat them and may go along for years thinking they have succeeded. Laios tried to sidestep the oracle by binding or piercing the feet of the baby and commanding that he be left on a mountainside to be eaten by wild animals. The exposure of children was a fact of Greek life: girls especially were sometimes unwanted and were "returned to the gods" or sold. Although it must have been the usual fate of these

---

8. This would mean that we have a play by a fifth tragic playwright of the fifth or fourth century, if *Prometheus* is also wrongly attributed to Aeschylus.

babies to perish or be trafficked and enslaved, when they get into a legend, they survive and are ultimately recognized. Laios was not cautious enough. He entrusted the baby to a servant who felt sorry for him and, instead of leaving him to die of exposure or mangling, gave him to a servant from another city (Corinth). The child was brought up far from his parents and, it would seem, safe from the oracle. There are stories in which dire oracles can end benignly, but these rarely appear in tragedies.[9] In comedies misplaced children are discovered often through tokens, freed from bondage if necessary, and returned to their families. Tokens (a footprint, lock of hair, garment, signet ring, or childhood scar) are used in the recognition of Orestes in *Libation Bearers* and both *Electra* plays. Euripides' tragedy *Ion* features such a recognition and happy ending.

Jocasta's baby was called Oedipus (usually interpreted as "swollen foot," from the old injury inflicted by his father) and he grew up to manhood. One evening, according to Sophocles (in *Oedipus the King*), he overheard a man in his cups say that Oedipus was not the legitimate son of his parents. In Euripides' version, the origin of his suspicion is left untold. The young man brooded over this slur and finally set out to ask the oracle who his parents were. In the meantime back in Thebes, Laios, for some reason, whether he had bad dreams or something else made him uneasy, set out to ask the oracle whether he had escaped that terrible warning of years ago. It was pure coincidence, but the kind of coincidence that makes people believe that there is a higher power (not necessarily benevolent) overseeing their affairs, and very compatible with Sophoclean irony. Oedipus is heading away from the oracle (as he tells after the fact in Sophocles' version, though not in Euripides' *Phoenician Women*), having heard a terrible thing: not the answer to his question (perhaps, "Who are my parents?" or "Am I the son of Laios and Merope?"), but a warning that "You will kill your father, you will sleep with your mother!" He is naturally horrified and eager to get as far away from Corinth and his family as he can and as fast as possible. Laios is hurrying toward the oracle, more and more anxious to find out if he succeeded in ridding himself of the cursed child. The road is narrow. Laios from his royal carriage

9. In *Oedipus the King*, after he has learned that the man he believes to be his father has died, apparently of natural causes (961–63), Oedipus suggests such a benign outcome when he says "unless he died of longing for me" (969–70). Of course it is not to be.

brutally tries to drive Oedipus out of the way; but Oedipus is young, strong, and proud. He hits the old man with his staff and kills him along with all his retinue (all but one: to have killed them all would spoil the plot). He has killed his father, not quite an accident, though to kill one's father even by accident is a terrible thing and in ancient sentiment, brings pollution. Furthermore he did kill these people on purpose. He continues along his way, putting his past behind him.

Now it happened that at this time there was a murderous monster plaguing the city of Thebes (another coincidence that seems like fate). It was the Sphinx who asked a riddle of passersby and killed those who could not answer. So far that had been all of them. Of course Oedipus met the Sphinx and of course he was asked the riddle. "What moves on four legs in the morning, two at midday, and three at night?" The answer came to him: "man," who crawls as a baby, strides upright in the prime of his life, and walks with a cane when he is old or blind. The Sphinx killed herself and Oedipus strode on. He is welcomed into Thebes as a hero, and since there is a vacancy on the throne, he is made king and given the queen, Jocasta, as his wife. She may be older than he, but basking in his victory, this man without a country and without a past—who has just reinvented himself—cannot resist or even understand the good fortune that is now being heaped upon him.

It is at the prime of his life when he has been king for many years that *Oedipus Tyrannus* opens. It is not a play about doing the terrible things that he has done, but about finding out that he has already done them. Oedipus and his mother had four children, two sons (Eteocles and Polynices) and two daughters (Antigone and Ismene). In horror at finding out what they had done, Jocasta hangs herself (in Sophocles and in a brief reference to the tale in Homer; in Euripides she remains in the palace) and Oedipus blinds himself. In Sophocles' version of the last stage of his life (*Oedipus at Colonus*), Oedipus goes into exile and his brother-in-law, Creon, rules until the boys are of age. In Euripides, he remains confined to the palace and only later becomes a refugee.

The two sons, however, are unable to live in harmony as joint rulers. So they agree to rule by turns, Eteocles will rule first. Polynices will go into temporary exile for one year until it is his turn to be king. But Eteocles finds that he likes being in power and refuses to give up the throne when his year is out. His brother is also unwilling to yield his birthright. Polynices gathers up an army of foreigners at Argos, his place of exile, and sets out to attack his native city, a great impiety, even though he was the one who suffered the first wrong. Classical tragedy rarely presents a clear black and white picture. The tragedy here is that both parties have a just claim on their side. This is the story told in Aeschylus' *Seven against Thebes* and in Euripides' *Phoenician Women*. Euripides' *Suppliants* enacts the grief of the women who have lost their sons in that battle.

The two brothers kill each other, saving the city but leaving a vacuum on the throne. This is filled by Creon, brother of Jocasta. His first act as king is to decree that Eteocles is to be honored as a patriot with a state funeral, but Polynices is to be left unburied, to rot or be mangled by the dogs and eaten by carrion birds. In this way he would, at the end of the line, suffer the fate intended for Oedipus. It is an abominable way to treat a man's body, but not unknown in the Greek world, both legendary and historical. Creon has made this proclamation for political reasons, to discourage plots against his new authority. The punishment for anyone who attempts to honor the body of Polynices is death by stoning. But Oedipus left two daughters as well as two sons, and for them the defilement of their brother's corpse is too appalling to endure. The story of these girls and Creon's one day as king in his own right is dramatized in *Antigone*, an early play of Sophocles. Creon is a benign figure in Sophocles' *Oedipus the King* and an intelligent adviser to Eteocles in Euripides' *Phoenician Women*, but in the latter play, after the death of his son and nephews, he becomes more like the Creon of *Antigone*. In *Oedipus at Colonus* he is one of the tormentors of Oedipus, by then a frail refugee, old and blind.

Euripides' *Suppliants*, like *Antigone*, takes place after the defeat of the expedition of the Seven against Thebes but from the point of view of the other side in the conflict. Creon has decreed that the bodies of the attackers are to lie unburied, probably to discourage future foreign assaults on his territory. The mothers along with the children of the fallen warriors and Adrastus, who led the expedition, have come to Eleusis to beg Aethra, mother of the Athenian king, Theseus, to intercede with her son to come to their aid. After some hesitation Theseus agrees to consult the citizens and elicit from them a declaration of war. When diplomacy fails, Theseus leads the army of the Athenians into battle to recover the bodies. He is victorious, and the bodies are brought back for cremation. One war leads to another in endless progression: Athena, speaking in the exodos, predicts and commands a war of revenge to be carried out against Thebes by the heirs of the slain attackers once they come of age.

The legend of the generations of the house of Laios is as powerful as that of the house of Atreus. The order in which the plays described above were written is: Aeschylus' *Seven against Thebes*; Sophocles' *Antigone* and *Oedipus the King*; Euripides' *Suppliants* (the exact dates of *Oedipus* and *Suppliants* are uncertain) and *Phoenician Women*; and, finally, Sophocles' *Oedipus at Colonus*. They are all independent of each other. Events in one play are not transferable to another, though they may be referred to or reactivated intertextually. The scene between Eteocles and Creon in *Phoenician Women*, for example, comments on Eteocles' leadership ability and may bring to mind the opening scene of *Seven against Thebes*. There, Eteocles is so firmly in charge that he merely mentions that he sent out a spy and the spy appears on stage. In the later play, Eteocles is about to send for Creon, but Creon anticipates him by coming on his own. The older man is the better strategist, diminishing the brilliance that Eteocles' Aeschylean counterpart had displayed, militarily and morally.

4. The Legends and the City of Athens

Often in tragedy the legends of other cities are connected with Athens, which was known in both mythical times and more recent history as a place of asylum for displaced persons from many cities. Medea, for example, is to be conveyed from Corinth to Athens (at the end of Euripides' *Medea*), where she has been promised asylum by King Aegeus, who is unaware that she intended to murder her children. Orestes is tried and acquitted in an Athenian court in Aeschylus' *Eumenides* and allowed to return to rule over his native Argos. Heracles is rescued from despair by the Athenian king Theseus, after he has, in a fit of madness, killed his wife and sons. He, too, will be received in Athens after the end of Euripides' *Heracles*. In Euripides' *Heraclidae* (*Children of Heracles*), Theseus' sons protect the hero's mother and children from persecution by Eurystheus, the enemy and tormenter of Heracles and his family. Oedipus (in Sophocles' *Oedipus at Colonus*), is treated graciously by Theseus after he reaches Colonus as a refugee. Both Heracles and Oedipus become heroes and protectors of the land of the Athenians. The mothers of the fallen attackers of Thebes seek redress from Athens, when their sons' bodies are denied burial, which is carried out by Theseus and the people of Athens, and Euripides'*Suppliants* ends with Adrastus making a promise that Argos will never attack Athens. This legend was also treated in *Eleusinians* (*Eleusinioi* or *Men of Eleusis*), a lost play of Aeschylus, in which Theseus succeeded in recovering the bodies through diplomacy.[10] It is a bragging point in Herodotus, *Histories* 9.27.3, and a frequent topic of the orators.[11]

It may look as if these legendary stories, of heroes contemporary with the Trojan War or even earlier, are far removed from the life of fifth century Athens. But, in fact, contemporary issues are treated through those heroic figures: a dialogue is carried on with the past. Stories of lethal family enmities, and of terrible deeds done to loved ones, of the individual against the state, or state interference in private matters, of the decision to lead one's country into war, of humans relating to their gods or to grand historical movements are universal. There was an incident in the Peloponnesian War (the long and costly war of Greeks against Greeks) of the Thebans refusing burial to the bodies of the fallen enemy, considered an act of barbarism then as now.[12] The plague at the beginning of *Oedipus the King* may be a reference to the plague at Athens in the second year of the Peloponnesian War which more than decimated the population. Some of the ideas voiced by Phaedra and her Nurse in *Hippolytus*, by Eteocles and Jocasta in the *Phoenician Women,* and by Theseus, Adrastus, and the Theban Herald in *Suppliants* are clearly related to the topics discussed heatedly by the fifth-century sophists and by Socrates. Some plays celebrate recently made treaties, others deplore current policy (*Trojan Women* and numerous comedies, for example). *Phoenician Women* was said by an ancient critic to be a "play full of many excellent maxims." *Suppliants* from the earliest times has been burdened with the label "an encomium of Athens." The former likely refers to the catchy political phrases

10. According to Plutarch, *Theseus* 29.4; see Mills 1997: 230.

11. See Tzanetou (2012) on the suppliant plays as a defense of Athenian democracy and moral hegemony over her allies (esp. 67–71); also Daneš (2011) on Athenian ideology and political theory, Michelini (1994 and 1997) on contemporary political references in *Suppliants*, and Toher (2001) on the relation of *Suppliants* to the function of Athenian public funerals for those killed in war.

12. See Thucydides, *History of the Peloponnesian War*, 4.97.1–101.1.

used in the debate and the latter to unabashed use of the Athenian legend of winning burial for those killed at Thebes.

Though Theseus is a character in several other tragedies (Sophocles' *Oedipus at Colonus*, Euripides' *Hippolytus* and *Heracles*), it is in Euripides' *Suppliants* that he is fully realized as (probable) protagonist and, furthermore, as inventor of Athenian democracy:

> When I liberated Athens I established the people
> as sovereign with equal suffrage for all citizens. (352–53)

He starts as undemocratic when he smugly condemns Adrastus, but after Aethra persuades him to help the mothers, he changes his whole outlook and becomes a champion of democracy and of the city-state as "a republic of equals" (Walker 1995: 147). As Michael Walton says (1980: 12), "In no era was the relationship between the theatre and public life so marked as it was in fifth-century Athens."

In Aristophanes' *Frogs*, a comedy about tragic playwrights, which takes place after the deaths of Euripides and Sophocles, Dionysus goes down to Hades to bring back one of the playwrights, either the venerable classic, Aeschylus, or the subversive but beloved modernist, Euripides. In order to decide which one would be best for the city, a contest is staged between Aeschylus and Euripides. It is a comic masterpiece, especially amusing in the parts that parody the styles of the two writers. On a more sober note, however, at one point Aeschylus asks Euripides, "What is a poet admired for?" The younger poet's answer is, "For wise counsels which make the citizens better." This, I think, should be taken somewhat seriously. The poets were teachers: in fact, the word for "to produce" a play is "to teach" that play. In the comedy, before lapsing into Aristophanic silliness, the character Euripides claims to have taught his fellow citizens how to think rationally:

> . . . I taught my audience how to judge, by introducing the art of reasoning and considering into tragedy. Thanks to me, they understand everything, discern all things, conduct their households better and ask themselves, "What is to be thought of this? Where is that? Who has taken the other thing?" *Frogs*, 970–79

Aeschylus, on the other hand, claims to have made the citizens braver and better soldiers, "by composing a drama full of Ares"

(*Seven against Thebes*) and, by producing the *Persians*, to have "taught them how to conquer their enemies," and further, never "to have placed an amorous woman on the stage." The question of the moral worth of literature is not a new one, and even in democratic Athens, censorship was not unknown. Euripides could have used the two plays in this volume to make the same assertions: *Phoenician Women* is a drama full of Ares and *Suppliants* is about Athenians defeating foreign foes. Arguing with a joke, however, is the part of a humorless pedant.

5. Conventions of the Greek Tragic Theater

Familiarity with the details of ancient theater production is useful in visualizing the plays as they were seen and heard by the original audience.

We sometimes hear it said that the ancient Greek theater was a theater of convention rather than a theater of illusion, and such a truism is true, but hardly enlightening without details about performance. Greek plays in some ways present reality, though not often everyday life. Consider some of the conventions we must accept before we can take even the most realistic modern plays as a "slice of life": we sit in a darkened auditorium, with one end lighted, watching people in a room of which one wall has been removed. We accept them as people talking in loud (or at least carrying) voices about the most intimate details of their lives. We hear people giving speeches to themselves and make it acceptable by naming it a soliloquy. In short, we accept on the stage behavior that in real life we would consider odd. And we would be more than a little annoyed if a naive person in the audience took the actions on stage to be real and tried to participate.

The conventions of the Greek theater were different from ours. First, all dramas took place outside in the daytime without artificial lighting. Time of day can be indicated only by verbal reference or by props, such as torches, used to suggest that it is night. The dramas were staged in large outdoor theaters, and the action that the audience saw was represented as taking place out of doors. There was a building, the *skēnē* (temporary at first, but later built of stone), in front of which the actors played their scenes. This building usually represented the palace of a king or a temple, although it might also be a private house, a military hut, or even a cave or cliff face. In Euripides' *Phoenician Women*, as in some other

Theban plays (such as Sophocles' *Oedipus the King* and *Antigone*, and Euripides' *Bacchae*), the *skēnē* represents the royal palace of Thebes (the *Cadmeion*, named after Cadmus, the city's founder). Important events that are unseen by the audience may happen inside this building: the suicide of Creon's wife Eurydice in *Antigone*, the suicide of Jocasta and the self-blinding of Oedipus in *Oedipus the King*, for example. Inside it Oedipus, blind and old before his time, has been confined for years by his sons in *Phoenician Women*. *Seven against Thebes* takes place on the Theban acropolis, but the *skēnē* is not prominent, if it was there at all. *Suppliants* is set in the temple precinct of Demeter at Eleusis, but the play opens with a tableau scene, and it is likely that no entrances or exits are made from or into the *skēnē*, a sacred place not suited to the funereal action of this play.

The ancient Greeks were an outdoor people more than we; much of their public business, commercial and political, was conducted out of doors. Dramas that concern the public, as do many tragedies, treating as they often do the fates of kings, are not unrealistically played out of doors. Intimate scenes of family life, on the other hand, may need more explanation. In *Antigone*, for example, the prologue displays the pathos of the two small figures of the sisters, meeting before dawn to discuss their family tragedy, ending with the brave decision of one of these girls to defy the law and bury her brother despite the ban and sentence of death: this scene gains in pathos by the very fact of the two girls being dwarfed by the vast setting. In *Phoenician Women*, Jocasta enters from the palace and introduces herself. Besides situating the story, she lets us know that she has arranged a truce between her sons and is acting on behalf of her family, but also in the public interest. When her young daughter, Antigone, makes her entrances, more explanation needs to be given because of the seclusion of women in Greek life; in her first scene she comes out onto the rooftop to look for her brother in the landscape outside the city walls, and later, her mother summons her to help save her brothers. Sophocles' *Oedipus the King*, Aeschylus' *Seven against Thebes*, and Euripides' *Suppliants* open with tableau scenes (or cancelled entrances, where the audience is asked to forget seeing characters, even large groups, enter and take their places). Eteocles (on the acropolis of Thebes) in *Seven* and Oedipus (before the royal palace) in *Oedipus the King* both address assembled citizens in the prologues of their plays. In *Suppliants*, Aethra (Theseus' mother) goes to the temple of Demeter for the celebration of autumn planting (an action appropriate to women) and is immediately surrounded by the women of the chorus with their branches of supplication; Adrastus with a crowd of young boys also enters before a word is spoken.[13]

(1) Verse and Song

All the surviving classical Greek plays are poetic dramas. The characters speak, chant, or sing in verse; this is true of both dialogue and choral song. The dialogue parts are mostly in iambics (⏑ _: iambic trimeter in dipodic units, that is, six iambs in groups of two), which is the meter closest to conversational speech in Greek. In fact, we are told by one of the ancient critics that "many people speak in iambics without realizing it." Other spoken or chanted parts are in anapests (⏑⏑ _) or trochees (_ ⏑). The choral passages, in various lyric meters, were sung and accompanied by dance. Actors sometimes have singing parts, both solo (in monodies) and with the chorus or with the chorus and other actors. Jocasta apparently sings and dances around her son, Polynices, when they are reunited in the first episode of Euripides' *Phoenician Women*. The presence of a formal chorus is certainly uncommon in modern plays, but we know that it was a constant feature in Greek plays. If, while *reading* a play, you wonder sometimes what the chorus is doing there, remember that it was probably the original feature of the plays. Besides, the theater is built around the dance floor, called the *orchestra*. This circular area is believed to be the origin of the theater and the only necessary part: seats for the audience, a stage-building, and various forms of scenery are later developments.

(2) Chorus

Every tragedy has a chorus, although in some of the later plays its part is curtailed, or at least it seems less integral to the play's structure. When a tragedian's set of plays was chosen for the festival, he was said to be "awarded a chorus." The chorus was made up first of twelve and later of fifteen men, citizens of Athens trained at public expense. It may represent either men or women, young or old. Aeschylus' choruses are female in the surviving plays, except for *Agamemnon* and *Persians* where the choruses are of old

---

13. It is possible that these actions are done separately: see Storey (2008: 107–8).

men. Sophocles prefers a chorus of men, except in his *Electra* and *Trachinian Women*. Euripides uses female choruses in most of his tragedies: the exceptions are *Alcestis*, *Heraclidae*, and *Heracles*, all of which have choruses of elderly citizens, and *Rhesus* (of questioned authorship), which has a chorus of soldiers. In all of Sophocles' Theban plays the chorus is of male citizens: Theban in *Antigone* and *Oedipus the King*, Athenian in *Oedipus at Colonus*, which takes place in the Attic deme of Colonus near Athens. In Aeschylus' *Seven against Thebes*, a female chorus contrasts with the strong male protagonist, Eteocles, and sets the fears and concerns of the city in opposition to the leader's brilliant strategy and cursed family history. Euripides' *Suppliants* moves away from Thebes to Eleusis in Attica and represents the mothers of the fallen warriors as the chorus of suppliant women. *Phoenician Women*, by using a chorus of foreign women, alienates the Theban royal family from the citizens more than any other Theban tragedy.

Since the chorus is a necessary part of the plays, but for the most part foreign to our experience, it is natural to ask what it does and how it performs. The chorus sings and dances between episodes. These songs (called *stasima*, singular *stasimon*) are divided into *strophes* and *antistrophes* (stanzas and matching stanzas, literally, "turnings" and "opposite turnings"), that is, each has the same metrical pattern. It is generally believed that the chorus did the same steps or dance pattern twice in opposite directions.

What are some of the things the chorus adds to the plays? It comments on the action, participates in the dialogue, and shares the action. The chorus of Euripides' *Suppliants* for example, sets the plot in motion by pleading for the intervention that brings on a new war. In Sophocles' *Antigone* the chorus of citizen elders is there in part to give the play its political theme. It is interesting to note that, for whatever reason, this chorus remains for a very long time on the side of Creon, but once it is too late, they advise Creon on the right course he should have taken. In Euripides' *Phoenician Women*, the chorus criticizes Eteocles' sophistry in presenting a bad case in fine words, but, as a band of foreign women, is somewhat removed from the action. At the same time it is part of the broader picture that encompasses the history of Thebes from its founding.

The chorus may also provide background material, as in Sophocles' *Antigone*: here the chorus enters singing of Thebes' victory over its attackers, showing us that this is more than a family drama and letting us know what that victory means to the citizens.

The chorus of *Phoenician Women* extends the action further back in time to the Phoenician origins of the city's founder, Cadmus, and fills in the mythological and cultic background. The chorus thus serves as both another actor and as a narrator.

If we look at the place of the chorus in the acting area between the tiers of seats and the stage-building, we see another of its roles: it stands between the audience and the actors, showing how heroic age doings affect the people. If the affairs of princes and kings and heroes (both male and female) are removed from the lives of ordinary people, the chorus can make them a concern of the public. In Sophocles' *Oedipus the King*, the opening tableau represents a crowd of citizens petitioning their king, which shows that the drama starts out as one affecting the people very closely, because there is a plague blighting the land, its people, herds, and crops. We learn that it is caused by the unsolved murder of the former king and his murderer having gone unpunished. Imperceptibly the focus changes to the search for the origin of Oedipus himself, and we watch the chorus move from admiration for their present king who saved them in ages past, to horror and withdrawal as they find out what he has done. The chorus of Aeschylus' *Seven against Thebes* is of citizen women, frightened by what is happening outside the walls. With them we watch the focus shift from the city to the family and the two warring brothers. The women bring home the life and emotions of those inside a city under siege. *Phoenician Women*, with its chorus of foreign women caught up in the war, offers a different perspective: the play ends with the death or departure of the last remnants of Cadmus' line as well as the end of the "Sown men" or *Spartoi*, the native-born Thebans, who sprang from the Dragon's teeth (sown at the founding of Thebes) and began their existence in mutual slaughter (see *Phoenician Women*, 657–675). The chorus of Phoenician women will now make their way to Delphi, their intended destination. Without a chorus of Theban men or women there is no one to mourn the loss of the line of Laios' father, Labdacus.

The chorus provides what may be called lyrical relief: a song may relieve the tension of a highly emotional episode. In *Oedipus the King*, for example, just before the protagonist finds out the horrible truth of his parentage, there is a moment when he has no idea who he is. He knows that he is not the son of the Corinthian couple who reared him, and he is delighted to think of himself as fortune's child, a man who came from nowhere and became king of two city-states, having just learned that the man he thought was his father has died and he has inherited the kingdom of Corinth. At this point (1086–1109) the chorus sings a short song in a joyous meter to match Oedipus' high spirits. This is typical of Sophoclean irony: the fortune of a man at the very height of his success and happiness is given an added boost by the chorus' impossible dream (that their king is sprung from the gods), which only serves to make his fall greater. In the opening song of *Phoenician Women*, the chorus wishes to be away dancing in Delphi (235–38), an escape from the war that threatens the city and from the drama itself that promises disaster within the confines of the city. Much later, after the departure of Menoeceus to self-immolate, they sing a dirge for those dead and those yet to die, forming a bridge between the present and past of Thebes as well as between the scenes before and after their song. Even in the midst of their unrelieved suffering and grief, the mothers, who form the chorus in *Suppliants*, wish for flight on wings, if only to carry them to battle so they will not have to wait for news (618–25).

The music of the chorus also provides a guide to our emotions. In *Antigone*, for example, after a chilly scene between Creon and his son, Haemon (who is Antigone's fiancé), in which the young man tries to persuade his father not to kill Antigone on political grounds, the chorus sings of the power of love. Haemon had not said a word about his love for Antigone, and his father had referred to it only in the crudest (but typically male and typically classical Greek) terms. For the subsequent action, however, we need to know that Haemon does love Antigone, and the choral ode fills in that gap. In *Phoenician Women* the chorus harps on the past, always showing a connection between the darkness at the heart of Thebes since its violent foundation and the present horrors. Their last two songs are short and intense, leading to the climax. In *Suppliants* the chorus gives voice to a wish never to have married and produced children (786–93), as a prelude to the scenes of Evadne celebrating her wedding and self-immolation and her father Iphis wishing he had never had children. In *Seven against Thebes*, the choral entrance is in a rhythm that indicates extreme agitation. We might think of the chorus as being something like the sound track in a movie: it tells us how to feel—scared, sentimental, angry, elated, grieving, in despair. If we were not familiar with the cinematic convention of the audience hearing music that the characters do not hear it could—and sometimes does—seem very odd.

The chorus is also one of the actors, and sometimes crucial to the plot. This is true of Euripides' *Suppliants* and, indeed, of all suppliant drama, in which a person or a group comes to petition for help, usually from a ruler (or, in the case of Orestes in Aeschylus' *Eumenides*, from a god). This request leads to a major action in the play when the requested help is provided.

(3) The Parts of a Play

Greek tragedies alternate between dialogue and choral song.

Prologue: The part of a play before the entrance of the chorus. In Aeschylus and Euripides this is usually a monologue, or a monologue followed by a dialogue. Sophocles' extant plays open with a dialogue. In Aeschylus' *Persians* and *Suppliants* there is no prologue: these plays open with the chorus entering in procession or in flight.

Parodos: The entrance song of the chorus. This is sometimes shared by the chorus and one of the actors (as in Euripides' *Electra*, *Orestes*, and *Iphigenia among the Tauri*). The side passages along which the chorus and characters from the outside enter and exit are called *parodoi* or *eisodoi*. In Euripides' *Suppliants*, the chorus is already in the orchestra, surrounding Aethra at the altar during the prologue.

Episodes: The dialogue portions of the play, consisting of speeches and back and forth conversation, between the choral odes. Dialogue in which single lines are spoken in turn by two or more characters is called *stichomythia*. A section of a play in which two (or three) characters deliver formal opposed speeches is called an *agōn*: in *Suppliants* there are two, in the first and second episodes; in *Phoenician Women* there is a three-person *agōn*. There are usually between three and five episodes in a tragedy.

Stasimon (pl. stasima): A choral song and dance between the episodes.

Exodos: The part of the play after the last choral song. This usually ends with a tag line from the chorus.

(4) Actors, Masks, Roles, and Messenger Speeches

Masks were worn by both actors and chorus in classical dramas. Thespis is reported to have whitened his face and Aeschylus to have been the first to add color and to have used frightening masks. But grotesque masks are much older than either playwright. Terra cotta masks from the seventh century have been found at Corinth and Sparta in sanctuaries of the goddesses Hera and Ortheia (a local Spartan goddess). These are life-sized masks believed to have been used in ceremonies in which the goddess and her attendants were personified.[14] The masks used in the tragic theater covered the entire face and had a wig attached. They were made of linen soaked in plaster and then sewn to a cap for the wig. The mouth was only slightly open: the distortions that we see in representations of Tragedy and Comedy—with the high peak of hair in front and the wide open mouth—are from a later era.

The use of masks means that detailed facial expressions cannot be shown, though these are sometimes referred to in speech. In fact, the wide distances between actors and audience would have the same result. On the other hand, the clear outlines of the masks make the features of the character more easily discernible. Different expressions can be shown by shifting the tilt of the head. Emotions can be shown equally well by body movements, postures, and gait, and, of course, by the sounds of sorrow or joy or anger, along with musical accompaniment. Certain postures and gestures are associated with certain feelings and attitudes, as we know from vase paintings. An actor needed versatility in voice and gesture, especially since actors very often had to play several roles in the same play. We speak of the "rule of three actors," meaning that only three actors were available to each playwright for his trilogy. To put this another way, all the tragedies we have were written in such a way that they can be performed by a maximum of three actors.[15]

---

14. The terra cotta examples were most likely the molds on which the masks (probably made of linen) used by the celebrants or performers were formed. The molds were later painted and dedicated to the goddess. One theory of the purpose of frightening masks is to chase away evil spirits who could spoil the work of fertility. Or possibly they could have represented the evil spirits being beaten back by the forces of good.

15. See Appendix A for suggestions and speculations on the distribution of roles in the three plays in this volume.

The use of masks makes the swift change of roles practicable. A change of head and face and clothing is a change of person. Both mask and character have the same name in Greek (*prosōpon*, as they do in Latin, *persona*). The mask *is* the character. There are masks for young men and young women, old women and old men, slaves and kings, and other variations in age, gender, and class or status. Once the actor dons the mask, he (all the actors in the original performances were men) becomes that role, which imparts certain expectations for the character. When Jocasta enters from the stage-building at the start of Euripides' *Phoenician Women*, she is immediately recognized, not yet as Jocasta but as a mature and regal woman. She has to identify herself specifically as Jocasta (12). When Polynices enters (at line 261), we know immediately who he is from the mask and costume of a young soldier, from his stealthy gestures, and from the fact that both Jocasta and the old servant have told us he was coming.

The three actors in a play are called *protagonist* (first actor), *deuteragonist* (second actor), and *tritagonist* (third actor). All the roles have to be divided among these three. We do not know what criteria were used in matching roles with actors, except that all three would have to be used in three-person scenes. It is obvious in a play like *Oedipus the King* that Oedipus is the protagonist in both the technical sense of "first actor" and in the more modern use of "leading character." In plays like *Antigone* and *Phoenician Women*, it is not so obvious which role or roles belong to the protagonist in either sense. In *Antigone*, Creon has the larger part, and since Antigone leaves the play so early, never to return, the actor who plays her would have to take on other roles, one of them being her betrothed, Haemon. (On the possibilities of role division in *Phoenician Women*, see Appendix A.) In speaking of the cast of characters in a Greek play, it is best to avoid the term "tragic hero," because "hero" is not used in Greek as equivalent to a protagonist. "Hero" is a special term in Greek for semi-divine men and women, between *daimones* (divinities, great spirits) and *anthrōpoi* (human beings), who were worshiped after death. Some were founders of cities. Often the heroes did terrible things in life, especially crimes against the family, breaking society's taboos: such as Oedipus, or Heracles who killed his wife and children, or Medea who killed her two sons, or Orestes who killed his mother. They became averters of evil and their tombs are centers of hero-cults (see, for example, the end of Sophocles' *Oedipus at Colonus*).

Some scholars connect the limitation in the number of actors to a supposed preference in the Greek theater for violence offstage rather than in front of the audience: for example, in Aeschylus' *Oresteia* all the murders (four altogether) take place inside the palace. We hear the victims' cries but do not see them act out their deaths. In Sophocles' *Oedipus* and *Antigone* and Euripides' *Hippolytus*, the scenes of violence all take place offstage. The actual stage death of Hippolytus near the end is in full view, and the result of the earlier offstage suicide of Phaedra is displayed for us (see below on the *eccyclēma*). It has been suggested that no one could die on stage early in a play because the actor was needed for another role later, though there are ways of removing bodies. Another reason suggested for the lack of much violence is that the Greeks were technically incapable of the necessary special effects. There was, however, an actor nicknamed "the leaper" because of his ability to commit suicide on stage in revivals of Sophocles' *Ajax*. His body must have been removed so that the actor could take on another role. It is possible also that the playwrights and their audience realized that violence could be more effective unseen. Screams are heard behind the scenes. The results of the action can be revealed on the *eccyclēma* (see below) or in the bloodied mask Oedipus wears when he lurches on stage in his last scene (in *Oedipus the King*), for example, or in the unattached mask, representing the head of Pentheus after he is torn apart, that is carried from Cithairon by his mother in the *Bacchae*. These props are as deeply moving as the grotesque doings that we are told about.

The offstage violence is necessarily connected to the messenger speech. In *Oedipus* and *Antigone* a messenger reports what happened offstage: deaths, self-mutilation, and mangling. In *Agamemnon*, Cassandra's role is in part to be a messenger before the action: as a prophet she knows what is going to happen to her. After her speeches, we do not need any detailed messenger speech. Similarly, in *Seven against Thebes*, the long scene in which Eteocles sends a defender to each gate to face a specific attacker makes a long messenger speech after the battle unnecessary. In *Phoenician Women*, on the other hand, there are two full messenger speeches, each giving exciting narratives about the battles. We see the results in the moving tableau of the bodies being carried back and then laid out in front of the stage-building. *Suppliants* also has a vivid description of a battle; the result is the return of the bodies, followed by funeral rituals that take up the rest of the play.

Messenger speeches often contain some of the most brilliant and exciting writing in the plays. Of course there was not the technical means nor personnel to depict a battle. Could it be that, as poets, the tragedians preferred writing these messenger parts to staging the action, even when it involves just a single death? If, as some scholars believe, tragedy developed not only from choral songs but also from epic recitations, there is an added explanation for messenger's speeches, which are the closest thing in tragedy to epic narrative.

(5) Stage Devices and Levels of the Acting Area

The original theater consisted of a round, smooth area called the *orchestra*, in which the chorus sang and danced. Nearly all the ancient theaters were later altered, with the orchestra cut down to a semi-circle, because in post-classical times the chorus had lost its central role and eventually was cut altogether. In the magnificent theater at Epidaurus the full circle has been left intact. There was an altar somewhere in this area.[16] It plays a role in the opening scene Sophocles' *Oedipus the King*, when the citizens come to supplicate their ruler, and later in the play, when Jocasta comes out to make sacrifice. In Euripides' *Suppliants*, as in all suppliant plays, an altar is a place of asylum. It is also the place where Aethra goes to sacrifice and is surrounded by the petitioning mothers. In Euripides' *Phoenician Women*, Polynices refers to the altars of his city's gods, and in Aeschylus' *Seven against Thebes*, the chorus prays at the altars of various gods in succession. That may have been all that was needed by way of stage furnishings before Aeschylus. But as tragedy became more dramatic and complex, some kind of building was necessary. At the back of the orchestra, facing across the playing area to the audience, was a building called the *skēnē* ("military lodging," "hut," or "tent," hence our words *scene*, *scenario*, and *proscenium*). Usually it represents a palace or temple, but may also be a private house, military lodging, or even a cave. To and from this building the actors made exits and entrances. Here the actors dressed and changed their masks and costumes to become other characters.

---

16. In Aeschylus' *Persians*, the same structure may represent the royal tomb from which the ghost of Darius is evoked. In Aeschylus' *Libation Bearers*, it becomes the tomb of Agamemnon at which offerings are made, though this tomb is off-stage in the later Electra plays of Sophocles and Euripides.

It is possible that there was also a slightly raised stage in front of the stage-building that separated the actors from the chorus, but not raised so high that it would prevent easy interaction between the two. There may also have been moveable painted scenery. In the *Poetics*, Aristotle says that Sophocles "invented" scene painting. This sounds straightforward enough, but the word for scene-painting (*skenographia*) is also the word for painting in perspective. In any case, a moveable painted scene could have been placed in front of the stage-building. There may also have been *pinakes* or plaques to suggest details of scenery that could have been turned for changes in scene, though these are rare in Greek tragedies, where messenger speeches narrate actions that happen elsewhere. Characters sometimes tell us that they are hiding. Such plaques would facilitate their concealment.

The top of the scene-building was a third level of action besides the stage and orchestra. Aeschylus' *Agamemnon* opens dramatically with a watchman on the roof. Probably he was hidden from view, and we would naturally be watching the door of the stage-building for the first entrance when—all of a sudden—a voice from the roof cries *theous* ("ye gods!") and grabs our attention as the actor reveals himself.[17] The second part of the prologue of *Phoenician Women*, the charming scene of Antigone and her old attendant looking out over the plain to identify the warriors, is played on the rooftop or *theologeion* or "god-dais," so called because the characters of divinities sometimes used it for making proclamations. In Euripides' *Suppliants*, Evadne, the widow of Capaneus, one of the seven fallen commanders, makes a surprising appearance probably on the rooftop or a piece of scenery representing a craggy outcrop attached to the scene-building, from which she leaps to her death onto her husband's funeral pyre, which must be out of the audience's sight line.[18]

From the top of the stage-building the gods often made their appearances: Artemis probably appears there at the end of Euripides' *Hippolytus*. She is unseen by Hippolytus and his father and would not be likely to come down from the roof. At the end of Euripides'

---

17. The messenger in Euripides' *Suppliants* may be modeled on this character. He too is watching from above (652); after the rout of the Thebans, like Aeschylus' watchman, he cries out in jubilation, claps his hands, and dances a victory jig (719–20).

18. See Storey (2008) on "the vertical dimension" of *Suppliants*: "People kneel down, lie down, leap down, look down in this play" (120).

Suppliants Athena appears suddenly on the rooftop. There was a device for lifting actors playing gods from the roof to the stage. This was the famous *mēchanē* or flying machine, as in the expression *deus ex machina*, which is a Latin translation of Greek *theos apo mēchanēs*, "the god from the machine." This was, apparently, a crane with counterweights that could be used to fly in gods at the ends of the plays. It is not needed in many of the extant tragedies, but it would be effective in Euripides' *Medea* for the heroine's exit to Athens on a chariot drawn by flying serpents. It was probably used in Euripides' *Electra*, *Orestes*, and *Iphigenia among the Tauri*. Its use in comedy was more extensive. Since Athena makes her appearance in *Suppliants* only to give orders and does not declare her intention to go anywhere, the flying machine was not necessary.

There was another device of even greater usefulness: the *eccyclēma*, or "thing rolled out." This was used for showing the result of actions that had taken place in the house and could simply have been a platform on wheels rolled out through the double central doors of the stage-building or possibly a revolve.[19]

The plays in this selection deal with deaths on the battlefield rather than in the palace so the *eccyclēma* is not used. *Phoenician Women* does not use either of these devices: the bodies of the dead are carried back from the offstage battlefield. It is likely that the *eccyclēma* was used to reveal the offstage indoor suicides of Eurydice (Creon's wife) in *Antigone* and Jocasta in *Oedipus the King*. Euripides makes reference to both these plays in his version, by having Creon return from the dark den, carrying in his arms not Haemon (as he does in *Antigone*), but his other son Menoeceus, and by having Jocasta uncharacteristically kill herself out of doors and with a sword. Suicidal women usually hang themselves indoors in Greek tragedies. Furthermore, in *Phoenician Women* we are told

---

19. The bodies of Cassandra and Agamemnon were wheeled out on the *eccyclēma* in Aeschylus' *Agamemnon*. Clytemnestra speaks of her husband's corpse as if it were there when she says, "this is Agamemnon, my husband . . . well, he's dead." The bodies of Clytemnestra and Aegisthus were revealed on it in Aeschylus' *Libation Bearers* after Orestes has killed them, when he holds up the cloth used as a net to snare his father. In Aeschylus' *Eumenides*, the *eccyclēma* could have been used for the entrance of a few members of the chorus, who are sleeping in the stage-building, which at the beginning of that play represents the temple of Apollo at Delphi.

that Creon's wife has been dead since Menoeceus' birth. Oedipus sees Jocasta's dead body hanging by her neck just before he blinds himself in *Oedipus the King*. In *Phoenician Women* he must be guided by his daughter to touch her face. Likewise in *Seven against Thebes*, the dead brothers' bodies are carried on stage for the final scene of mourning by the chorus and their two sisters. In *Suppliants*, the bodies of the fallen attackers of Thebes are carried in for mourning and are eulogized by Adrastus, as if to undo the noisy arrogance attributed to them in Aeschylus' version. *Seven* actually makes little or no use of the stage-building and, therefore, has no use for the *eccyclēma*, which was probably not even in use at the time of the play's production. In *Suppliants* the stage-building is an exterior presence, but it is not used for entrances and exits. Though Eleusinian motifs of maternal mourning and the earth's fertility are constant in *Suppliants* (see Mendelsohn 2002: esp. 135–48), the setting is alien to the theme of war, death, and burial. The temple remains closed to this desecration.

II. Three Other Theban Plays—Comparisons and Interpretations

Though the various Theban plays cannot be fit together into a continuous narrative, they are related and the later ones refer frequently to the earlier ones. A look at the three tragedies collected in this volume in the context of the whole Theban saga as it appears in the tragic tradition will be useful for more specific interpretations. As subjects for tragedy the stories from the Theban cycle were second in popularity only to those about the Trojan War. Because little is known of the content of the lost early Theban epics (*Oidipodeia*, *Thebaid*, *Epigonoi*), the tragedies are our best sources for the legend. While the ending of *Phoenician Women* covers some of the material treated in Sophocles' *Antigone*, the main event in Euripides' play, the war of the Seven against Thebes had been treated by Aeschylus in *Seven against Thebes* (467 BCE), a single-minded drama in which it is clear from the beginning that Eteocles is the protagonist, with his life and death the focus of the play.[20] *Phoenician Women* (probably around 410 BCE), on the other hand, goes off in a number of directions, and it is less clear

20. Winnington-Ingram (1983: 16–54) provides a good discussion of Eteocles, "the first Man of the European stage."

what its focus is at the end. Aeschylus' *Seven* was the last in his Theban trilogy (that is, three plays written to be performed together at the same festival), of which the first two, *Laios* and *Oedipus*, are now lost. What is sometimes referred to as the Theban trilogy of Sophocles is in fact three plays produced at widely different dates: *Antigone* (about 442 BCE), *Oedipus the King* (probably after 429 BCE), *Oedipus at Colonus* (Sophocles' last play, written around 406 BCE, but produced posthumously in 401). *Oedipus the King* is about Oedipus finding out that he has already killed his father and married his mother, the background referred to again and again in *Phoenician Women* and to a lesser extent in *Seven against Thebes*. The earlier *Antigone* treats the day after the battle of the Seven, and it is concerned with Creon's refusal to bury Polynices and Antigone's determination to perform the necessary rites for her brother despite the danger, themes taken up in *Suppliants* (probably from 424 or 423 BCE) and in the last scene of *Phoenician Women*. *Oedipus at Colonus*, Sophocles' last play and our last surviving Greek tragedy, covers the exile and death of Oedipus, events announced at the end of *Phoenician Women*.

1. Laios, Oedipus, and Oracles in the Theban plays

(1) The Oracle Given to Laios

All three playwrights treat an oracle pronounced to Oedipus' father Laios at Delphi by Apollo. The marriage of Jocasta and Laios has been childless (13–14). Jocasta fills in this detail in *Phoenician Women*, before quoting the oracle that tells Laios not to have a son, because if he does, his son will kill him:

> . . . "King of Thebes, keeper of fine horses,
> do not try to plant a crop of children against gods' will,
> for if you father a child, he that is born will kill you
> and your whole house will wade in its own blood." (17–20)

In Aeschylus' *Seven against Thebes* we hear that Laios was told three times to "to die without offspring / and save his city" (748–49). In Sophocles' *Oedipus the King*, Jocasta reports the oracle as saying that it is fated that "he [Laios] die by his son's hand, /one who would be born from me and him" (713–14): here there is no *if* as in Euripides and Aeschylus, and, therefore, no escape. In the same play Oedipus himself has received an oracle which he repeats (791–93), not realizing what it has in common with his wife's.

In Aeschylus the oracle to Laios is political, referring as it does to the city's preservation. In disobeying it, Laios ignores the common good of his people and acts heedlessly. We see the consequences of his failure in the direction of the play's movement from the city to the family to the individual brothers. The city is saved because the brothers are killed, leaving the line without male issue. In Sophocles, the prediction is only personal. The play itself, however, is political from its opening tableau of citizens petitioning the king, and only gradually turns personal as Oedipus looks into himself. Oedipus' quest for the killer is undertaken for the common good, to save the city: this is why we recognize him as a great man, a king who rules for the good of the citizens and not for himself. In Euripides the oracle is personal and extends to the whole family, but it does not refer to the city, although in the next generation the city's survival is at stake because of the warring brothers, who put their selfish interest above the state, the people, and even their kin. The implicit comparison of the self-centered brothers to their altruistic and patriotic cousin Menoeceus serves to underscore the futility of their pursuit of power, the waste of their lives, and the threat to the lives of the men they lead into war. The oracle given to Laios says nothing about incest in any of these versions. In Aeschylus (*Seven* 745–46, 750) and Euripides (*Phoenician Women* 21–22), Laios is said to disobey the oracle through lust.

Laios tries to escape the oracle by getting rid of the baby. As often happens in ancient lore, this effort to outrun the oracle—indicating the simultaneous belief and disbelief in its finality—leads to its inevitable fulfillment. Of Aeschylus' *Laios*, which is believed to have treated the death of Laios, there are no fragments of which scholars can be certain. In both *Phoenician Women* and *Oedipus the King* we are told that Laios first pierced his son's ankles (*Oedipus* 717–22; *Phoenician Women* 26) and then gave the infant to a herdsman to dispose of. The baby was passed on to another herdsman and taken to Corinth, to King Polybus and his wife (*Oedipus* 1022–40; *Phoenician Women* 28–31).

(2) Oedipus at the Crossroads

Oedipus spent his childhood safe in Corinth with parents who were not his blood kin, living in ignorance—the necessary condition of his doing the unspeakable deeds that he eventually commits. The Euripidean Jocasta is unable to fully explain why her son left the safety of his home in Corinth, whether he heard something or had a vague suspicion about his origins (*Phoenician Women* 32–34). Sophocles' Oedipus is more explicit (779–93): at a banquet a man who had drunk too much wine blurted out, "you are not your father's true son." The slander grew and Oedipus went away in secret to consult the oracle. Apollo sent him away "dishonored" (*atimon*, 789), he says, with respect to what he had come for, but the god uttered terrible prophecies, saying:

> That I was destined to sleep with my mother
> and bring into the light progeny unbearable for men to see,
> and be the murderer of the father who engendered me.
> (Sophocles, *Oedipus* 791–93)

At this Oedipus fled, avoiding Corinth, and reached a place where three roads meet. A herald and an old man in a wagon try to cut him off and Oedipus strikes the charioteer, at which the old man hits him on the head with the goad (794–812). "And," says Oedipus, "I killed them all" (Sophocles, *Oedipus* 813). In all the versions Laios and Oedipus meet at a crossroads: a fragment from Aeschylus' *Oedipus* says, "we were coming to a place where three highways branch off." Again, Euripides is vague about the actual killing, but makes some significant changes (*Phoenician Women* 35–45). Jocasta fills in the detail that Laios was going to the oracle to assure himself that the child was dead, but in this version neither man reaches the oracle. Oedipus never heard that he was destined to kill his father and marry his mother. The cruelty of Laios resurfaces, and the old wounds are reopened. Oedipus kills Laios, and in an act of filial piety takes the spoils back to his (foster) father Polybus (*Phoenician Women* 44–45). In Sophocles, Oedipus is told that he will kill his father. He hurries away thinking he can outrun the oracle by never seeing his parents again, and in all innocence he kills the first man he meets on the road. It is as if the oracle had said to him, "the man you will kill is your father; the woman you will marry is your mother." This is the deadly irony of Sophocles and his Apollo. In Euripides' version, Oedipus *is* innocent. Only Laios has heard the oracle; Oedipus never hears it. In her recitation of the tale Jocasta is vague about how Oedipus found out that he had married his mother, but when he did he blinded himself. The series of events as told in *Phoenician Women* seems random when compared to the tight and cruel plot of Sophocles' play, where every coincidence is strictly controlled by the playwright and his gods.

(3) The Curse of Oedipus

In Aeschylus, the curse of Oedipus is prominent, invoked by Eteocles in moments of decision:

> Oh Zeus and Earth, gods who keep our city safe,
> my father's curse, potent Fury of revenge. (*Seven against Thebes* 69–70)

And when he knows that he will meet his brother in combat:

> Oh, maddened by gods, by the gods deeply hated.
> Oh, our race of Oedipus, overflowing with tears.
> Ah me! Curses of my father now to be fulfilled! (*Seven against Thebes* 653–55; also 695, 705)

Again and again after Eteocles' departure for battle the chorus brings up the curse, making explicit what exactly Oedipus prayed for:

> And on his sons for their cruel care
> he cast vengeful curses, alas,
> from his embittered tongue,
> that they divide his possessions
> armed with swords in their hands. (*Seven against Thebes* 785–89; see also 818–19, 832, 892, 898, 944, 951)

In Euripides' *Phoenician Women*, too, the curse is not only described but repeated. Oedipus inherited it from his father and passed it on to his children (1611); Polynices repeats it just before his single combat with his brother (1364–68). Everybody talks about it: Jocasta (67, 70, 335, 624), Polynices (475), Eteocles (765), Tiresias (876), the Chorus (1053, 1426), and Creon (1355).

The other surviving play concerned with the legend of Oedipus, his progeny, and the fight over his inheritance is Euripides'

Suppliants, which takes place after the battle of Oedipus' sons and treats the Athenian expedition to recover the bodies of the dead and the mourning over them. It, too, speaks directly of Oedipus' curse: this is what drove Polynices out of Thebes (150). Adrastus undertakes a war to reclaim Polynices' patrimony, led on by another oracle of Apollo (138–46, the same one that is given to him in *Phoenician Women* 409–23). Of his fate the chorus, connecting the two legends and their victims, sings:

> The Fury full of grief
> has left the house of Oedipus deserted,
> has come now to haunt you. (*Suppliants* 834–36)

Oedipus' house is deserted by the Curse because all the sons are dead. Not only Adrastus but outsiders like Iphis and his family and even the city of Argos (as the chorus sings to Iphis, the father and father-in-law to two of the Seven) are contaminated by the curse of Oedipus:

> Yes, your life is tragic.
> You have had your share of Oedipus' luck,
> you, along with my unhappy city. (*Suppliants* 1077–79)

2. Jocasta's Story (*Phoenician Women*)

A feature that sets Euripides' *Phoenician Women* apart from other Theban plays is the unique prominence given to Jocasta. Jocasta is not named as a character in Euripides' *Suppliants*.[21] No reference is made to her by name in Aeschylus' *Seven against Thebes* nor in Sophocles' *Antigone* or *Oedipus at Colonus*. In *Seven against Thebes*, seven (926–32) lines are devoted to her marriage and mothering in the long ode that is sung after the deaths of her sons have been announced. There she is named the unhappiest of all women

---

21. Jocasta is the mother of one of the warriors being denied burial, but it is hard to imagine her as one of the suppliants who make up the chorus of women who have journeyed from Argos. See Storey (2009) for problems relating to the size and composition of the chorus of *Suppliants*. An acceptable solution to the problem of a chorus of fifteen composed of seven mothers is that the chorus is made up of the mothers and their companions and/or attendants, or that it includes mothers of the commanders and other slain warriors.

who have been called "mothers of children." Earlier, before the battle, in the ode about the trespass of Laios, her unfortunate coupling with her son is mentioned (753–54). Her character, however, has a strong supporting role in Sophocles' *Oedipus the King.* Jocasta leaves the stage when she—having one more piece of the puzzle than her son has—realizes the unbearable truth. The actor who played her comes back as the second shepherd, the one who pitied the infant and saved his life. The parental love that was missing from the baby's natural parents finds a place in the lowly slave.

Euripides' fullest treatment of the Theban saga, on the other hand, has no single character of the stature and prominence of Oedipus in *Oedipus the King* or of Eteocles in *Seven against Thebes.* Is *Phoenician Women* just a series of episodes with one character after another dominating the scene and then departing? Is there anything to mesh the pieces together, either the characters or the events that make up the plot? In this brief investigation I will look at the role of Jocasta to see whether she supplies such a unifying element. (See also the section on division of roles in Appendix A.)

From the opening lines of the play Jocasta's perspective is prominent. What she chooses to tell and what to leave out and where she chooses to give a little more or less detail are significant. Furthermore, she bears a close relationship to everyone in the play. True, all the members of the royal house are related, but she is closer to all of them than anyone else. Like other women in drama (and like Antigone in this play) she is a mesh of relationships (daughter, sister, wife, mother, aunt, foster mother, grandmother), and her connection to others may be seen as her major role.

In the course of the play her complete biography (at least enough for an obituary) is given, from her birth to her death. Her point of view prevails because—standing alone in front of the scene-building—she tells the story. Unlike some tragic narratives, however, hers is not the story of a lonely heroic woman or man standing up to defy the world, the gods, or the elements, though at the end of her speech she does suggest to Zeus that it would help if he eased up on the suffering of Oedipus (84–87). No, hers is a tragedy of too many relationships. Her heroism is the quiet courage of endurance and survival against all odds, even against a strong literary tradition from which she is absent by this time in the legend. In the powerful finale of *Oedipus the King*, she hangs herself on learning the truth of her relationship to Oedipus.

In her telling of the story events are less prominent than relationships. There is a concentration of words with the root *phy-* (a basic root for *grow, bring to birth, engender*, 8, 9, 11) early in her account. These relationships make this a woman's story. She includes details that are not usually mentioned by men. For example, she adds her own family tree to that of Cadmus and the orderly succession of kings that follow him. Once she reaches the name of Laios (10), though the words in Greek mean simply "but I," it is as if to say, "this is where I come in."

She names her father and brother and even refers to her mother (10–13), though without giving her name. The feminine touch may also in part explain the many references to naming, in particular the naming of herself (12) and her children, the girls specifically named by father or mother (57–58). Only Oedipus is left unnamed.

Her natal relationships (of lines 10–13) are surrounded by references to Laios (9, 13). For women, the marital relationship overwhelms the natal. The first lines are about Laios and his genealogy back to Cadmus, into which she now interposes her own family. When she gets to Laios she has chronologically reached her generation and the beginning of the current ills. Laios, her cruel first husband, defines that part of her life. In three lines she situates herself in her own family as daughter of Menoeceus, sister of Creon, her "own mother's son" (11), and ends again with her father who named her. This family will later become more prominent than we might expect at this point. Creon always plays a part in the aftermath of the war of the Seven against Thebes, but Menoeceus, his son and the grandson and namesake of Jocasta's father, is little known elsewhere, and may have been an invention of Euripides.[22]

As her marital family takes over, things begin to break down. Laios is childless. Laios (not Jocasta) is the subject of the series of verbs and participles that follows (13–16), making her less prominent and less responsible in the fate that defines her in Theban legend. Laios receives the oracle; in spite of it he gives in to pleasure, realizes his mistake, pierces the baby's ankles, and gives him to herdsmen to expose. In the rest of the narrative Jocasta continues to harp on the relationships in her family, moving from place to place and including details of the story that she must have heard after the fact from others: "my son" (33), "my husband" (35), and "son

22. In *Seven against Thebes*, Eteocles sends Creon's son, Megareus, to face Eteoclus at the third gate (474).

killed father" (44). At the next phase, she continues, "And with my husband dead" (46), "my brother Creon" (47), "my son Oedipus" (50), and ends with the complicated mother-child relationship of lines 53–54 with its concentration of words from the root *tek-* relating to birth. Oedipus is not called husband: "I bore two sons to my son" (55). Of her two daughters by Oedipus she says: ". . . Ismene [was] named by her father, Antigone—I chose her name" (57–58). Finally, she refers to Polynices and Eteocles by the relationship they bear to her rather than to each other (82), son to son.

In the play everybody (except the servants) is related, but only Jocasta has a close, primary relationship to all the royal characters: Creon is her brother. Antigone (and Ismene, though she is not a character in this play), Polynices, Eteocles, and Oedipus are her children. Menoeceus is her nephew, but the relationship is closer than that because she nursed him after his mother died, and he is almost a son to her. He feels close to her too. He tells his father that he is going to see her before he leaves. He does not do so because—displaying the unselfishness recommended by Jocasta to her own sons—he wants to save the city that her natural sons are threatening to destroy. It is as if he is the true son to his foster mothers, Jocasta and Thebes.

In the opening monologue, then, Jocasta emphasizes the power that her natal family members had over her, as first her father and then her brother, in the capacity of her guardians, in turn arranged her marriages. She does not express the horror of the Sophoclean Jocasta at the discovery of her incestuous marriage, but seems almost to accept it. Oedipus reacts as he does in Sophocles by blinding himself. In the first episode she refers to her marriage to Oedipus and the birth of her children as a misfortune rather than wrong-doing (381). That is, wrong was done, but—as is common in Greek tragedy—blame cannot be firmly and unambiguously affixed to those who carried it out: in this case, Jocasta was given in marriage to the wrong person. Throughout she is careful to place and to remove blame and to make sure that knowledge and volition are requisites for the full application of blame. For example, Laios had knowledge of the consequences and acted with diminished capacity. Acting on the knowledge he had, he abused and disfigured his son and tried to do away with him, and then, because he was ignorant of the outcome of his attempted infanticide, he sped to his death, which was, in Jocasta's telling, the result of a coincidence. In the marriage both she and Oedipus are innocent through their ignorance, even more so than in Sophocles' play, where a confluence of oracles has given them clues through which they finally recognize what they have done. Jocasta's speech in the Euripidean version makes it perfectly clear that Oedipus had no reason to believe that he was in danger of killing his father or marrying his mother. But the self-blinding and cursing of his sons are his responsibility. The sons in turn abuse their father. Jocasta attributes all or most of this to the gods or to human suffering, as does Oedipus near the end of the drama (1610–14).

Jocasta assumes for herself more of a role than that imposed on her. She is needed as a mother. Oedipus has become, through self-blinding and ill treatment, an absent parent to his sons. Jocasta continues to treat him with maternal concern and kindness (1088–89, 1616–17). Her influence is felt in all the scenes, even when she is not present. Antigone is able to come out to view the troops because her mother has given permission. Jocasta's two sons hold their debate because she has arranged it. The second episode is between her son and her brother and the third among Tiresias, her brother, and her surrogate son. She herself returns in the fourth episode to hear about the fates of her two sons and leaves with her daughter in a final, futile attempt to save them. In the exodos her brother is looking for her when the messenger comes to tell of the deaths of her sons and of her own death. Her body is brought back with those of her sons, in a grim reunion of characters from the first episode and the doomed attempt at reconciliation. Her first son (second husband) and her daughter mourn those deaths.

Jocasta provides an emotional and rational center, at least loosely holding the complex plot with its many characters together. At the end, without her, even the plot falls apart. Creon turns cruel and stubborn, reverting to the roles of other Creons in other plays. Oedipus and Antigone, both long confined inside the palace, break out into a chaos of mourning and too many choices. Jocasta can be seen as a unifying element, though the randomness of events is also a counterforce that militates against unity of action. The known end of the story also weighs against her efforts, as if, try as she and her author might, they cannot overcome the forces of death and destruction.

3. The City of Thebes in *Phoenician Women* and *Seven against Thebes*

Chief among old friends we see again in Euripides' *Phoenician Women*, the last of our plays, is Thebes itself. In *Seven against Thebes*, the rivers and especially the gates, walls, and towers are prominent, but it is in *Phoenician Women* that we get a fuller picture of Cadmus' city than in any of the other tragedies, not only its history but its monuments and topography, which are inextricably connected because of their associations with persons and events in the play.

The natural landmarks outside the walls begin with "Hera's sacred meadow on craggy Cithairon" (*Phoenician Women* 25) where Oedipus was exposed, a place fraught with emotion and tragic consequences. Mount Cithairon comes up at various crucial times: as the place of Oedipus's exposure and hoped for death (*Phoenician Women* 802, 1604), and again as the unnamed mountain of the maenads (*Phoenician Women* 1753). The two rivers of Thebes, Ismenus and Dirce, together or one at a time, are named again and again to remind us of why the city was situated in this exact spot (*Phoenician Women* 101–2, 131, 238, 347, 368, 648, 730, 794, 826–27, 931, 1028; *Seven* 273, 307, 379). It is, of course, this near distance that is filled with the enemy soldiers. By mentioning the famous rivers, hills, mountains, plains, and meadows, Euripides and, to a lesser extent, Aeschylus make the place more real. This is the eternal history and geography in which today's tragic events take place. In Euripides' *Suppliants*, which is set in Eleusis, the references to Thebes are less intimate: they occur in the chorus' request to Theseus (61); in Theseus' directions to his herald (383); in the messenger speech about the battle (637, 655, 660, 663); and in Athena's proclamation of the next war (1215).

In *Phoenician Women* and *Seven against Thebes* the offstage exteriors are both within the walls and beyond them. Thebes is enclosed behind its walls and locked gates with a host of armed warriors gathered on its plain; but all we see with our own eyes is, as always, the *skēnē* with the spaces in front of it and the passages on the sides, or in the case of *Seven against Thebes*, the orchestra with its altar(s) and statues, whether real or notional. Jocasta's opening monologue offers a more internal palace history. Antigone looks beyond the palace to the plain and the sites of monuments that hint of the stories of other Thebans, not named in Jocasta's carefully edited genealogy. The famous sites of Thebes are given their due, in the scene from the roof, for example, in Polynices' greeting and farewell to the haunts of his youth (367–68), and in Menoeceus' site-specific sacrificial suicide (1009–11). This act brings together the long ago founding of the city with its present dangers.

Jocasta's genealogy reveals two strains of the royal family of mythological Thebes: the Cadmeians and the Spartoi (or Sown Men). Jocasta mentions her own marriage to Laios (who was himself born of a mother from the Spartoi). This twofold ethnicity comes back later, in the central scene, in which Tiresias points out that Creon and his sons are the last of the unmixed Spartoi and that, therefore, his son Menoeceus must be sacrificed to the serpent from whom he is sprung. The Cadmeians are already mixed, at least in their royal family. The double origin of the citizens is also reflected in the alternative versions of Thebes' foundation, which come out in the second scene of the prologue (see Goff 1988: 144) where Antigone and her aged slave look out over the plain.

The most commonly mentioned features of Thebes are the seven gates and the walls which form a unit representing the security and vulnerability of the city.[23] The seven gates are listed by name in *Phoenissae* (1105–34) and in Aeschylus' *Seven against Thebes* (375–676), though the names are not exactly the same and do not have the same attackers or defenders, except that Capaneus is killed at the Electra gate in both versions and in the account by the travel writer Pausanias (*Description of Greece* 9.8.4–7; 9.5.2–4). The messenger in *Suppliants* watched the battle from the Electra gate (651). If the Ogygian is the same as the gate near Onca Athena, Hippomedon also has the same position in both tragedies of the War of the Seven. Euripides even moves Polynices from the Seventh (where he faces his brother in Aeschylus' *Seven against Thebes*) to the Krenaian gate and posts Adrastus (who is not one of the seven attackers in *Seven*) at the last (Seventh or Highest). These gates remained a tourist attraction into Pausanias' time (second century CE, 9.8.4–7; for a clear plan see Demand 1982, fig. 2: 46–47).

23. *Phoenician Women* 79, 113–115, 180, 239, 244, 261–2, 287, 366, 449, 451, 593, 720, 739, 741, 744, 748, 752, 798, 809, 823–4, 974, 1009, 1058, 1078, 1090, 1094, 1098, 1103–1138, 1150, 1180, 1357, 1475; see *Suppliants*: gates 12, 101, 142, 402, 498, 503, 588, 651, 720, 753, 1221; walls 274, 664, 724.

Within the gates are generic monuments of civic life that are found in all Greek city-states: altars and shrines of the gods and gymnasia. Most prominent in *Seven against Thebes* are the shrines and images of the gods, which are approached, prayed to, and embraced by the chorus in the parodos. Reference to these suggests a Thebes with a civic life outside the palace, even in *Phoenician Women*, a play that unlike *Seven against Thebes,* in which the connection of the defenders to their land is emphasized, is devoid of citizen participation. The single, but powerful exception in *Phoenician Women* is the final battle in which the citizen army—without their king—routs the occupying force. It also adds poignancy to Polynices' words in the first episode, where he addresses these buildings and shrines at the beginning, middle, and end of his stage life (274–75, 367–68, 604, and 630–32), emphasizing his loss of homeland and reminding us of the lost innocence of his boyhood:

> my eyes at long last gazing on gods' shrines and altars,
> the gymnasia where I spent my youth, and Dirce's stream. (367–68)

At his entrance he comes into a world of enemies and strangers in spite of being among the familiar places he has missed during the time of his exile. These are the things that would be his if he wins. But the familiar faces are not to be seen again, except those of his mother and the brother who hates him, the brother he hates. He is denied a last reunion with his sisters and father.

The wall itself was built by Amphion and Zethus (sons of Antiope a member of the Spartoi and sister of Labdacus' wife; *Phoenician Women* 113–15). Thebes' past is hinted at through reference to historical monuments, against which the enemy leaders and contingents are seen by Antigone as she peers from the palace roof in the second part of the prologue to *Phoenician Women.* The associations of these monuments are ominous. The monument of Zethus (which he shared with his brother Amphion, 145) is pointed out because the frightening Parthenopaeus is passing by (*Phoenician Women* 145–50; see *Suppliants* 663, and *Seven against Thebes* 528). In the ancient rivalry between the Sown Men and the Cadmeians, Zethus and Amphion led an army against Lycus, who was acting as regent for Laios (see Pausanias 9.5.3–9). The tomb of Niobe's children is where Polynices is sighted (*Phoenician Women* 159). Niobe was the wife of Amphion, whose children died of a plague (Pausanias 9.5.9) or were shot by Artemis and Apollo. The brothers collaborated not only in founding the city but also in invading and conquering it (Goff 1988: 144), making their contrast to Polynices and Eteocles more ambiguous. They are given credit for building the wall around the city:

to the sound of Amphion's lyre
the walls of Thebes rose and the towers rose to his lyre
at the crossing between the twin rivers
where Dirce waters the green-growing plain
opposite Ismenus. (*Phoenician Women* 823–27)

The stones moved miraculously to his playing. Though the double founding myth remains a mystery to many scholars, the scholiast (in his note to line 115 of *Phoenician Women*) rationalizes it simply by saying that Cadmus founded the city, but Amphion and Zethus walled it.

In addition to these solid landmarks are more mysterious places associated with the founding and its more magical and darker aspects, mentioned in the first stasimon and in Tiresias' exegesis. In the first stasimon the chorus sings of the place where Cadmus' cow lay down:

. . . for him the four-footed
heifer, not forced to its knees,
lay down, fulfilling
the oracle that told him where to settle
the wheat-bearing plains of his new home.
The divine voice proclaimed:
"where the beautiful stream of water
comes over the land,
the green-bearing, deep-sown
fields of Dirce." (*Phoenician Women* 639–48)

Pausanias says that this place is still pointed out (9.12.2), and he situates it near an altar and statue of Athena, the Athena Onka (also spelled Onga or Onca).

More sinister is the place where Cadmus went for water:

There it was, the blood-thirsty dragon
of Ares, cruel-minded guard,
watching over the running streams
and green runnels with its

> eyes darting everywhere.
> And this creature, when Cadmus the monster-killer
> came for ritual water,
> he killed it with a rock, crushing
> its murderous head
> with weapons hurled from his hands. (*Phoenician Women* 657–66)

Pausanias identifies the fountain of Ares with the spring of Ismenus (near the Ismenion, below the Electra gate), but Euripides says the serpent was "the watcher of Dirce's waters" (*Phoenician Women* 932; see also 1009 and 1090, where the self-sacrifice of Menoeceus is said to take place from the highest tower which for both Euripides and Aeschylus is the seventh gate; *Suppliants* mentions the Ismenion hill and the spring of Ares at 655 and 660). Cadmus sowed the dead serpent's teeth and men rose up who killed each other. Some survived to become the Spartoi. In the third episode, Tiresias declares that one of the Sown Men must be sacrificed to atone for the long distant killing of the serpent and to appease Ares (931–35; 1009–12). This is Creon's young son Menoeceus who lives his stage life between two choral odes on violence and monsters bred in the earth—from whom he is in fact descended. That he has evolved into a better, more publicly-minded man of peace is not as optimistic as it might have been had he been spared. The darkness of the dragon's lair suggests irrational terrors, monstrous imaginings, such things as have plagued Thebes since its founding. It has taken yet one more life. More men will fall outside the walls. We realize at the end of the play, with its concentration on the palace and the release of Oedipus and his exile with his daughter, that Jocasta was right in thinking that the day of Thebes' founding was indeed a tragic day for its founding family.[24]

4. War Plays

"The world's everlasting grief and glory"
(Laird Hunt, Neverhome, *2014)*

The three plays in this volume are about war. Wars are going on offstage during the time of all three dramas. In *Seven against Thebes*

24. Zeitlin (1990) writes of Thebes that it "provides the negative model to Athens' manifest image of itself with regard to its notions of the proper management of city, society, and self" (131).

and *Phoenician Women* the famous war of the Seven is fought. Closure is reached in Aeschylus' play with the final scene of mourning in which the two sisters (or two parts of the chorus) keen in equal measures beside the corpses of their two brothers. *Phoenician Women* ends less symmetrically with further suffering, exile, and loss for Oedipus and Antigone, and with the question of tending to the body of Polynices left unresolved in a chaos of grief (which may be more chaotic because Euripides' ending is lost or mangled). *Suppliants* takes place after that notorious war, but a new war breaks out when the Thebans refuse to bury the bodies of the fallen captains, an event that was an important part of Athens' legendary history. A third war, the revenge of the sons of the Seven (the Epigoni or Epigonoi), is in the offing, once the boys grow up. This war seems to us, as modern readers, unjustified, considering the fact that the Seven were the unjust aggressors and were justly defeated.

Not every war play is an anti-war play. In Euripides' two plays the wars are presented as wars of choice. Not so in Aeschylus. In *Seven against Thebes*, the war is seen from Eteocles' point of view and that of the Chorus of Theban women (see below). The city is already under siege, and there is no possibility of avoiding the battle. In *Suppliants* the war of the Seven is over. Adrastus, the Argive king, admits that Eteocles offered favorable terms (739–40) and that he had the opinions of the seers against undertaking the expedition (155–59, 230–31; cf. 210–12), but he chose to ignore them, surrendering to the war fever of impetuous young warriors. The play's central war is deliberated in dramatic time. We see Theseus first reject undertaking it because he has no respect for Adrastus, and then accept it, giving in to the persuasion of his elderly mother. He makes his decision on the basis of what is right (to honor the Panhellenic law regarding the proper treatment of the dead) and what will bring glory to himself and the city. Athens is not under attack. This, too, is a war of choice. The third, predicted war is for vengeance, and it is also a war of choice. In *Phoenician Women*, the setting is once again the city of Thebes under siege. Jocasta, however, in the hope of preventing the war even at this late date, has arranged a truce so there can be eleventh-hour peace talks between her two sons, offering a rare glimpse of Polynices and his point of view. The first episode is like a flashback in which we see the two brothers refusing to yield and instead choosing war. In *Seven against Thebes*, Eteocles is the hero, defending his homeland. After he leaves to take his station at the battlements, the focus shifts to the history of the family curse, with its mixture of inevitability and choice. Oedipus cursed his sons deliberately and with full knowledge. Choice is presented most dramatically in Eteocles' choice of himself to face Polynices. The city is saved, but the dramatic focus turns to the brothers' deaths and the sisters' grief.

From Homer on, in Greek war narratives and dramas, the civilians' side is presented. Inside the city under siege life goes on, even if normal living is disrupted. The *Iliad* goes back and forth from scenes of brutal war outside the walls to the attenuated life of the Trojans hemmed inside their doomed city. Aeschylus' *Persians* (his earliest extant tragedy) dramatizes the Persian War from the Persian point of view, inside their capital, as the queen and the elder citizens wait for the messenger with news from the front. The great Panhellenic but especially Athenian victory (in the particular battle of Salamis) is presented as a monumental defeat for Xerxes and his empire. Empty beds and mourning women are an inevitable result. In similar fashion, through its chorus of women terrified of the enemy at the gates, *Seven against Thebes* presents the war from two sides within Thebes itself: Eteocles commands and controls his army, but he cannot control the female citizens who fear for their city and lives as they face slavery, rape, loss, and death. In *Suppliants*, the Argive mothers have been forced to leave their homes, not because their city was taken, but because the aggressor lost and the victorious Thebans refuse burial to the fallen enemy.

Mothers, then, both the bereft Argives and Aethra, Theseus' mother, are put in the position of arguing for war. The Argive mothers recognize their delicate position as the cause of it all (603–7). Will they be blamed if casualties mount up? In *Phoenician Women* more characters participate in the life inside the city: Creon (like Priam, a non-fighting king),[25] Antigone, the chorus of women (less in terror, because as gifts for Apollo they will still go to Delphi whatever the outcome), Jocasta and Oedipus, the seer Tiresias, and Creon's son Menoeceus, all give a fuller picture of the constrained existence in the besieged city. There is both an expansiveness, in the scene of Antigone on the palace roof, looking out over the battlefield (an incident reminiscent of *Iliad* book 3), and a feeling of claustrophobia in the stealthy entrance of Polynices, suspicious of everyone and in the dark hole at the heart of the city where

25. In Euripides' *Suppliants*, Creon takes part in the battle over the bodies (694–96).

Menoeceus sacrifices his life. With the messenger's first speech the war comes into the city and takes with it Jocasta and Antigone. The victory of the citizen army is followed by an emptying of Thebes. Of the characters, only Creon and Tiresias are left. Even the chorus will depart for Delphi.

A drama full of Ares (*Seven*), an encomium of Athens (*Suppliants*), a play full of excellent slogans (*Phoenician Women*)—all war plays, but in spite of victories, they are very sad songs. They all dramatize the tragedy of war. Ironically the strongest anti-war sentiment is expressed by the Theban herald in Euripides' *Suppliants*:

> Whenever war comes up for a vote of the people,
> no one any longer figures his own death is imminent;
> instead he lays this misfortune off on somebody else.
> If death were before their eyes when the vote is cast,
> war-crazy Greece would not now be destroying itself.
> And yet of the two points of argument, we all know
> which is better, both the good and the bad of each,
> how much better peace is than war for humankind.
> Peace: far and away the Muses' favorite, and enemy
> to Retribution, delighted by children growing up,
> happy in prosperity. . . . (481–91)

Is this Euripides letting even the least likable character have a say, or is the playwright expressing a deeply felt sentiment? Even in a democracy, war fever cannot be cooled. Monarchy, of course, fares no better, as Adrastus admits and Creon displays. Are we to conclude with Plato (*Laws* 1.626a) that "what the majority of people call peace is only a name, but in fact all cities are by nature ceaselessly engaged in undeclared war with all [other] cities"? Though one of Theseus' motives for going to war in *Suppliants*, is to bring credit to Athens, not much space is given to the glory of war in any of the plays. Even the funeral oration in *Suppliants* is taken by some critics to be a parody (Smith 1967: 162; Mendelsohn 2002: 187–96, cf. 215–23; Kornarou 2008: 35). Mourning takes over the ends of *Seven against Thebes* and *Phoenician Women*; grief and mourning are constants in *Suppliants*.[26] It would perhaps be anachronistic to call these tragedies anti-war plays, but they may yet instill in

---

26. Without the mourning ritual, the mothers cannot resolve their grief: see Toher (2001: 337).

us the longing to end the foolishness voiced too late by Adrastus (*Suppliants* 949–54) and in vain by Jocasta (*Phoenician Women* 559–85). As Mendelsohn (2002: 223) writes: "Like Theseus in the play the Athenians were beguiled. Like him they chose badly."[27] Even in this "encomium of Athens," however, there is another hand, as there is in most Greek tragedies. In upholding laws and customs that are common to all, in fighting for the helpless, in showing the sympathy that is essential to the survival of the city-state, King Theseus becomes an Athenian democrat, both humble and humane.[28] Tragically, the war's real (and only) justification in Athenian eyes is Athens' victory. Ideology, even the ideology of altruism, can be treacherous.

---

27. Though I do not agree with every detail of Mendelsohn's analysis of *Suppliants*, I cannot fail to admire his success in seeing and presenting a coherent integrity in this difficult play. He is particularly brilliant on the importance of gender and the "omnipresence of the feminine" throughout, especially pp. 135–70.

28. Walker (1995: 143–69, esp. 160–64).

Translator's Note

When I taught Greek Tragedy, the course was divided into two major sections, separated by a group of individual plays like *Alcestis*, *Medea*, and *Hippolytus*. The two major groups were Trojan War plays and Theban plays. The Theban series was, in order of discussion, *Seven against Thebes*, *Antigone*, *Oedipus*, *Phoenician Women*, and *Bacchae* for the grand finale. If I were to teach it again, perhaps, I would include *Suppliants* or *Oedipus at Colonus*. The justification for the selection of plays here is the convenience of having together in one volume works by Aeschylus and Euripides that treat elements of some of the same myths as the more well-known Sophoclean Theban plays, for comparisons of the tragedians' styles and world views. These plays offer other stories about Antigone, Jocasta, Oedipus, and their kin.

The translations are meant to be readable, both silently and out loud. When I feel they are presentable, my husband and I always read them together, taking the different parts. This saves them from the unspeakable.[1] I follow the lines of the Greek texts as much as possible without mangling the English and try to make the line numbering correspond to the Greek texts, which are the real plays. If at times the line numbers do not exactly match the translation, it is because they are aligned to the Greek, which may have a line missing or, in the case of lyric passages, the stichometry is awkward to reproduce in translation. Words sometimes have to be added or shifted to get the sense and rhythms right and to make unfamiliar names and terms immediately understandable. The notes provide background material, make suggestions about staging, and offer an occasional comment about the text.

When I came to working intimately on Euripides' *Suppliants* for the first time since my graduate student days in the late sixties to early seventies, the question asked years ago by a student in my Greek tragedy class, "Do these plays have any meaning for us?"

---

1. In an early version of my translation of *Alcestis*, for example, I used the word "pusillanimity," which is literally unspeakable, as became apparent in a classroom reading

seemed particularly relevant, more even than for the other two war plays in this volume. Most heartbreaking is the question of the just war as opposed to the war of choice which might come up in a discussion of any of the three plays but is especially prominent in the debate scenes of *Suppliants*. Whether we consider Theseus' decision to take his troops to war to be just or not, Adrastus' decision to lead the expedition against Thebes was certainly a war of choice, as is made abundantly clear in the play (especially at lines 739–41). Adrastus refuses the diplomatic option. There is the sheer awfulness of war: in a play so rich in agricultural metaphor, we might speak of the crop of dead bodies, some buried on the borders of Attica and others brought back to Eleusis. The horror of the disfigurement of the body is an eternal feature of military conflict. After the battle, Adrastus asks if those who picked up the bodies were disgusted by the task (762). Later Theseus refuses to let the mothers see and touch the bodies until after they have been cremated and inurned (942–45). A passage about the horribly mutilated body of a young soldier in Kevin Powers' powerful novel about the Iraq war, *The Yellow Birds: A Novel* made me think of Theseus:

> The body . . . would land in Dover, and someone would receive it, with a flag, and the thanks of a grateful nation, and in a moment of weakness his mother would turn up the lid of the casket and see her son, Daniel Murphy, see what had been done to him, and he would be buried and forgotten by all but her, as she sat alone in her rocking chair in the Appalachians long into every evening. . . . And we'd remember too, because we would have had the chance to change it.[2]

And then there are the eulogies for the fallen warriors in Euripides' *Suppliants*. Day after day in the news coverage of war casualties, we hear sound bites from their friends, neighbors, family members, fellow soldiers. Tragically, unless we knew the particular soldier, they all sound the same, like the comments of Adrastus and Theseus.

2. Kevin Powers, *The Yellow Birds: A Novel*, New York: Little, Brown and Co., 2012: 207.

A Eulogy, after *Suppliants* 857–932

Now say a few words about the dead.
It's the right thing to do.
You know, thank them for their service.
Everybody loved him.
Too bad he didn't make it.
He was an immigrant,
but he loved this country.
He was rich, but nice.
He was poor, but nice.
He was the class clown.
I can't believe he's gone.
He came to my house once.
He paid his debts.
Not much to say.
Not much left of him.
He had a sister.
He had a wife.
(She killed herself.)
He's survived by his mother.
His father is all alone now.
He left a son.

These dead warriors all left sons. The funeral oration begun by Adrastus and filled in by Theseus offers little more than clichés. The bodies have been recovered at considerable risk. They will be given a proper burial. Part of the funeral ritual is praise of the fallen heroes. This section of *Suppliants* (857–932) is the subject of much critical discussion and is the most difficult for me. Given the reputations of these men for hubris, is Euripides being ironic in praising them? Or is he asking the audience to take another look at these men? After all, they were brave men; they have paid the ultimate price; they must have had their good points; above all, there were people who loved them. Evadne, Capaneus' widow, sister of the late Eteoclus, is one of them. Also, of course, there are mothers and sons who hear the eulogies. For the most part the men's civic virtues are presented, and the eulogy has been seen in a positive light as part of the education of the young by a number of recent critics (Storey 2008: 98–100, Collard 1975: 308–310; for a summary of opinions see Morwood 2007: 209–10), though I still find it disturbing. In the translation of *Suppliants* and the other translations, I tried to use words and images that would make connections to our world.

One of the bright spots in working on these translations was discovering that Henry David Thoreau had published a translation of *Seven against Thebes*. It is not his most brilliant work, but it does have insights, a few of which are included in the notes.

Translations of other briefly cited ancient works are my own unless otherwise attributed.

I would like to take this opportunity to thank Hackett's editors and anonymous readers for their kind and helpful suggestions, my Facebook friends listed in the dedication for their encouragement, and my husband Lance, for everything.

AESCHYLUS

Seven against Thebes

Cast of Characters

Eteocles	son of Oedipus, king of Thebes
Messenger	Eteocles' Spy
Chorus	of unmarried Theban women The Chorus Leader speaks for the group in the dialogue sections
Antigone	daughter of Oedipus
Ismene	daughter of Oedipus
[Herald][1]	Creon's mouthpiece

Non-speaking parts

Extras to represent a crowd of Theban citizens, Eteocles' entourage, Eteocles' arms-bearer. Possible extras to represent the six other defenders of Thebes to face the seven attackers. Pallbearers to bring in the bodies of the fallen brothers.

Seven against Thebes is a two-actor play. It was first performed in 467 BCE.

---

1. With most other editors, critics, readers, and translators, I believe that the epilogue (lines 1011–83), which includes the part of the Herald, was added later. For a summary of the arguments and bibliography, see Hutchinson (1985: 209–11). Many editors believe the introduction of the two sisters is also an interpolation: for example, Dawson (1970: 24–25); see also Conacher (1996: 71–74).

Seven against Thebes

SCENE: *The action takes place on the acropolis of Thebes. The orchestra is decorated with altars and statues to the city's gods. The play starts with a tableau of Eteocles addressing a crowd of Theban citizens. Stage right represents the nearer distance (the town of Thebes); stage left the farther distance (the battlefield outside the walls).*

Prologue[2]

ETEOCLES:
Citizens of Cadmus,[3] to say what the times call for
is the role of whoever guides the ship of state,[4]
plying the tiller, never letting his eyes rest in sleep.
If we do well, the gods will get all the credit;
but if—heaven help us—disaster should befall us,
Eteocles is the one name that would be chanted

---

2. The Prologue is the part of the play before the entrance of the chorus. *Seven* begins with a monologue followed by a dialogue, which is also the usual practice of Euripides. In this case the scout's report is almost a second monologue, except that he delivers it to a specific person. Aeschylus' *Suppliants* and *Persians* begin with the entrance of the chorus; *Prometheus* opens with a dialogue between Hephaestus and Kratos (*Might*, personified); the three plays of the *Oresteia* begin with monologues.

3. *1:* "City of Cadmus" and "Cadmeians" or "citizens of Cadmus" are the usual terms in tragedy for Thebes and Thebans respectively. The presence of citizens in the opening tableau is also an effective part of the staging of Sophocles' *Oedipus the King*. Euripides' *Suppliants* begins with a tableau that includes the chorus. Eteocles grabs our attention with the urgency of this speech.

4. *2: Ship of state* and other nautical imagery, especially the enemy army as a swollen angry sea, are constants in *Seven* (for example, 62–4, 113–15, 207–10, 602–4, 652, 769–71, 854–60). See Thalmann (1978: 32ff.), Dawson (1970: 18–19).

by citizens all over the city in waves of loud harangues
and cries of woe. Zeus, our Protector, be true
to your name[5] and defend the city of Cadmeians.
Now, all of you—those still short of full maturity,
and those who are past the prime of life but still
strive to maintain full physical vigor, and all
who are in the springtime of youth—as you are able,
you must come to the aid of our city and the altars
of our country's gods and never let their worship
be blotted out; for your children and for Mother Earth,
your nurturer, who tended you as infants crawling
on her loving ground, welcoming all the burden of your
tender care so you would grow up to be householders
and bear arms,[6] be loyal to her now at this time of crisis.[7]
This much can be said: despite the long siege, to this day
Fate's balance has been on our side. Thanks to the gods,
the war for the most part has been going in our favor.
But now, the seer,[8] keeper of birds, with infallible skill
has given the word, making observation of the feathered flocks
with his ears and in his mind, without resorting to fire.[9]
Our master of such oracles has declared that
the greatest Argive onslaught has been debated
during the night and they are plotting to sack the town.
Make haste to the parapets and gates of our city wall,
go with all speed, arm yourselves in full panoply;
man the battlements and take up your posts

---

5. *9: True to your name*: cf. Latin, *nomen-omen*, the idea that the name expresses the essence of the person or thing (see lines 144–46, 405, 439, 536–37, 578–79, 828–30; Hogan 1984: 245, 255).

6. *19–20:* Thoreau translates, "shield-bearing colonists."

7. *16–20:* After the Ship of State, the second major theme is the Earth, as motherland, as nurturer, as source of the "Sown Men," and as receiver of the dead (see Dawson 1970: 19–22).

8. *24:* The blind seer, Tiresias, though not named in this play, was a well-known figure in Theban legend. The prophecy that Eteocles refers to is confirmed by the spy's report.

9. *25: Without fire*: a common method of divination was to examine the innards of sacrificed animals before putting them on the fire, but Tiresias' observation is from sound, the cries of birds and the noise of their wings in flight.

on the scaffolds of the towers; at the city-gates
make your stand with valor and do not fear
the assault of attackers. God will bring us victory.
I have myself sent scouts to spy on their army;[10]
I am confident that their mission is not in vain.
When I hear their report I will not be caught off guard.

(Assembled citizens exit stage right.)

(Messenger enters stage left.)

MESSENGER (SPY):
Eteocles, most valiant king of Thebes, I am here
to bring clear intelligence of the army outside.
All that was done I saw with my own two eyes.
Men, seven in all, their side's hot-blooded leaders,
slit a bull's throat into a black-rimmed shield,
dipped their hands into the victim's warm blood,
and swore an oath by Ares and Enyo,[11] spirit of war,
and bloodsucking Terror,[12] either to tear down the city
and by force to sack the Cadmeians' town,
or to die and drench this land with their blood.
With their hands on Adrastus'[13] chariot they wound
tokens for their parents at home to remember them by,
letting their tears fall, though not a sound of woe was heard.
There breathed in them a steely heart, glinting
with valor, like lions with battle in their eyes.
I have come at once to bring you this intelligence:
I left as they were casting lots to see where each one
by luck of the draw would lead his troops to the gates.
With all speed post our best warriors, the elite

10. *36:* This is Eteocles' way of announcing the messenger and letting us know to expect him.

11. *45: Enyo* is a goddess of war. In the *Iliad* she was a warrior goddess called "sacker of cities" (5.333) and along with Ares led the Trojans into battle (5.592).

12. *46: Terror*: this is the god Phobos (or *Rout*).

13. *49:* Adrastus is king and leader of the expedition, but not one of the seven attackers; see also Euripides' *Suppliants*, in which he is a major character; in *Phoenician Women* he is one of the attackers.

of Thebes, to face them at the outlets of our city-gates.
The army of Argives armed to the teeth is near;
it is on the move, it is raising dust, the white foam
dripping from the horses' mouths stipples the plains.
You, now, like a ship's unwavering helmsman,
fortify the citadel before the gales of war can shatter it.
A swelling surge of troops rumbles over the land.
Seize whatever chance is most opportune.
I will keep my eyes unblinking watchers by day
for what is coming; with clear intelligence, in safety,
you will be kept abreast of what is beyond the gates.

(Messenger exits stage left.)

ETEOCLES:

Oh, Zeus and Earth, gods who keep our city safe,
my father's Curse, potent Fury of revenge,[14]
do not, I pray, wipe out our city from stem to stern
in total ruin, prey to hostile forces. We are speakers
of Greek; do not destroy our hearths and homes.
Do not ever shackle under the yoke of slavery
a land that is free, the city built by Cadmus.
For our common good, be our mighty fortress:
a country that prospers gives honor to its gods.

(Eteocles exits stage right.)

Parodos[15]

*(The Chorus enters in terror from both sides
as if coming from all parts of the city.)*

---

14. *70:* The Curse and Fury (*Erinys*) seem to be identified as they are in Aeschylus' *Eumenides* (*Furies*): "Curses we are called in the halls below the earth" (417).

15. The Parodos is the entrance song of the chorus. Usually this is in an orderly procession along the side entrances (*parodoi* or *eisodoi*), as in Euripides' *Phoenician Women*, but here the chorus may make a scattered entrance. The first part is not divided into strophe and antistrophe. The meter is primarily dochmiacs (◡ _ _ ◡ _), which are used to express

CHORUS:

My cries shrill with panic.
The army is let loose. It has left camp and advances
in a mighty flood, a host on horseback streams in front.
The dust rising to the sky is what convinces me,
a herald clear and true without a sound.
And now the plains of our land pounded by hoofs
boom in my ears. It swoops, it bellows
like a torrent no force can resist crashing on the hillsides.
Oh, oh!
Oh, gods, goddesses, this swelling evil,
keep it back. The din rises above our walls.[16]
The horde, flashing white shields, sweeps onward,
stampeding toward the city.
What god, what goddess
will save us?
Who will hold it back?
Should we throw ourselves on
the statues of our fathers' gods?
Oh, blessed gods, throned on high,
it is time for us to cling to your images.
Why do we hold back
in our loud shrieks of woe?
Don't you hear? Are you deaf to the clanging of shields?
What time is better to make offering
of robes and wreathes to add to our prayers?[17]
The din—I see it! It's not the sound of one lone spear being shattered.
What will you do? Will you betray your own people,
Ares, ancient god of our land?[18]
Oh god of the golden helmet, look on us,
look on our city that you once loved so well.

---

extreme agitation (see Hutchinson 1985: 57–59 for a detailed metrical analysis).

16. *88:* Hutchinson's suggestion for this uncertain line (1985, note at 89ff.).

17. *102:* The offering of a new robe to a goddess is often part of an annual ritual (as in the Panathenaea; see also *Iliad* 6.269–79; 285–311), but there it is done in solemn, dignified procession.

18. *105:* Thoreau translates, "aboriginal Ares."

Guardian gods of our land,
come, all of you, come,
look at this band of girls!
On our knees we pray:
Save us from captivity.
A human surge with waving plumes
laps around the city,
driven on by Ares' squalls.
Oh Zeus, father,
perfecter of all,
save us, keep us
from hostile hands.
Argive men circle the city Cadmus built.
Their weapons of war make us shiver in terror.
The bits in the horses' jaws
let out a rattle of death.
Seven proud chiefs towering above the army,
shaking spears, take their stands as allotted
at the seven gates.
And you, daughter of Zeus,[19]
powerful war-lover,
save our city,
Pallas Athena. And you on horseback,
lord of the sea,
Poseidon of fish-spearing trident,
grant us deliverance,
deliver us from this terror.
And you, Ares, protect
the city named for Cadmus,
care for the city,
show yourself in person
to honor your kinship.
And Cypris Aphrodite,
first mother of our people,[20]
hold back the hordes. We are born

19. *127–65:* Members of the chorus run from statue to statue of the gods they call upon.

20. *140–41:* Aphrodite's daughter Harmonia became the wife of Cadmus, founder of Thebes. Aphrodite is called Cypris because at her birth she rose from the sea near Paphos on the island of Cyprus.

of your blood. We draw near you, reciting
litanies, invoking the gods.
And you, Wolf King Apollo,
be a wolf to the enemy army, make them pay for our pain.[21]
And you, maiden goddess, daughter of Leto,
ready your bow, dear Artemis.

[Strophe 1]

Ah, ah, ah, ah,
I hear the clattering of chariots all around the city.
Oh, goddess Hera!
The fittings rattle
under the loaded axles.
Oh, dear Artemis. Ah, ah, ah, ah.
The air is wild with the shaking of spears.
What harm will our city suffer? What will become of us?
What doom will the gods bring down upon us?

[Antistrophe 1]

Ah, ah, ah, ah,
stones are raining upon our battlements,
hurled from far away. Oh, dear Apollo!
At our gates a ringing of bronze-fitted shields!
Son of Zeus, you who
settle the final hallowed
outcome in war!
And you, oh blessed queen, Athena Onca,[22] for our city
preserve your seven-gated home!

---

21. *145–46: Lykeios* ("of a wolf" or "wolflike," from *lukos*, "wolf") is an epithet for Apollo, possibly referring to Apollo as "wolf-slayer" or "Lycian," "from Lycia." In Argos his main cult was that of *Apollo Lykeios*. At *Iliad* 4.101 he is called *Apollo Lukēgenēs*, which is interpreted as "wolf-born," "born in Lycia," or "light-generating."

22. *164:* Onca is a title of Athena, derived from the name of a Phoenician goddess. Her temple and cult were established by Cadmus when he founded the city (Scholion, Schwartz, 1887 (1966): to line 1062 of Euripides' *Phoenician Women*).

[Strophe 2]

Oh, gods all-powerful,
gods sublime, sublime goddesses,
protectors of this land,
do not forsake our city circled by war
to an army of alien speech.[23]
Hear the maidens,
hear our prayers,
our arms stretched out with justice.

[Antistrophe 2]

Oh, gods most cherished,
redeemers, encircling our city,
show that you still love our land,
that you care for the people's sacrifices,
and preserve us with your care.
Remember, we implore you,
the city's devotion,
and our rich offerings.

First Episode

(Eteocles enters stage right.)

ETEOCLES:
You preposterous women,[24] do you think this is
the best way to keep our city secure and instill
courage in our troops blockaded inside the towers,
throwing yourselves at the images of our gods,
baying and bawling, and subverting civic stability?
I pray to god never to live in a house full of women,
whether in hard times or blessed with prosperity.

---

23. *170:* Both Thebans and Argives spoke Greek, but different dialects.

24. *182–202:* Eteocles' misogynistic tirade is part of a pattern of his distrust of the female. Of course, the Sphinx is one of the dreaded female monsters of Greek mythology. Eteocles' own mother Jocasta has broken the taboo against incest. The women of the chorus, though they are reduced to despair, are not the enemy within, in the larger context of Eteocles' situation in family and city.

If they get their way they make life unbearable,
but if they're anxious it's still worse for home and city.
And now with your frantic running this way and that,
you spread despair and cowardice among the citizens,
while giving aid and comfort to our enemies outside
the walls, making us destroy ourselves from within.
This is what you get from living among women.
And if there are any who do not obey my command,
whether man or woman or anything in between,[25]
a sentence of death by public stoning will be cast
against them, and they will not escape their doom.[26]
Foreign affairs are men's concern. Women's opinions
are not wanted. Stay inside and keep out of trouble.[27]
Did you hear me or not? Or am I speaking to the deaf?

[Strophe 1][28]

CHORUS:
Oh, dear son of Oedipus, I was terrified
when I heard the din, the din of rattling chariots,
the clang of the wheels spinning,
the jangle of reins, their bits forged in fire,
straining in the horses' mouths.

ETEOCLES:
So then, do sailors by careening from stem
to stern find a means of saving their skins
when the ship is foundering on the swelling seas?

---

25. *197:* Eteocles' intention is probably to be rhetorically inclusive rather than to propose a third gender.

26. *198–99:* Hecht and Bacon (1973: 75) translate, "the public shall drop its fatal weight on his name," explaining in the note: "The pebbles which convicted a man of treason are here assimilated to the stones with which the sentence was executed."

27. *200–201:* The notion that woman's place is in the home is typical of Greek thought, not specific to Eteocles (see also *Iliad* 6.431–41, 490–93, where Hector tells his wife to go back home to her weaving, "war is the concern of men," 492).

28. *203–41:* The choral parts are sung; Eteocles speaks in iambics.

[Antistrophe 1]

CHORUS:
In my frenzy I came to the gods'
ancient images, trusting in the divine, when I heard
the pounding of rocks hailing down on our gates;
then I was whipped by terror to pray to the gods
to shield our city from harm.

ETEOCLES:
Pray that our towers hold back the enemy's spear.
The gods will see to this. But the saying goes
that the gods desert a city when it is captured.

[Strophe 2]

CHORUS:
Oh no! Never in my lifetime let this congress
of gods abandon us. Let me never see
our city overrun in the chaos of war and enemy troops
setting it ablaze with ravishing fire.

ETEOCLES:
When you summon the gods do not anticipate evil.
The mother of success is Obedience, and
that is where salvation lies, as the proverb goes.

[Antistrophe 2]

CHORUS:
True, but the gods' might surpasses all;
in dire times it often raises the helpless
out of deep misery, as clouds are hovering
over their eyes.

ETEOCLES:
That is men's work, to perform blood sacrifices
to the gods, when we are beset by hostile forces.
Yours is to keep silent and stay inside the house.

[Strophe 3]

CHORUS:
Thanks to the gods the city we live in is unconquered
and our towers shelter us from the enemy hordes.
What reason have you to threaten us with punishment?

ETEOCLES:
I do not begrudge your worshiping the gods;
but keep calm and do not give in to panic and
cause the men of the city to be disheartened.

[Antistrophe 3]

CHORUS:
I heard a startling chaos of noise
and came in terror here to the citadel,
our revered sanctuary.

ETEOCLES:
If you hear of men being killed or wounded,
do not take in the news with shrill outbursts—
that is Ares' supper, the blood of dead men.

CHORUS:
What I hear now is the snorting of horses.

ETEOCLES:
You hear it, but try not to hear it so noticeably.

CHORUS:
From the very ground the city groans under siege.

ETEOCLES:
It's my job, mine alone, to deliberate on these issues.

CHORUS:
I am so afraid. The crashing at the gates gets louder.

ETEOCLES:
Will you be quiet? Your words are doing the city harm.

CHORUS:
Congress of gods, do not forsake our battlements.

ETEOCLES:
Damn you! Can't you endure your fate in silence?

CHORUS:
Gods of our city, do not let me be taken into slavery!

ETEOCLES:
It is you who are making slaves of me and the city.

CHORUS:
Zeus, almighty god, turn your thunderbolt against our foes.

ETEOCLES:
Oh, Zeus, what a breed you have given us in women.

CHORUS:
An unhappy breed, the same as men whose city is taken.

ETEOCLES:
With your hands on the holy images such words bring ruin!

CHORUS:
Yes, fear takes hold of my tongue along with despair.

ETEOCLES:
I have one small favor to ask of you—please listen.

CHORUS:
I will know it if you tell me as quick as you can.

ETEOCLES:
Keep quiet, you wretch, and do not dishearten our side.

CHORUS:
I am quiet. I will suffer the same fate as the rest.

ETEOCLES:

I much prefer this to what you were saying before.
And now one more thing, move away from the shrines;
make this your petition, that the gods fight on our side.
First hear my vow and then add your own voices,
raising in joy the sacred shout of praise and victory,
the sacrificial cry that is the custom of the Greeks,
instilling boldness in our side, quelling fear of war.
I swear to the gods of this country who protect our city
dwelling on the plains or watching over the market,
and to the springs of Dirce and the waters of Ismenus,[29]
if we meet with common success and the city is saved,
the gods' altars will run red with the blood of sheep
[and with the blood of slaughtered cattle—that is my vow],[30]
and I will set up trophies of victory and deck the holy
temples with spear-won spoils stripped off the enemy.[31]
You pray to the gods in this way, too, not with outcries,
not with vain and inarticulate barbarous mutterings.
You will not any more escape your fate by doing that.
Now I will go and post six men with myself the seventh
to oppose our enemies, like the soldiers we are,[32]
stationed at the seven entrance gates to the city
before messengers arrive in hot haste bringing
swift-running rumors to inflame us with urgency.

(Eteocles exits stage right.)

---

29. *273:* Dirce and Ismenus are the two rivers of Thebes.

30. *276:* Considered spurious on stylistic grounds.

31. *279:* Line 279 is considered spurious by most editors, since it repeats much of 277–78.

32. *283:* Hutchinson (1985) believes a line is lost after 283 and that the second half of the line means "that proud manner of theirs."

First Stasimon[33]

CHORUS:

[Strophe 1]

I hear his words, but cannot calm the fear in my heart.
Cares, my heart's constant neighbors,
kindle terror's fire,
terror of the army encircling the walls,
like an anxious dove
in dread of snakes, nightmarish bedmates,
for her young brood in the nest.
Right now against the walls
in a great swelling surge, with wave upon wave of troops,
they are coming. What fate is in store for me?
More men are hurling
jagged rocks
at our citizens, bombarded from every side.
Help us, gods,
born of Zeus, whatever way you can
help the city, the people born of Cadmus.

[Antistrophe 1]

What place on earth braver than this will you take up
if you abandon to the enemy
our rich-soiled land,
and the waters of Dirce,
most sustaining of all rivers
that Poseidon,
cradler of earth,
and Tethys' river children[34] send forth?
And so, oh gods,
protectors of the city, cast

33. *287–368:* This ode is full of epic allusions and even includes several instances of Homeric phrasing, making the comparison to the fall of Troy more explicit.

34. *311:* Tethys is the wife of Oceanus. Her children are the rivers of the world.

upon those outside the walls
man-slaughtering death and the doom of panic
to throw away their weapons,
and win glory for yourselves in the people's eyes.
Be saviors of the city;
stay in your fine abodes
in answer to our wild, wailing prayers.

[Strophe 2]

What a pity to cast a city so ancient
down to Death's dominion, captive slave
of the spear, crumbling to dust,
ruthlessly devastated
by the Argive host through gods' will,
and the women subdued, oh no, not that!
young and old to be dragged away
by their hair, like horses,
their garments torn to shreds. Wailing goes up
from the city as it is being emptied,
a confused cry from the ravaged human plunder.
This is the heavy fate I fear.

[Antistrophe 2]

What grief for innocent girls plucked unripe
from their homes before their wedding day
to reach the end of a journey so hated.
No, I say a dead man
is better off than these.
When a city is overpowered, oh god, no!
it suffers so many, many disasters.
One man hauls off another, or kills him,
or brings torches to set it ablaze, and the whole city
is choked with smoke.
Maddened Ares, subduer of people,
storms against the city, polluting all that is sacred.

[Strophe 3]

Ear-splitting turmoil through the city and around it
a towering circle of men. Man sets upon man—
lays him low by the spear.
Blood-curdling bleatings
of babies nursing at the breast
blast the air.
Brothers are seized by running soldiers:
looter falls in with looter;
an empty-handed man calls to another,
looking for a partner in crime,
eager for no less or even equal share.
What is there left to guess from this?

[Antistrophe 3]

Provisions of every sort, strewn on the ground
cause distress, a bitter sight
to householders.
The bounty of earth
turned into waste is swept along
in worthless waves.
Young women now enslaved feel new grief:
the wretched captive's bed
crushed by a triumphant enemy
in place of her happy husband:
this is what they have to hope for every night,
a new burden of sorrow and pain.[35]

Second Episode

HALF CHORUS:
Look, the army's scout is here, I think,
my friends, bringing us new intelligence,
moving his feet like wheels driven in his haste.

(Messenger enters, stage left.)

35. *369:* See Hecht and Bacon (1973: 76), "The sack of the city is imagined as an inverted marriage ritual whose consummation is rape and death."

HALF CHORUS:
And here, too, is our king, the son of Oedipus,
just in time to hear the messenger's report:
his haste makes his feet outrun each other.[36]

(Eteocles enters, stage right, with six champions.*)*[37]

MESSENGER (SPY):
I am here to give an eye-witness account of the enemy,
how each leader has his allotted post at the gates.
At this moment, Tydeus is ready to storm the Proetid
gate, but the seer will not permit him to cross
Ismenus, because the sacrifice does not bode well.
This Tydeus raging and ravenous for war
squalls like a snake's hissing at noontime;
spits out abuse at the seer, the wise son of Oecles,[38]
accuses him of whimpering in fear of death and battle.
With such shrieks he shakes his triple-shadowing
plumes, the helmet's crest. From inside his shield
bells made of bronze ring out terror and flight.
He bears on his shield this arrogant device:
a design of the heavens blazing with stars,
and in the middle, all aglow, the full moon,
oldest of the stars, the eye of night, stands out.
Roused to such a pitch by his cocky trappings,
he bellows beside the river bank, hungry for war,
the way a horse, chafing at the bit, stands waiting
impatiently for the sound of the trumpet.
Whom will you pick to face him, what champion
to stand at the Proetid gate when the bars are loosed?

ETEOCLES:
A man's trappings do not make me quiver:
insignia have no power to wound their enemy;

---

36. *374:* The line literally reads, "does not allow his feet to move evenly"; see Hutchinson (1985: 107) on line 374.

37. Some scholars do not agree (see Dawson 1970: 63, Taplin 1977: 149–50) that the Theban champions are present, but believe that Eteocles would have already dispatched them.

38. *382:* The son of Oecles is Amphiaraus, a seer who was tricked by his wife into joining the expedition. See below, 568–96.

no crests, no bells can stab without the spear.
And this night you speak of plastered on his shield,
embellished with the twinkling stars of heaven;
possibly his lunacy will prove prophetic to him.
Yes, if night falls on his eyes when he is dead,
for the man carrying this bombastic device,
it would well and rightly be true to its name and
his insolence will prove prophet of his own doom.
My answer is to post opposite this Tydeus
the steady son of Astakos to defend this gate,
a true-born man who respects the throne of honor
and loathes language that is full of arrogance.
He's a man of courage and a stranger to wrong-doing.
His roots go back to the Sown Men spared by Ares,[39]
a true son of our land, is Melanippus here. Ares himself
with a throw of the dice will determine the outcome.
Yet Justice runs in his blood; it is she that sends him forth,
to drive back the enemy's spear from his mother Thebes.

CHORUS:

[Strophe 1][40]

To our defender may the gods
grant success, as he sets out, with justice,
to fight for our city. I shudder to see

---

39. *412:* Sown Men (*Spartoi*): Cadmus was told by an oracle to follow a heifer until it collapsed and to found the city of Thebes on that site. A dragon, descendant of Ares, guarded the spring of Ares and other waters. Cadmus needed water and killed the dragon with Athena's help. Athena advised Cadmus to sow the teeth of the slain dragon in the earth. When he obeyed, grown men sprang from the earth fully armed. These are the *Spartoi* (Sown Men). They fought each other and all but five were killed. (See Euripides, *Phoenician Women* 638–75 and 934–44.) Only some of the Thebans are descendants of the Sown Men. Creon and his family are among them. This would make Oedipus and his children part *Spartoi* through their mother Jocasta, Creon's sister. Laios, Oedipus' father, was a descendant of Cadmus and Harmonia (see Euripides, *Phoenician Women* 7–8).

40. *417, etc.*: The chorus sings between the descriptions of the sets of attackers and defenders.

the bloody deaths of men
dying for those they love.

MESSENGER (SPY):
Yes, may the gods grant him the success he deserves.
Next, Capaneus[41] has been allotted the Electra gate,
another giant of a man even bigger than the last,
his boast is beyond human reason—against our towers
he threatens such outrage—which I pray the gods avert.
He swears, whether the gods are willing or not,
he will destroy the city: even Zeus, counterattacking
with the fiery bolt, striking the ground at his feet,
would not hold him back. Lightning and thunder
he compared to the warmth of the midday sun.
On his shield he holds the device of a naked man
carrying fire, armed with a blazing torch in his hands.
In gold letters it makes the claim, "I will burn the city."
Dispatch against such a man—uh, who will face him?
Who can, without fear, await this man's insolence?

ETEOCLES:
This second gain compounds the first with interest.
Against men's vain and empty imaginings,
the tongue turns out to be a true accuser:
Capaneus threatens and is ready for action,
blaspheming the gods, giving his tongue a workout,
in his empty glee, a mere man, he utters against heaven
a sea swell of words loud enough for Zeus to hear.
But I have confidence that on him, with justice,
the fiery thunderbolt will crash down, not at all like
the warm rays of the sun at the midday lull.
Against him, however loud-mouthed he may be,
a man fiery in temperament, strong Polyphontes,
is posted, a trusted guardian, who has earned
the favor of protecting Artemis and the other gods.
Tell me who is the next, allotted the next gate?

---

41. *423:* Capaneus' name means "Smokey," which turns out to be prophetic of his fate: he is, in fact, struck by the thunderbolt. For a graphic description of his death see Euripides' *Phoenician Women* 1180–86.

[Antistrophe 1]

Chorus:
Death to him with his grandiose boasts against the city.
I pray a blast of thunder will stop him
before he can leap into my home
and with insolent spear drag me out
of my maiden's chambers.

Messenger (Spy):
Now I will tell of the one who drew the next lot
at the gates: to Eteoclus third the third lot
sprang from the helmet wrought of solid bronze,
to attack with his contingent at the Neïstan gate.
In a circle he wheels his horses heaving angrily
in their bridles, eager to fall upon our gates.
Their muzzles, filled with breath snorting from
their nostrils, whistle an outlandish noise.
His shield is decorated by no insignificant sign:
a man in full armor climbs the rungs of a ladder
up to the enemy's battlement, bent on destroying it.
And in the letters' configuration he bellows
that not even Ares could throw him off the towers.
To face this man send someone you can trust
to drive away the yoke of slavery from our city.

Eteocles:
Here's the man I would send now, a happy choice:
he's already gone, holding his boast in his two hands,
Megareus, son of Creon, from the race of the Sown Men,
who will not budge from his post at the gate. He will not be
frightened by the roar of the horses' furious snorting,
but either in death he will pay back the earth for his nurture,
or he will capture two men and the city on the shield
to ornament his father's house with these spoils.
Boast me the next, do not shy away from the telling.

[Strophe 2]

CHORUS:
I pray that he will succeed, ah,
defender of my home, and that they will fail.
Just as they utter ugly boasts against the city,
with maddened mind, so may Zeus
the Avenger cast the evil eye upon them.

MESSENGER (SPY):
Next, the fourth, having the gate right by the side of
Onca Athena, with battle cry makes his way
forward, the massive figure of Hippomedon:
that huge orb,[42] I mean the circle of his shield,
I shuddered as he whirled it—I cannot deny it.
The designer who applied this work to the shield
was no second-rate craftsman: on it Typhon[43] was
depicted belching out dark smoke, glowing
sister of fire, through his fire-breathing mouth.
The surface of the hollow-bellied circle of the shield
is filled in with coiled serpents. The man himself
lets out a battle-cry; possessed by Ares, like a Bacchant,
he raves for the battle, terror shoots from his eyes.
We must guard well against the onset of such a man:
Panic is already swaggering at our gates.

ETEOCLES:
First, Onca Athena living near the city, a neighbor
to these gates, who hates this man's insolence,
will keep him like a deadly serpent from our young.
And beside her, Hyperbius, brave son of Oenops,
has been chosen to counter him, man to man,

---

42. *489: Orb*: the Greek word is *halōs*, "threshing floor" or "disk of the sun or moon." Thoreau, using the English derivative, translates as "the huge halo."

43. *492–4: Typhon*, the youngest son of Gaia (Earth), was the scariest monster in Greek mythology. He tried to destroy Zeus and, though he won an early battle, was ultimately defeated by Zeus. A hundred-headed snake grew from his shoulders. See Hesiod, *Theogony* 820–68; Aeschylus, *Prometheus Bound* 351–72.

ready to test his destiny in fortune's time of need,
beyond reproach in body and spirit and in bearing
of his arms: Hermes[44] has matched them perfectly.
For the man is an enemy to the man he will face,
and on their shields they will bring together gods
hostile to each other: the one holds fire-breathing
Typhon, but on Hyperbius' shield sits Father Zeus,
poised with the blazing thunderbolt in his hand;
never in all of time has anyone seen Zeus defeated.
This is how the goodwill of the gods shows itself:
we are on the winners' side, they on the losers'.
If Zeus is truly mightier in battle than Typhon,
it's likely the opposing men will fare the same,
and to Hyperbius, in keeping with the sign's meaning,
Zeus, who appears on his shield, will prove his savior.

[Antistrophe 2]

CHORUS:
I feel confident that the man bearing
Zeus' hated enemy on his shield, the image
of the earthborn monster, likeness hateful to mortals
and to the long-lived gods,
will lose his life in front of the gates.

MESSENGER (SPY):
This is my hope too. Now I will name the fifth,
posted to the fifth gate, called the Northern,
right beside the monument to Amphion,[45] son of Zeus.
He swears by the spear he carries, in his brazenness,
honoring it more than a god, more than his own eyes,
that he will pillage the Cadmeians' city in spite of Zeus.
So boasts this pretty-faced progeny of a mother

44. *508: Hermes*, the god of transitions and the guide between human and divine worlds, is also the god of the lot and bringer of good luck.

45. *528: Amphion* with his twin brother Zethus ruled Thebes and built the walls around the city to the accompaniment of Amphion's lyre (see *Phoenician Women* 115 and note). In Euripides' *Phoenician Women* it is referred to as the monument to Zethus (145). Zethus was the strong athletic brother, Amphion the musician and artist.

who roams the mountains, this man, this boy-soldier.[46]
The first downy beard just now spreads over his cheeks
in the springtime of his youth, the thick hair sprouting up.
But his heart is cruel, unsuited to his maiden's name,
and with a Gorgon's glaring eyes he takes up his post.
He stands by the gate not holding back his boast:
on his bronze-studded shield, the circling defense
of his body, he brandishes our city's shame,
the Sphinx, eater of raw human flesh, fashioned
with heavy bolts, its polished form worked in relief,
and under her body she carries a lone Theban man,
so most of our spears and arrows will fall upon *him*.
He has come from far away and is not likely to make light
of the war nor bring shame on the long journey he made,
Arcadian Parthenopaeus, "Virgin-face." This is what he is,
a resident alien, and to repay Argos for its foster care,
he makes threats against our towers—may god avert them.

ETEOCLES:
I pray the gods cause them to meet with what
they intend for us with these blasphemous boasts,
and then they would meet an evil and awful end.
Against this man, the Arcadian you speak of,
will go a soldier without boast, but his hand sees
what must be done—Actor, brother of the man
I just named, who will not let talk without deeds
stream through the gates and multiply our evils,
nor allow a man carrying the image of a murderous
hated beast on an enemy's shield to pass inside.
Outside, *she*[47] will blame him for trying to bring her in
when she meets constant hammering blows under
the city walls: god willing, I hope I speak the truth.

46. *532–33: Parthenopaeus* ("maiden-faced") is the son of Atalanta, the famous huntress who was raised by a bear.

47. *560: She* is the Sphinx.

[Strophe 3]

CHORUS:
These words stab my breast,
my hair stands on end,
when I hear the noise of those loud-mouthed
blasphemous men. May the gods
strike them dead in our land.

MESSENGER (SPY):
Sixth I name a man most modest and wise,
a prophet brave in battle, valiant Amphiaraus;
at the Homoloid gate, taking up his allotted post;
again and again he utters imprecations against
mighty Tydeus: "You murderer, disturber of peace
in the city, worst teacher of evil in all Argos,
summoner of the Fury of revenge, servant of death,
adviser to King Adrastus in his ruinous policies."
After that, addressing your very own brother,
mighty Polynices full of strife, turning up his eyes,
he dwells twice on the last syllables,[48] reviling
his name. And this speech issues from his mouth:
"A deed like yours, of course, is pleasing to the gods
and noble for future generations to hear and tell of:
that you are laying waste the city of your fathers
and ancestral gods and letting loose upon them
a foreign army. Dirce's spring, mother that gives you life,
what claim to justice will dry it up? Your fathers' land,
in your zeal, taken captive by your spear, how will it
be your ally? But what of me? Will I, god's prophet, enrich
this soil, laid to rest under ground in enemy territory?
Into the fray then! I do not foresee death with dishonor."[49]
This is what the seer said, calmly holding his shield
made of solid bronze. On its circle it bore no sign,
for he wishes not to seem but to be most noble,
reaping a harvest in the deep furrows of his mind

48. *578: -nices* of Polynices means "strife." See below, line 830.

49. *589:* During the battle the earth opened up and Amphiaraus, chariot and all, was swallowed whole. The spot where he was engulfed became a sacred site and he a chthonic hero.

from which sprout his careful considerations.
Against him I advise you to send a wise and noble
opponent. A man who honors the gods inspires awe.

ETEOCLES:
Ah! When men's fortune brings together
a just man against those without the fear of god!
In every matter nothing is more evil than evil
association: its fruit is not to be harvested;
the field of doom yields a crop of death.
For if a god-fearing man gets on board ship
with sailors hot for some kind of felony,
he goes down with the god-forsaken crew;[50]
or a just man living among fellow-citizens
who hate strangers and are unmindful of the gods
unjustly slipping into the same trap, being struck
by the gods' indiscriminate lash, he falls with them.
So it happens with the seer, I mean Oecles' son,
a wise man, honest, noble, and god-fearing,
a great prophet, but, by associating with ungodly,
arrogant men, against his better judgment,
men who draw out a march too long to get back,
Zeus willing, he will be dragged down with them.
In fact, I think he will not even attack our gates,
not because he lacks spirit or is a coward at heart,
but he knows he will meet his end in battle
if the oracles of Apollo Loxias[51] are to come to fruition.
[But the god keeps silent or speaks as need requires.][52]
Still, against this man, I will station mighty Lasthenes,
a man at the gates who will not welcome a stranger;

---

50. [49]*602–4:* The usual story pattern is the opposite: an impious man (such as the polluted rapist Ajax the Lesser) gets on board with a shipload of fair to middling men and takes the whole ship down with him. Amphiaraus' situation fits the story Eteocles tells, but the story pattern invites us to think of the opposite.

51. *618: Loxias* is a cult title of Apollo as god of prophecy.

52. *619:* This line is suspected of being an interpolation added to explain the condition in line 618, which does not need explanation since it is only formally conditional. Line 620 takes up the idea expressed in 615. The interruption of 619 is therefore unnecessary and even vapid.

mature in mind but young in body, his eye is quick
and his hands will not be slow to catch his opponent
with his spear where he's left defenseless by the shield.
In any event, human success is a gift from the gods.

[Antistrophe 3]

CHORUS:
Oh gods, hear our righteous prayers
and grant their fulfillment, that our city succeed
and turn away from our land evils brought by the spear;
turn them on the invaders. And Zeus, we pray, strike them
with the thunderbolt and kill them outside the walls.

MESSENGER (SPY):
The seventh man at the seventh gate, I will name
him now: it is your own brother. Against our city,
here are the disasters he prays and calls for in curses:
that he breech the battlements and be heralded in the land;
then raising his voice in a wild paean of triumph,
that he meet you and kill you and die by your side,
or, if you survive, that he will pay you back, as a man
without rights driven from home in exile, as he was.
Such noises he snarls, and he calls upon the gods
of his people and his ancestral land to be keepers
of his prayers—this is the mighty Polynices.
He carries a shield, circular and newly made,
with double insignia artfully fashioned for it:
a woman, modest in her bearing, leads a man,
a soldier in full armor, overlaid in beaten gold.
She claims she is Justice, that's what the letters
spell out: "I will bring this man home, and he will
have a city and the run of his fathers' estates."
This is my full description of all their devices.
[You, now, must know whom to send to face him.][53]

---

53. *650:* Another interpolated line. The messenger has just concluded his description of the attackers with a summing up (649), and this frigid line breaks in before the messengers' conclusion by asking us to return to the individual attacker. Half of line 650 is also found in 652, literally "but you yourself know." Perhaps the line was added because the messenger's other speeches end similarly.

You will never find fault with me for my report.
You alone know how to guide the ship of state.

(Messenger exits, stage left.)

ETEOCLES:
Oh, maddened by gods, by the gods deeply hated.
Oh, our race of Oedipus, overflowing with tears.
Ah me! Curses of my father now to be fulfilled!
No, it does not suit me to cry out or shed tears,
lest a sorrow harder to bear be brought to birth.
To Polynices, so true to his name, I have this to say:
soon we will know what effect his symbol will have,
whether letters worked in gold babbling on his shield
will bring him home, with his mind so unbalanced.
If Justice, Zeus' maiden daughter, were present
in his deeds and in his heart, this might have been.
But not when he escaped the darkness of the womb
nor in his growing up, not ever in his boyhood,
nor in the gathering of the first beard on his chin
did Justice look on him and find him worthy;
and now, I think, in the devastation of the land
of his fathers she will not take her stand by his side.
Truly then Justice would in every way be false
to her name if she stood by a man ready for any evil.
Relying on this I will go and I will stand to face him
myself: What other man has a better right than I?
Ruler against ruler and brother against brother,
hater against hater, I will face him. Quick, bring
me my greaves, defense against spear and stones.[54]

CHORUS:
Oh no! My dear man, son of Oedipus, do not
be like that man who voices ugly words in anger.
It is enough that Cadmeians will go into the fray
with the men of Argos—that blood can be expiated.

54. *676:* Eteocles is clearly unarmed until this point. The greaves (leg armor) are put on first, then the breastplate, and finally the helmet. See Dawson's stage directions (1970: 90–92).

But self-inflicted death by men of the same blood
like this: that brings a taint that never grows old.

ETEOCLES:
If one is to suffer evil, let it be without disgrace,
for among the fallen this is their only gain:
nothing good can be said of death with dishonor.

[Strophe 1]

CHORUS:
My son, why are you so eager? Do not let Doom,
greedy for war, filled with wrath, carry you away.
Cast off the first evil inkling of lust for war.

ETEOCLES:
Since god is in such a hurry for the outcome,
let the whole race of Laios, hated by Phoebus,
go down on the wind, fated to Cocytus'[55] waves.

[Antistrophe 1]

CHORUS:
Too fierce a desire urges you on
to taste the bitter fruit of killing a man
whose blood you must not shed.

ETEOCLES:
The hideous tragic curse of the father I loved
sits upon my dry unweeping eyes, telling me
of something gained first and later of death.

[Strophe 2]

CHORUS:
Do not let it push you on. You will not be called
coward: you have led a life beyond that reproach.
Will the black-robed Fury of revenge never leave this house
when the gods receive sacrifice at your hands?

---

55. *691: Cocytus*, one of the rivers in Hades, was the river of wailing.

ETEOCLES:
Long, it seems, we have been disregarded by the gods.
The only pleasure they want from us is our demise.
Why should we still shrink from the doom of death?

[Antistrophe 2]

CHORUS:
Doom now stands at your side; but the spirit,
at the last minute, might alter its mood
and come on with a gentler blast.
Now it is still boiling.

ETEOCLES
Oedipus' curse brought it to the boil.
Too true the visions from the phantoms
of my sleep, dividing my father's estate.

CHORUS:
Listen to us women, though you do not like to.

ETEOCLES:
Say something possible, but don't make it long.

CHORUS:
Do not take that journey to defend the seventh gate.

ETEOCLES:
Honed[56] as I am, you will not blunt me with speech.

CHORUS:
Victory, even of a coward, is what the gods honor.

---

56. *715: Honed*: Eteocles becomes one with the sharpened iron of his sword. It is likely that he arms on stage, beginning with his call for his greaves (676, leg-armor that he would have to put on before his breastplate). At this line he puts on his sword, in the next (717) he hoists his shield, and then at 719 he would take up his spear (see Bacon 1964: 34–36). This would have the effect of turning Eteocles into the living embodiment of the figure that is described on his brother's shield (644–45).

ETEOCLES:
No man-in-arms could put up with that sentiment.

CHORUS:
Do you want to reap your own brother's blood?[57]

ETEOCLES:
There is no escape from disasters sent by the gods.

(Exit Eteocles, stage left.)

Second Stasimon

CHORUS:

[Strophe 1]

I shudder at the demon,
poison to this house, not like other gods,
too true a prophet of evil,
Fury of revenge, invoked by the father's prayer
to bring to pass the angry curses
of Oedipus, tormented in his mind:
strife, lethal to his sons, stirs it up.

[Antistrophe 1]

A stranger pays out the inheritance,
a Chalybian immigrant from Scythia,[58]
bitter divider of possessions,
cruel-minded iron,
allotting the land to dwell in
as much as will hold them when they are dead,
without a share of all their broad acres.

---

57. *718: Reap*, or as Verrall suggests "make a prize of" (1887: 86, note to his line 705).

58. *728: The Chalybians* (or Chalybes), discoverers of iron, are here said to be Scythians.

[Strophe 2]

But when in suicidal murder
they lie dead, killed by each other's hands,
and the dry dust of earth drinks
their black-clotted bloody gore,
who could provide expiation?
Who could cleanse them?
Ah, new troubles of the house
mixed with the evils born long ago.

[Antistrophe 2]

Ancient is the trespass I tell of
but swift in retribution when it comes;
it remains into the third generation,
from the time when Laios against the will of Apollo,
who told him three times
at Delphi's central navel
in Pythian oracles[59] to die without children
and save his city.

[Strophe 3]

Overpowered by his lustful urge,
he fathered a doom for himself,
patricidal Oedipus,
who lived to sow his seed
in his mother's sacred field where he was nurtured,
and planted a root with tainted blood.
Madness brought together
that crazed wedding couple.

[Antistrophe 3]

A sea of evils brings the surge,
one wave falling as another rises
triple-crested, which even now pounds
against the ship of state.
Our defenses extend with just a narrow space

---

59. *745–48:* Delphi, the site of Apollo's major oracle, was considered the center and the navel of the earth.

in between: the width of a tower.
I fear our city will be overwhelmed
along with our rulers.

[Strophe 4]

Curses uttered long ago, now fulfilled,
are trafficked with peril. And deadly deeds
once done do not pass away.
The wealth of sea-faring men
grown too heavy
is thrown overboard from the sinking ship.

[Antistrophe 4]

What man was so admired
by the gods and those sharing the city's hearth,
the crowded assembly of mortals,
as Oedipus was honored then,
when he freed the land
of its doom that preyed on men?

[Strophe 5]

When the unhappy man
became aware of his tragic marriage,
in his pain, grief-stricken,
with madness in his heart,
he dealt a double evil:
with his patricidal hands
he struck out his two eyes, dearer than his own sons.

[Antistrophe 5]

And on his sons for their cruel care
he cast vengeful curses, alas,
from his embittered tongue,
that they divide his possessions
armed with swords in their hands.
And now I am afraid that
swift of foot, she will bring them to pass, the Fury.

Third Episode

(Messenger enters, stage left.)

MESSENGER:
Lift up your spirits, you daughters of doting mothers.
Our city has escaped the yoke of slavery;
the boasts of big men have sunk into the ground.
Coming into fair weather now, after much crashing
of the surging sea, the city has not taken on water.
Our battlements hold and we have hedged the gates
with champions standing sure in single combat.
Matters as a whole have gone well at six of the gates.
The seventh, the sacred leader of sevens,[60]
Lord Apollo, has singled out, fulfilling for Oedipus'
race the ancient wrongs committed by Laios.

CHORUS:
What new deed is there to hurt the city more?

MESSENGER:
The city is saved, but the kings of the same seed—

CHORUS:
What is it? Your words make me crazy with dread.[61]

MESSENGER:
Be calm and listen to me. The sons of Oedipus—

CHORUS:
Oh no! I am so sorry. I find myself a seer of evils.

---

60. *800: Hebdomagetēs*, "leader of sevens" is an epithet for Apollo. Apollo is associated with seven (see, for example, Herodotus 6.57 on sacrifices to Apollo on the seventh of the month). Apollo's birthday is on the seventh.

61. *805, 807:* In stichomythia (dialogue in which single lines are spoken in turn by two or more characters) it sometimes happens that news is drawn out by the inane interruption of one of the interlocutors.

MESSENGER:
Without a doubt: they lie low, fallen in the dust.

CHORUS:
Out there, do they lie dead? It's grim, but tell us.

MESSENGER:
Dead. By their own hands they killed themselves.

CHORUS:
By brothers' hands were they killed together?

MESSENGER:
Closely, too closely, the same fate was shared by both.
Their destiny on its own squandered the ill-fated race.
Such deeds give us reason to be glad and to grieve:
that the city fares well, but the commanders,
the two leaders, have apportioned the total
of their possessions with the beaten Scythian iron.
They will keep as much land as they receive for a grave,
carried off, ill-fated by their father's curses.
[The city is saved; the blood of the two kindred kings
has fallen on the ground, each murdered by the other.][62]

(Exit messenger, stage right.)

Third Stasimon

CHORUS:
Oh, great Zeus and gods,
who keep our city safe, who saved
Cadmus' towers,
do I rejoice and raise the victory cry
for the survival of our city intact,
or shall I weep for the tragic, ill-starred
childless warrior kings
who, true to their name,

62. *820–21:* These telegraphic lines are suspected of being taken from another text and copied into the margin (see Hutchinson's note on 804).

both men full of strife,[63]
have died through their own impious intentions?

[Strophe 1]

Oh black curse of Oedipus
working its destruction on the race,
an evil chill falls over my heart.
For their tomb I make my song
in a frenzy when I hear
of the bloody corpses, dead
by tragic destiny. Of evil omen
comes this flute-accompanied song of the spear.

[Antistrophe 1]

They accomplished their end and did not renounce it,
the father's words uttered in prayer.
The wayward decisions of Laios have prevailed.
I am anxious for the city.
Divine oracles are not blunted.
Ah, full of grief, you have performed
this deed beyond understanding. There have come
sorrows to cry over and that is fact.

Exodos

(The bodies are carried into the orchestra, stage left.)

These are self-evident: the messenger's tale revealed to our eyes;
cares times two, two soldiers killed
tragically by their own hands, both doomed:
their suffering is complete. What more to say?
What else than more sorrows on top of those sorrows
that have settled in the house?
My friends, over the sighing of your laments,
with hands about your head slap the stroke

63. *830: Men full of strife*, in Greek *poluneikeis*, as if they were both named Polynices.

that sends them on their way, crossing Acheron[64]
in the black-sailed convoy
to the land where Apollo does not set foot,
the sunless, unseen country
where all men are welcomed home.

(Antigone and Ismene enter stage right.)

And here come Antigone and Ismene
to this bitter business,
to sing the dirge for their brothers. Equally for both,[65]
I think, they will sing from the lovely deep folds
of their bosoms, a song of sorrow that is their due.
For us it is right, before they raise their voices,
to sound the harsh hymn
of the Fury of revenge
and to sing to Death
its hated song of triumph.
Ah, most unhappy in your brothers of all
who tie a twisted cord around their women's robes.
I weep, I sob, and without deceit
from my heart I raise the shrill sad sound.

[Strophe 1]

Ah, ah, out of your minds,
untrusting of friends, never wearying of woe,
you have taken ownership of your father's house
tragically by spear point.
Tragic men who met tragic deaths
to the grief of the house.

[Antistrophe 1]

Ah, ah, overthrowing the walls
of the house and looking

64. *856: Acheron* is a river in Hades, the river of woe or pain. It is also a swamp in Aristophanes' *Frogs*.

65. *864:* Or "without distinction," "unambiguously": that is, the sisters will honor their brothers without distinguishing them as patriot and traitor (see Verrall 1887 on line 849 in his edition).

toward poisonous single rule,
now you are reconciled by the iron.
The demonic Fury of revenge of your father
Oedipus has come true, too true.

[Strophe 2]

Struck through
the left sides,
yes, struck clear through
flesh born of the same womb.
Alas god-inspired,
alas curses
of death
requiting death.
You speak of a blow struck through—
through the house, through their flesh,
by inutterable wrath
by the doom of their father's curse
shared with undivided mind.

[Antistrophe 2]

A wail passes through the city,
the towers groan,
the land that loves its people groans.
But possessions remain for those who come after,
those doomed to a bitter fate:
through them strife has come
and its end is death.
In their hearts' bitterness they divided
their possessions, an equal share for each.
For those who loved them the mediator
is not blameless: Ares receives no thanks.

[Strophe 3]

Struck by the iron they lie here.
Struck by the iron this awaits them.
What? Someone may ask.
Shares of their fathers' graves.

Shrill sounds of the house echo around them:[66]
a heartrending wail attends them,
its own cry, its own pain,
with woeful mind, truly joyless,
shedding tears from the heart,
which wither away as I weep
for these two lords lying here.

[Antistrophe 3]

It may be said of the two wretched men
that they did much harm to the citizens
and much to the foreign foe,
fallen row on row in the war.
Unhappy the mother who gave them birth
more than all women called
mothers of children.
She took as her husband her own child
and bore these, who ended their lives
with hands that murdered each other,
men of the same seed.

[Strophe 4]

Of the same seed, yes; utterly destroyed
in loveless division,
with maddened strife
their conflict ends.
Their hatred has ended. With the earth
soaked in blood, their lives
are mingled. They are now truly one in blood.
A cruel conciliator of their quarrels, the stranger
from beyond the sea let loose from the fire,
sharpened iron: bitter was the evil divider
of their property, Ares, making their father's
curse come true.

66. *915:* "The text of this line cannot be recovered" (Hutchinson 1985: 197).

[Antistrophe 4]

The tragic brothers have their allotted portions
of Zeus-sent sorrows.
Under their corpses will lie
a bottomless wealth of earth.
Ah, with countless toils
you have festooned your house.
The curses, now fulfilled, raise
their shrill triumph song, the family
turned in rout this way and that.
At the gates stands a trophy of Doom
where they struck each other. The evil spirit
has defeated them both and is gone.

(Antigone and Ismene at the biers of their brothers sing the dirge.)

ANTIGONE:
You struck, you were struck.

ISMENE:
You killed and you died.

ANTIGONE:
By the spear you killed.

ISMENE:
By the spear you died.

ANTIGONE:
Sad toils.

ISMENE:
Sad troubles.

ANTIGONE:
Sounds of grief pour forth.

ISMENE:
Tears of grief flow forth.

ANTIGONE:
You lie dead.

ISMENE:
By your hand he died.

ANTIGONE:
Eh, eh.

ISMENE:
Eh, eh.

ANTIGONE:
My mind is distraught with grief.

ISMENE:
My heart sobs inside my breast.

ANTIGONE:
Ah, ah. You, full of lamentation.

ISMENE:
And you, full of sorrows.

ANTIGONE:
By your own kin you were killed.

ISMENE:
And yes, you killed your own kin.

ANTIGONE:
Twofold to tell.

ISMENE:
Twofold to see.

ANTIGONE:
Their woes are beside them.

ISMENE:
Brother lies beside brother.

CHORUS:
Oh, tragic fate, giver of grief.
mighty shade of Oedipus,
dark Fury of revenge, your power is great.

ANTIGONE:
Eh, eh.

ISMENE:
Eh, eh.

ANTIGONE:
Sorrows hard to look at—

ISMENE:
—he showed to me when he came home from exile.

ANTIGONE:
But he did not come back after he had killed.

ISMENE:
He survived and then he lost his life.

ANTIGONE:
Yes, truly, he lost his life—

ISMENE:
and deprived *him* of his.

ANTIGONE:
Tragic family.

ISMENE:
Tragic suffering.

ANTIGONE:
Grievous cares of blood kin—

ISMENE:
drenched in triple sorrows.

CHORUS:
Oh, tragic fate, giver of grief.
Mighty shade of Oedipus,
dark Fury of revenge, your power is great.

ANTIGONE:
You knew as you reached your goal—

ISMENE:
—and you learned at the same time.

ANTIGONE:
When you came home to the city—

ISMENE:
—you faced him, spear in hand.

ANTIGONE:
Deadly to tell.

ISMENE:
Deadly to see.

ANTIGONE:
Ah the toils.

ISMENE:
Ah the troubles.

ANTIGONE:
To home and country.

ISMENE:
And most of all to me.

ANTIGONE:
And more than that to me.

ISMENE:
Ah for the pain of grief, oh king.

ANTIGONE:
Most grievous of all mankind.

ISMENE:
Ah, ah, god-possessed by Doom.

ANTIGONE:
Ah, ah. Where will we lay them in the ground?

ISMENE:
Ah. Where it is most honored.

ANTIGONE:
Ah. One more burden to lay by father's side.

[Epilogue[67]

(Herald enters, stage right.)

HERALD:
I am here to proclaim the decisions of the people's
council of the city of Cadmus: it is decreed
that Eteocles, for his good service to the country,
will be buried in this land with proper rites.
He hated our enemies and chose death in the city;
he was free of offense against our fathers' sacred
places; he died where young men die with glory.
That is what I was sent to say concerning his remains,
but his brother, Polynices, lying dead beside him,
is to be cast outside the city, unburied, prey to dogs,
because he intended the overthrow of Cadmus' land,
if one of the gods had not blocked his way
with his brother's spear. Even dead he will carry the stain
of his ancestral gods, whom he held in dishonor

67. *Epilogue*: Most editors believe this is the end of the play Aeschylus wrote. The whole epilogue (1011–83) was probably added by a post-Aeschylean producer to make this tragedy fit the story as dramatized by Sophocles in his *Antigone* and by Euripides at the end of *Phoenician Women*, both of which had become very popular. For a thorough analysis of the interpolated scene, see Taplin 1977: 180–91.

when he tried to capture the city at the head of a foreign army.
Therefore it is decreed that he receive the distinction
of being "buried" without honor by the winged birds.
And he is not to get a funeral mound raised by hand,
nor be honored with the high keening songs of lament,
but to be cast out without the rites of burial by his kin.
So it was decided by decree of the Cadmeians.

ANTIGONE:
I have this to say to the leaders of the Cadmeians:
unless anyone else is willing to join me in burying him,
I will inter him myself and risk the danger
of burying my brother, and I am not ashamed
if the city considers me disloyal or subversive.
Sacred is the common womb of our suffering mother
from which we were born and from an unhappy father.
Therefore, my willing heart will share in misfortunes
with one whose will is gone, the living with the dead
with a sister's love. His flesh no hollow-bellied wolves
will tear to pieces. Do not proclaim your decree to me.
Yes, I will dig a grave for him and contrive for him
a means of covering his body, though I am a woman.
I will carry it in the folds of my linen garment.
I will cover him myself. Decree me no other decrees.
Be strong, my heart. The means to do it is at hand.

HERALD:
I am warning you not to defy the city in this way.

ANTIGONE:
I am warning you to stop making proclamations to me.

HERALD:
After the recent brush with disaster the people are harsh.

ANTIGONE:
Let them be harsh. This man will not go unburied.

HERALD:
But will you honor with burial a man the city hates?

ANTIGONE:
His affairs have not been honored by the gods of late.

HERALD:
He was not dishonored until he put this land in danger.

ANTIGONE:
He suffered wrong and answered it with wrong.

HERALD:
But this deed was carried out against us all, not one alone.

ANTIGONE:
Strife, last of the gods, brings the story to an end.
I will bury him. There is no need to over talk it.

HERALD:
Well, you will do as you wish. I advise against it.

(Herald exits, stage right.)

CHORUS:
Ah, ah.
Oh, far-famed bringers of ruin,
spirits of Death, Furies of revenge, who brought down
Oedipus' race, root and branch.
What to do, how to go on, what to contrive?

(To Polynices.)

How will I have the heart not to grieve for you,
not to accompany you to the tomb?
But I am afraid and I turn away
in dread of the citizens.

(To Eteocles.)

You, at least, will have
many mourners. But *he*, poor man, without lament
will go with only his sister's mournful dirge.
Who could agree to that?

Half-Chorus 1:
Let the city punish or not punish
those who mourn Polynices.
We will go and join in burying him
in the funeral procession. For to our race
this grief is in common, and the city
approves as right now one thing, now another.

Half-Chorus 2:
And we will go with this one just as the city
and Justice approve.
For second only to the blessed gods and Zeus almighty,
he protected the city of Cadmus
from going down and being overwhelmed
by a surge of men from another land, he more than anyone.

(The two funeral processions file out.)]

EURIPIDES

Suppliants

Cast of Characters

Aethra	mother of Theseus
Chorus	the suppliants: mothers of warriors who fell attacking Thebes
Theseus	king of Athens
Adrastus	king of Argos, leader of the expedition against Thebes
Herald	from Thebes
Messenger	an Argive soldier, taken captive in Thebes
Evadne	widow of Capaneus, struck down at Thebes
Iphis	father of Evadne
Athena	goddess, patron of Athens
Children	a secondary chorus: sons of the fallen warriors

Extras are needed as temple servants, the Athenian Herald, pall-bearers, and attendants of Theseus.

The date of the first performance of *Suppliants* is in doubt. It has been dated between 425 and 416 BCE (around 425 to 423 is favored).

A short fragment of the Hypothesis of *Suppliants* by the scholar Aristophanes of Byzantium (257 to the 180s BCE) survives:

> The scene is in Eleusis. The chorus is of Argive women [the mothers of the champions who fell at Thebes]. The drama is an encomium of the Athenians.

Suppliants

Scene: *The action takes place in front of the temple of Demeter in Eleusis, in Attica. Stage right represents the nearer distance (the town of Eleusis and Athens); stage left the farther distance (Argos and Thebes). Aethra, the Chorus, Adrastus, and the secondary Chorus of children have already taken their places before Aethra speaks. Aethra is standing at the altar in the orchestra, the Chorus is kneeling around the altar, and Adrastus and the children are lying or sitting on the ground near the scene building.*

Prologue

Aethra:

Demeter, keeper of the hearth in Eleusis' land,
and you servants who tend the goddess' shrines,
I pray to be happy along with my son Theseus
and the city of Athens and Pittheus' country,[1] where
my father raised me in a wealthy home and gave me,
his daughter Aethra, in marriage to Aegeus,
Pandion's son, as bidden by oracles of Apollo.[2]
This is my prayer as I look at these old faces
of women who have left their homes in Argos
and fall here at my knees with suppliant branches.[3]

---

1. *4:* Pittheus, one of Pelops' sons, was king of Trozen (or Troezen) in the Peloponnese, across the Saronic gulf from Athens.

2. *7:* On Apollo's oracle to Aegeus, see Euripides, *Medea* 679–81, where it is revealed that Aegeus was forbidden to have sex until he returned home to Athens. On the way he stopped in Trozen to consult the "pious Pittheus," who seduced him with wine into sleeping with his daughter, Aethra. Aethra cleans up the story for this version.

3. *10:* Olive branches still bearing leaves, with tufts of wool tied onto them, are carried by suppliants.

They've suffered a terrible blow: around Cadmus'[4]
city-gates, their seven noble sons have died.
They are childless now. Adrastus the Argive king
led them, in a vain attempt to reclaim a share
of Oedipus' royal inheritance for his son-in-law,
Polynices. They lie dead there, fallen in the battle.
Their mothers want to lay their limbs to rest,
but the victors forbid it and, defying gods' law,
will not even let the bodies be lifted off the ground.[5]
Adrastus, too, has need of me, a burden he shares
with them. He lies here, weeping his eyes out,
regretting the war he started and the ill-fated troops
he led into harm's way, far from their homes.
He begs me to persuade my son with prayers
to agree to gather up the bodies for burial,
either through diplomacy or by force of arms.
This is all he asks of my son: with the city of Athens
to perform this service.[6] I came from my home here
to this sacred space to sacrifice for the land's yield.
It was here that the bountiful stalk of grain first
appeared: its ear bristling up from the ground below.[7]
Bound by their boughs, no bond at all,[8] I wait
here beside the holy altars of the two goddesses,

---

4. *12:* That is, Thebes, the city founded by Cadmus.

5. *18–19:* See Sophocles, *Antigone* 454–55, and Euripides, *Phoenician Women* 1320–21; and for a heart-wrenching look at the gods' concern for Hector's body, Homer, *Iliad* 22 and 24.

6. *27–28:* "This is all" (or "only this") represents the manuscript reading: that is, Adrastus asks only for help in recovering the bodies, not in avenging the defeat of his army. Other editors suggest that "only" refers to Theseus, who alone is in a position to help them. (See Adrastus' explanation of why he has come to ask for Athens' help, 184–92.)

7. *30–31:* Demeter taught the Eleusinian hero Triptolemus to plow and plant the first grain. On Demeter's gift, see also Euripides, *Bacchae* 275–77.

8. *32:* The women surround Aethra with their boughs, an effective use of the prop, but the bond is moral rather than physical, the obligation due to all suppliants (like persons seeking asylum at shrines or altars). In tragedy, suppliants' requests are usually granted.

Demeter and her daughter,[9] feeling pity for these
gray-headed mothers who have lost their sons,
out of respect for their sacred wreaths. A herald
has gone to town to summon my son Theseus here
so that he will release the land from their sorrow
or relieve their suppliant needs, doing what is right
and holy towards the gods. Women who are wise
do everything through their men: that is our custom.[10]

Parodos[11]

CHORUS:

[Strophe 1]

We implore you, old woman
through our old women's lips,
and fall at your knees.
Recover our sons!—Lawless men have left the flesh
of those who died in bone-crushing death
to be carrion for beasts that roam the hills.

[Antistrophe 1]

You see the bitter tears of despair
in my eyes and this wrinkled
faded old flesh gouged
by my nails. What else can I do?
I did not lay out my dead sons at home.
I do not see their funeral mounds piled high.

[Strophe 2]

You are a mother too, Oh queen, you have a son.
Through him you sweetened your marriage

---

9. *34:* Persephone is Demeter's daughter, but when she is named with her mother she is called in Greek Korē ("girl," "maiden," "daughter").

10. *40–41:* Here Aethra bows to male superiority, but only after hinting at her own opinion (39–40) that granting the women's plea would be the right and pious thing to do. Later she persuades Theseus to intervene (297–331).

11. The Parodos is usually the entrance song of the chorus, but in *Suppliants*, the chorus is already present from the opening scene.

for your husband. Share with us now
the feelings of your heart.
Feel the depth of our grief
as we mourn for our lifeless sons.
Persuade your son, this we implore you,
to go to the river Ismenus and put into our arms
the bodies fallen in their prime, wandering now unburied.

[Antistrophe 2]

Not in reverence, but under duress I come to kneel
in prayer at the sacrificial altars of the gods.[12]
We have right on our side, and you,
you have the power as a mother blessed in her child
to relieve our unhappy fortune.
In our deep suffering we implore your son
to put their bodies into our poor hands,
so we can embrace the sorry limbs of our sons.

[Strophe 3]

This second bout of grieving
follows on top of the last. Hands of servants pound the beat.
Come, sounding in response,
come, grieving together,
to the dance Death honors.
Across your cheek drag your white nails
and redden your skin with blood. Woe, woe!
The rites due the dead bring glory to the living.

[Antistrophe 3]

The pleasure of grief, full of pain,
never enough, transports me, like water running in drops
from a steep rugged rock,
without surcease in its mourning.
When children are lost,

---

12. *63–64:* The chorus' funereal attire and sounds of mourning are inappropriate to the festival and rituals for the land's fertility. The ground as both nurturer of life and keeper of the dead creates one of the play's tensions.

a woman's painful lot
is wailing tears of grief. Woe, woe!
I wish I could end this pain by dying.

First Episode

(Theseus enters stage right, from Athens.)

THESEUS:
What is all this mourning and beating of breasts,
these threnodies for the dead I hear, this solemn din
issuing from the temple? Anxiety sets me on edge—
I have come for my mother. Has something happened
to her? She has been away from home such a long time.
Aha! What's this? A strange subject hits my eyes:
my elderly mother sitting at the altar, surrounded
by old women who are strangers to me, beating out
not just a single strain of grief: from their aged eyes
piteous tears stream to the ground. Their hair is cut
in mourning, and they are not dressed for our festival.
What is this, Mother? It's up to you to inform me
and to me to hear you out. I suspect something's not right.

AETHRA:
My son, these women are the mothers of sons
who met their deaths attacking the gates of Cadmus
—those seven commanders. With suppliant boughs,
as you see, they hold me here encircled, dear son.

THESEUS:
And who is that man raising a din at the temple doors?

AETHRA:
They say his name is Adrastus, king of the Argives.

THESEUS:
And these children around him, are they theirs?

AETHRA:
No. They are the sons of the men killed in battle.

THESEUS:
So, why do they come to us reaching out a suppliant's hand?

AETHRA:
I know their story, but it should come from them.

THESEUS: *(addressing Adrastus)*
You there, wrapped in your shawl, answer my questions:
uncover your head, cease your mournful noise, and speak.
Except through discussion, no decision can be made.

ADRASTUS:
King of the Athenians' land, Theseus, glorious
in victory, I am here as a suppliant to you and the city.

THESEUS:
What have you come after? What do you ask of us?

ADRASTUS:
You know the disastrous expedition that I led?

THESEUS:
Yes I do; you did not pass through Greece in secrecy.

ADRASTUS:
That's how I lost the best and the brightest men in Argos.

THESEUS:
That kind of disaster is often the result of brutal war.

ADRASTUS:
I went to ask the city for the men who had died there.

THESEUS:
Relying on Hermes' sacred heralds, to bury the bodies?

ADRASTUS:
Yes, but those responsible for their death won't allow it.

THESEUS:
What was their reason, when what you asked was right?

ADRASTUS:
What do you think? Their success did not make them wise.

THESEUS:
Have you come to me for advice? Or what do you want?

ADRASTUS:
Theseus, I want you to bring back the Argive men.

THESEUS:
Where is your Argos now? Are her boasts for nothing?

ADRASTUS:
Defeated. We are utterly defeated. We have come to you.

THESEUS:
Was this your private decision or did the public consent?

ADRASTUS:
All the people of Argos[13] supplicate you to bury the dead.

THESEUS:
Why did you lead the seven companies against Thebes?

ADRASTUS:
I was doing it as a favor for my two sons-in-law.

THESEUS:
Which of the Argive men wooed your daughters?

ADRASTUS:
I did not make an alliance with any native Argives.

THESEUS:
Are you saying you gave Argive girls to outsiders?[14]

---

13. *130:* In Greek the "people of Argos" are here called *Danaidai*, the descendants of Danaus, who are referred to as Danaids and Danaans.

14. *135:* In Athens after the Periclean reforms of 451 BCE, to be enrolled as an Athenian citizen both parents had to be of native Athenian stock. This explains the Athenian's surprise (anachronistic for him, but not for the audience) that Adrastus married his daughters to foreigners.

ADRASTUS:
Yes, one to Tydeus and one to Polynices, a native of Thebes.

THESEUS:
What made you want to bring these men into your family?

ADRASTUS:
Phoebus' confusing riddle caught me off my guard.

THESEUS:
What did Apollo say about making matches for your girls?

ADRASTUS:
That I should give my two daughters to a boar and a lion.[15]

THESEUS:
So, how did you unwind the god's inspired utterances?

ADRASTUS:
One night two refugees came to my palace gates.

THESEUS:
Who were they? Tell me. You mention two men at once.

ADRASTUS:
Tydeus and Polynices: they got into a fight with each other.

THESEUS:
You gave your daughters to them as if they were wild beasts?

ADRASTUS:
Yes, I thought they fought like two savage animals.

THESEUS:
How did it come about that they had left their homelands?

---

15. *140:* In Euripides' *Phoenician Women* (411–23) Polynices tells a similar story of how he and Tydeus came to blows over a place to spend the night.

ADRASTUS:
Tydeus was in exile for spilling the blood of a kinsman.[16]

THESEUS:
And Oedipus' son? What caused him to leave Thebes?

ADRASTUS:
His father's curses. He was afraid he might kill his brother.[17]

THESEUS:
It was a good idea for him to accept that voluntary exile.

ADRASTUS:
But those who stayed mistreated those who went away.

THESEUS:
Was his brother trying to deprive him of his birthright?

ADRASTUS:
Yes. To avenge that wrong I set out. That's how I was ruined.

THESEUS:
Didn't you consult with seers, look at the sacrificial flame?

ADRASTUS:
Alas. You indict me where I made my biggest mistake.

---

16. *148:* Who was Tydeus' victim? Sources vary. Some say it was his father Oeneus' brother or his own brother or an assortment of other relatives. Adrastus promised to restore Tydeus to his homeland in Aetolia, after he has restored Polynices. A sentence of exile was common in cases of homicide.

17. *150:* Oedipus' curse was that his sons would divide his possessions with the sword (see Aeschylus, *Seven against Thebes*, 785–90 and 818–19 and Euripides, *Phoenician Women* 67–68). To avoid the curse, the brothers agreed that each would rule for a year in turn. Polynices went into voluntary exile first, but his brother Eteocles refused to yield the royal power at the end of his year (see *Phoenician Women* 71–76, 474–83, 624).

THESEUS:
You did not, as it seems to me, set out with the gods' favor.

ADRASTUS:
Even worse, I set out despite the advice of Amphiareus.[18]

THESEUS:
Did you find it so easy to brush aside the gods' will?

ADRASTUS:
Yes, my mind was muddled by young men's clamor.

THESEUS:
You acted with a stout heart rather than a sound mind.

ADRASTUS:
Something that has brought many commanders to ruin.
You, who are most valiant throughout all Greece,
king of Athens, I feel ashamed to kneel on the ground
as a suppliant and grasp your knees in my hands,
a gray-haired man, a king once, favored by heaven;
yet I must yield to my reduced circumstances.
Bring the bodies back to me, I beg you. Take pity on
my mistakes. Pity these mothers of dead sons:
gray-headed old age has come on them bringing
childlessness in its wake. They have dared to come here
and set foot on foreign soil, their limbs cramped
by old age, not on a mission to Demeter's mysteries
but to bury their dead sons, though they are the ones
at an age ripe to receive this service from them.
It is wise for the rich man to look at poverty
and a poor man to take an interest in the wealthy
so that a desire for prosperity will take hold in him,

18. *158:* Amphiareus was the Argive seer, a man of integrity, who was tricked by his wife into participating in the expedition of the Seven which he knew was doomed.

and those without misfortune to regard[19] others' misery.[20]
. . .
[And the poet, when he produces a poem, takes joy
in its creation. Yet if he does not feel this pleasure,
he can not bring comfort or joy to his audience
when he is in personal torment: it would not be right.]
Then, perhaps, you'll say, how is it that you ignore
Pelops' land and come to lay this burden on Athens?
This explanation I have to offer by way of justification:
Sparta is harsh and is known for a deceitful character.[21]
The other states are small and impotent. But your city
is the only one that has strength to withstand this labor,
for it is attentive to others' suffering and can claim you
as its young shepherd, something many cities lack
and are lost because they are in want of such a leader.

---

19. *179:* or "to fear" as the manuscript has it. Collard argues for "regard," because he believes Theseus is being asked to look upon the unfortunate in order to help them (1975: 154); but see Walker (1995: 150), who suggests that the rich "should be filled with fear of failure" at the sight of the poor. Adrastus completes his appeal to Theseus on the mothers' plight at 175 and turns to a more general argument on mutual understanding. Unlike Theseus (238–45), Adrastus does not see the classes as fixed, but the poor by striving can improve their lot and bad luck can ruin the rich.

20. Between 179 and 180 some lines are missing. Lines 180–83 are considered an interpolation, perhaps a quotation from another play, by many editors; but see Collard (1975: 154–55) on their relevance to Adrastus' argument, as an illustration of the previous general words, and suggesting that Adrastus is comparing himself to the broken-hearted poet whose words fail to please. To fill in the gap before line 180, Morwood (2007: 158, note to lines 176–83) suggests it could have been something like, "<Forgive me if I do not speak with the eloquence for which I am famous . . . it is necessary for an orator to be successful and confident to be persuasive> and for the song-maker to . . ."

21. *187:* According to the fragmentary Hypothesis (or blurb), *Suppliants* is an "encomium of Athens." "It is easy," the proverb goes, "to praise Athenians in Athens." Similarly, it is not difficult to criticize Sparta in Athens. Sparta had a reputation for not caring about anything but war. Athens had the reputation for taking on labors and helping the oppressed to the point of being considered meddlesome (the world's policeman, as we might say). For a Euripidean rant against Sparta, see his *Andromache* 445–53.

CHORUS LEADER:
I, too, add my voice to his,
Theseus. Take pity on our tragedy.[22]

THESEUS:
I have struggled over this question in debates
with others. I've heard it suggested that the bad things
in our lives are more numerous than the good.
Well, I have the opposite opinion to this: I say
that mortals have more that's good than bad;
if not, we wouldn't be able to get on with life.
I have nothing but praise for that god who set
our lives in order out of chaos and brutality:[23]
first instilling reason and then bestowing speech,
the give and take of words, so we understand each other;
then the growing of crops[24] with the life-giving drops
of rain falling from the sky, so that earth's bounty
gives food and drink for our bellies; after that, defense
against winter weather, protection from the sun's heat;
and sailing across the sea so that we can carry on
trade with each other for whatever we lack at home.
And if something is obscure and we don't see it,
by looking into the fire or down at the folds of entrails
or from watching birds' flight, seers make it known to us.
Isn't it arrogant on our part—when god has provided
so well for the needs of life—to find it insufficient?
Our self-importance strives to get us power greater
than god's, and, obsessed with pride in our intelligence,
we deem ourselves to be more clever than the gods.

---

22. *193–94:* The chorus often speaks between speeches in an *agon* (formal debate scene that is a characteristic of tragedy, favored especially by Euripides), as much to mark the transition as to make a meaningful assertion.

23. *201–13:* Speculation on the beginnings of civilization was popular in the fifth century; see, for example, [Aeschylus,] *Prometheus* 442–506 (in which the god who taught humankind all the arts is Prometheus); Sophocles, *Antigone* 332–72; Plato, *Protagoras* 320c–322d. Note that Theseus leaves out law and war: he seems to miss the inappropriateness of his argument under the circumstances, in front of the bereaved mothers and sons.

24. *205–7:* Grain is Demeter's gift to humanity.

You, it's clear, belong to this company: foolishly,
you gave your daughters in marriage to outsiders,
following oracles, as if you believed in gods' power,[25]
and, by mixing your splendid family with society's dregs,
you tainted your house. A man of sense should not bring
good people into contact with persons of low character,
but should ally his house with those blessed by god.
Gods do not make such fine distinctions: the man
contaminated by the disease—even if he has done
no wrong—is destroyed by the troubles of the sick.
Next you led the Argive forces on a military expedition.
You had the seers' prophecies but disregarded them;
you defied the gods and destroyed your city, led on
by young men who are greedy for glory and build up
war fever with no regard for right and wrong: causing
loss of life among the citizens, one for military command,
another to seize power and live a life of luxury,
another for profit, without a care for whether or not
the people as a whole will be harmed by his actions.
Citizens fall into three categories:[26] the super-rich
are unproductive—all they care about is getting more;
the have-nots, those in need of a livelihood,
give us reason to fear them because they live in envy—
they make the rich targets of their slings and slanders,
brainwashed by the mouthings of vicious leaders.
Of the three, the middle class is our salvation,
defending the good government established in the city.
And then, you want me to become your ally in war?
What good reason can I put before my citizens?
I bid you goodbye. If your plans have failed,
it is your lot to feel the crunch, but count us out.

25. *221:* The meaning is obscure and the text has been questioned. Literally, "As if the gods are real." Does Theseus mean that Adrastus followed the oracle (as he interpreted it), as if he believed the gods are real and have power in the world, but then ignored the clear warnings of the seers (prophecy being one of the gods' gifts to humanity) in leading the expedition against Thebes? An alternative reading has been suggested: "as if the gods gave them [in marriage]."

26. *238–45:* Theseus makes his point that Adrastus should have listened to more temperate voices by cataloguing the classes of citizens, in this undemocratic praise of the middle class to the exclusion of the less affluent.

CHORUS LEADER:
They made a mistake as young men often do.[27]
You ought to show him some compassion.
[We came here for relief from our troubles.][28]

ADRASTUS:
King Theseus, I did not choose you as judge
of my troubles, and if I am found to have done
wrong, I don't need you as my castigator-in-chief,
but I came for your aid. If you choose not to help me,
I must be content with your decision. What can I do?
Come, old women, let's go; leave this place. Put down
your pale green suppliant boughs wound with wool.
Call to witness the gods, and Earth, and Demeter,
torch-bearing goddess, and the sun's light,
that our prayers to the gods have come to nothing.

CHORUS: *(The Chorus leaves the altar to supplicate Theseus.)*
<Theseus, son of Aethra, daughter of Pittheus>[29]
who was the son of Pelops, and we, who come
from Pelops' land, have the same blood in our veins as you.
What will you do? Betray your heritage and drive out
gray-headed women and not treat them as you should?
Do not do this. A wild beast has its rocky refuge;
a slave has the gods' altars to turn to; a storm-tossed city
cowers to another city. For in all of mortals' affairs
nothing has the gods' blessing all the way to the end.[30]

---

27. *250:* The manuscript has the singular, "he [Adrastus] made a mistake." Since Adrastus is an old man, some editors accept the emendation of the plural form to refer to the young men who clamored for war (see 160); others understand these lines to refer to Theseus.

28. *252:* Perhaps an interpolation expanded from line 256. Choral remarks between speeches are usually two lines (see 193–94).

29. Between lines *262* and *263* a line is lost that is filled in with an address to Theseus, with reference to his ancestry to make sense of what follows.

30. *263–70:* these lines are in iambics, the rhythm of spoken dialogue. At 271 the chorus switches to dactyls, mostly dactylic hexameter, the meter of classical epic poetry.

Astrophic Lyric

—Go, now, old women, leave Persephone's sacred ground,
go now and beseech him, laying your hand on his knees
to recover for us the bodies of our slain sons, oh misery,
I lost my sons at the walls of Cadmus' city.
[Woe, woe! Take hold, support, conduct, decide <in favor of>. . .
our poor old hands.][31]

—By your beard I beg you, dear friend, most renowned in Greece,
in my grief I beg you,
falling at your knee and touching your hand.

—Take pity on me for my children, a wandering suppliant
letting out a mournful, mournful keening cry of woe.

—Do not allow our sons to go unburied in Cadmus' land,
tender morsels for wild animals' feast, I beg you, in your youth.

—Look upon the tears in my eyes, as I fall down
at your knees, to beg of you—a burial for my son.

THESEUS:
Mother, why are you crying and covering
your head with your fine cloak? Is it from hearing
their sorrowful laments? I felt something too.
Raise your white head. Do not sit in tears
at the sacred hearth of the goddess Deo.[32]

AETHRA:
It's so sad.

THESEUS:
Their grief is no reason for you to cry.

---

31. *275–76:* Probably an interpolation made for pathetic effect. We are, perhaps, to imagine several members of the chorus each voicing one of these exclamatory imperatives as they hold out their hands toward Theseus.

32. *290:* Deo is a poetic shortening of Demeter.

AETHRA:
Poor, poor women.

THESEUS:
You are not one of them.

AETHRA:
May I say something, son, that is a credit to you and the city?

THESEUS:
Yes, a lot of wisdom comes from women's words.

AETHRA:
Still, I hesitate to give the advice I'm holding inside.

THESEUS:
Shame on you, to hide useful advice from friends.

AETHRA:
I will not, then, be silent now and later blame
my silence because I kept silent to our harm,
nor in fear that it is useless for a woman to give
good advice will I dismiss mine out of timidity.
First, my son, I ask you to consider the gods' part
in this, so you don't slip up out of disrespect;
in all other ways you show wisdom, but not in this.
Besides that, if we did not need to show courage
on behalf of the wronged, then I would hold my tongue.
As it is, be aware of how much honor this brings you
and it causes me no fear in advising it, my son:
the violent men who are preventing the dead bodies
from obtaining the burial and funeral rites due them—
with your own hand you should force them to do this;
stop them from tainting the laws all Greeks share.
It is this, you know, that sustains human society,
when everyone preserves the laws scrupulously.
Then, someone will say that you had a chance to win
a crown of glory for Athens, but you stood back in fear
because you are a coward; yet you took part in

the struggle with the wild boar, a useless sport,[33]
but when you ought to take up this struggle in sight
of helmet and spear point, you proved a coward.
You are my son, Theseus. Do not do this.
Do you see how your country, ridiculed as lacking
in policy, turns a glaring eye at the scoffers?[34]
The city's reputation will grow through its efforts.
But those isolationist cities acting in obscurity
because of their caution also look darkly on others.
Will you not go, my son, and bring aid to the dead
and to these unhappy women in their hour of need?
I have no fear for you setting out with right on your side,
and though I see the people of Cadmus prospering now,
I am confident, there will some time be a different fall
of the dice. A god can turn everything on its head.

CHORUS LEADER:
Dear, dear woman, thank you for your kind words
to him on our behalf. Our pleasure in this counts twice.

THESEUS:
Mother, the words I have just spoken are right
as far as he is concerned, and I have made clear
my opinion on the decisions that tripped him up.
But I also understand what you advise me to do,
how it is not consistent with my inclinations
to avoid dangers. By performing many glorious feats,
I have displayed this character among the Greeks,
always to stand out as a scourge of wrong-doing.
It is not possible for me to repudiate toils.
What will those with ill feelings toward me say,
when my own mother who fears for me more
than anyone else is the first to urge this undertaking?
I will do it! I will go and gain release for the bodies,

---

33. *317:* Theseus took part in the Calydonian Boar Hunt with his friend Pirithous along with many heroes, including the huntress Atalanta (mother of Parthenopaeus, one of the seven attackers).

34. *321–23:* That is, as Walker (1995: 152) interprets these lines, "Athens, by her naive and altruistic policies is able to face the world . . . with a bold look that turns all opposition to a stony silence" (lit. "the Gorgon's eye").

using diplomacy, but if that fails, it will be done
by force of arms. And I will have the gods on my side.
Still, I need the whole city to approve of this,
and if I am for it, they will approve. Yet by sharing
the deliberation, I will have the city better disposed.
When I liberated Athens I established the people
as sovereign with equal suffrage for all citizens.[35]
I will take Adrastus as proof of my arguments and go
into the assembly of the people and convince them.
I will come back with a force of elite Athenian youth
and waiting under arms I will send Creon a message
requesting him to give up the bodies of the fallen.
Old women, remove your sacred boughs from my mother
so that I can escort her home to the house of Aegeus,
taking her by her loving hand. It is a thankless child
who does not repay his parents' kindness to him;
by giving this service he can expect to get back
from his own children what he gave to his parents.

(Theseus exits stage right with Aethra and Adrastus.)

First Stasimon[36]

CHORUS:

[Strophe 1]

Argos, pasture of horses, my fathers' ground,
did you hear this, did you hear it,
the king's reverence for the gods
and great deeds for our ancient land[37]
and throughout Argos?

---

35. *352–53:* Walker refers to this passage as Theseus' "declaration that he invented democracy" (1995: 143–69, esp, 153).

36. *365–80:* The First Stasimon, though one of the shortest in tragedy covers a long interval: Theseus takes his mother back to Athens, summons and addresses the assembly, persuades them to make the expedition to recover the bodies, musters an army, and returns to Eleusis.

37. *368:* "Ancient land" translates *Pelasgia*, named for Pelasgos, a traditional early king of Argos. *Pelasgia* can be used to mean Argos or Greece in general.

[Antistrophe 1]

If only he will reach the limit and beyond
of my suffering and bring back
a mother's gory prize,
and through his kindness
make Inachus' land his ally.[38]

[Strophe 2]

Pious struggle is a glorious prize
and has eternal thanks.
What will the city decide? Will it strike
an alliance. Will we achieve burials for our sons?

[Antistrophe 2]

City of Pallas, defend the mothers, defend us.
Do not pollute humanity's laws.
You revere what's right; you disdain the wrong
and you protect all the wretched of the earth.

Second Episode

(Theseus enters stage right with Adrastus and an Athenian Herald.)

THESEUS: *(to Athenian Herald)*
You use your Herald's craft to serve our city
and me in delivering messages when needed.
Go now across Asopus and Ismenus' water[39]
and say this to the Thebans' haughty despot:
"Theseus asks you, as a favor, to bury the bodies,
believing that as a neighbor this is his right,
and to make an ally of the people of Erechtheus."[40]
If he agrees, thank him and come back with all
speed. But if he refuses, offer this alternative:

38. *373:* Inachus was the first king of Argos, after whom the river Inachus was named.

39. *383:* Asopus and Ismenus are rivers in Boeotia.

40. *387:* Erechtheus was an early king of Athens.

"Then play host to my shield-bearing revel band.
The army waits, stationed and ready nearby,
fully armed beside the sacred spring, Callichorus."[41]
Tell him: "The city willingly, even gladly, accepted
this struggle when they saw I was in favor of it."
Oh, look![42] Who is this coming to interrupt our words?
A Cadmeian, a herald, from the look of him,
though I don't know him. Hold on, in case he will
save you the trouble, by agreeing to my decisions.

(Herald enters stage left from Thebes.)

HERALD:
Who is master here? To whom am I to deliver
the message from Creon who governs Cadmus' land,
now that Eteocles has perished at the seven-mouthed
gates, fallen at the hand of his brother Polynices?

THESEUS:
First, my friend, you used the wrong word to begin
your speech in looking for a master here. A city
that is free is not governed by one man acting alone,
but the citizens are sovereign, taking turns by yearly
succession, and it does not give the lion's share
to the wealthy, but the poor man has an equal part.

HERALD:
In our game of dice this is one point you cede
to our advantage.[43] The city I come from is governed

41. *392:* Callichorus was one of the sacred springs of Eleusis, near which Demeter rested in her search for her daughter.

42. *395:* The exclamation *ea* ("look there") is used to express surprise at a new arrival.

43. *409–10:* The game referred to here is *pessoi*, which may be a game of dice or a board game, such as the one Achilles and Ajax are pictured playing on numerous vases. There were several such games, ranging from simple to complex. See Leslie Kurke, "Ancient Greek Board Games and How to Play Them," *Classical Philology* 94 (1999): 247–67, quoting the thesaurus of Julius Pollux, a scholar of the second century CE (*Onomasticon* 9.98): "The game, which uses a large number of pebbles (as playing pieces), is a

by one man and is not in the hands of the mob.
There is no one to puff the citizens up with his words,
turning them this way and that for his own advantage:
one instant he's well-liked and gains popularity,
the next he causes ruin; then coming up with new lies,
he hides his earlier failures and gets off unpunished.
Anyway, how could the people, who aren't capable
of reasoning straight, guide a city on a straight course?
A better understanding is reached through time
than in haste. A poor man who toils on the land,
even if he has some education, could not look out
for the common good because he has work to do.[44]
For serious people this is an unhealthy situation,
if a worthless man rises in value by controlling
the people with rhetoric when he comes from dirt.

THESEUS:
Our herald is a braggart and, it seems, an amateur orator.
Well, since you are the one to have initiated the debate,
listen to me: you have set the terms of discussion.
There's nothing more corrosive to society than tyranny,
where, first of all, there are no laws established
for the common good, but one man holds all the power,
becoming a law unto himself. There is no equality.
Where the laws are written, the powerless poor
and the rich have equal justice before the law.[45]
If he is slandered, the less fortunate man can use

---

board having areas marked off in lines. The board is called *polis* ["city," used at 405 and 410]. Each one of the pebbles is a dog (*kuon*). The pebbles are divided into two sets according to their colors. The art of the game is to capture a pebble of the opposite color by hemming it in with two of the same color." Aristotle (*Politics* 1273a7) writes about the person who is *apolis* (cityless) being like an isolated piece in *pessoi*. In performance, one could translate *pessoi* as "chess" or another game of strategy.

44. *420–22:* For an opposite view, on the virtues of the working farmer and the value of his participation in public life, see Euripides, *Orestes* 917–22.

45. *433–34:* For a good summary (with bibliography) on democracy and the written laws, see Morwood's note to line 433 (2007: 178–79); see also Walker (1995: 160–62).

the same words as the one in better circumstances.
The weaker can defeat the stronger if his cause is just.
This is freedom: "Does anyone have a good suggestion
for the city's welfare that he wants to present to the people?"
Whoever chooses to do so is admired; whoever doesn't
is free to remain silent. What is more equitable than this?
And truly when the citizens are a country's masters,
they are happy to count many young people in their ranks.
A man who is king, however, finds this dangerous,
and the best of the citizens—any he thinks are clever—
he puts to death out of suspicion and fear for his power.
How can a city remain strong and secure when
the ruler eradicates enterprise and cuts down
the young like stalks of grain in a spring meadow?[46]
Why should we gain wealth and a livelihood
for our children only to toil for a despot's gain?
Or why bring up our daughters chastely at home
to be playthings for tyrants when they so desire
and get them ready for tragedy? May I end my life
if my children are to be subject to a tyrant's lust.[47]
These words I have aimed in answer to yours.
Tell me, what need has brought you here to our land?
If your city had not sent you, your ugly words would
make you regret the trip. A herald should say his piece
as he has been told and leave with all good speed.
Next time I hope Creon will send a messenger
to our city who is a man of fewer words than you.

CHORUS LEADER:
Ah, ah! When a god gives kind blessings to the evil,
they grow haughty as if they will always be on top.

HERALD:
Now it's my turn to speak. On the points under dispute
you trust in your opinion and I take the opposite view.

---

46. *447–49:* For the story of Thrasybulus, tyrant of Miletus, cutting down the tallest stalks of grain, to signify his elimination of the most prominent citizens, see Herodotus, *Histories* 5.92.

47. *444–55:* On the evils of one-man rule and the lusts of monarchs in general, see Herodotus *Histories* 3.80.2–5.

With the backing of all the people of Thebes, I forbid
you to allow Adrastus to set foot in this country.[48]
If he is already in the land, before the sun goes down,
break up his sacred ritual boughs of supplication
and drive him out. Do not try to take up the bodies
by force, since the city of Argos is no concern of yours.
If you go along with me, you will pilot your city
in calm waters, but otherwise, a great sea swell
of war will rise and overwhelm you and your allies.
Consider carefully and do not, out of irritation
at my words—because you believe your city is free—
puff up with pride and make your answer from weakness.
Hope is faithless: it sets many cities to join in battle
with each other, leading their spirit to deeds of excess.
Whenever war comes up for a vote of the people,
no one any longer figures his own death is imminent;
instead he lays this misfortune off on somebody else.
If death were before their eyes when the vote is cast,
war-crazy Greece would not now be destroying itself.
And yet of the two points of argument, we all know
which is better, both the good and the bad of each,
how much better peace is than war for humankind.
Peace: far and away the Muses' favorite, and enemy
to Retribution,[49] delighted by children growing up,
happy in prosperity. But brushing all this aside
in our delusion, we choose war and we enslave
the weaker, man against man, city against city.
You want to help our enemies—our *dead* enemies—
by taking up for burial men who were destroyed
by their own violence? Isn't it right that Capaneus' body
is still smoking[50] from the thunderbolt when he raised up
ladders to scale our gates and swore that he would
sack our city whether god was willing or not?
And that bird-watching seer, wasn't he swallowed up
when his chariot and team went down into earth's maw?

---

48. *467–75:* The Theban Herald is repeating his instructions from Creon.

49. *489–90:* Peace and Retribution (or Vengeance, in Greek, the *Poinai*) are personified.

50. *496–97:* Capaneus means "Smokey."

And the same for the other warriors lying outside
our gates, their bones crushed to smithereens by stones?
Be confident that you know more than Zeus himself,
or admit that the gods are right to lay low lawless men.
Men with good sense ought to love their children first,[51]
then their parents and country which they should increase
and not shipwreck. A rash commander is as dangerous
as a young sailor. A calm one is skilled when needed.
And this, discretion in a crisis, is the better part of valor.

CHORUS LEADER:
Zeus has already punished them enough.
There is no need to add insult to our loss.

ADRASTUS:
You vile, vile man—

THESEUS:
Be quiet, Adrastus. Hold your tongue.
And do not try to press your case in front of mine.
He has not come here to bring a proclamation for you,
but for me. So it is my prerogative to answer him.
In my response I will take up your first points first:
I did not realize that Creon was my master
and his power was so much greater that he could
compel Athens to do as he commands. Watch the world
spin backward if we are to be pushed around like that.
I am not the one who's bringing on this new war.
I did not go with these men into Cadmus' land either.
I am not trying to do damage to your city, or causing
the kind of struggle that comes at the cost of human life—
but the bodies of the dead—I have the right to bury them,
preserving the law of all Greeks. What is wrong with that?
Whatever you suffered at the hands of the Argives, they

51. *506–7:* In Euripides' *Medea* (328–29) the Corinthian Creon admits to loving his child more than his country, playing into Medea's hands. Is it ironic that the herald of the statist Theban Creon, who is keeping the mothers from their sons, urges Theseus to subordinate country to family? Is it equally ironic that Theseus risks the lives of young Athenians to recover the dead Argive sons?

are dead now. You defended yourselves against your foes
nobly, but disgracefully for them: your claims have been met.
It's time to allow their bodies to be laid to rest in the ground.
Let each of their parts return to that element from
which it came into the light: the spirit into the air,
the body into the earth. For we do not own our body
except to live our life in it and then, when we depart
this life, earth who supported it takes it back again.
Do you think you are hurting Argos by refusing burial?
Well, you are not. This matter concerns all of Greece,
when someone robs the dead of what they deserve to have
and keeps them unburied. Even the bravest soldiers
will turn coward if that custom becomes established.
Have you come here to give me an ultimatum and yet
you are afraid of the dead if they will be laid to rest?
What are you afraid will happen? That if they are buried
they will dig up your land? Or in the depths of the earth
they will father children from whom vengeance will come?
This is a foolish waste of words, yours and mine,
to voice fear of imagined chimeras in your mind.
Listen, you fools, learn the tragedy of human existence:
our lives are a struggle to the end. Some prosper soon,
some later, for others their luck has come and gone.
Fortune is a tease: it is held in the highest regard
by the unfortunate, who want to rise in the world,
and the well-off, afraid luck's favor will leave them,
hold it in high esteem. We know all this and so we must,
when wronged, bear it not with anger but moderation,
and avoid doing what will bring harm upon the city.
What should be done then? Allow us—we just want
to do the right thing—to bury the bodies of the fallen.
Or accept this truth: I shall go and bury them by force.
It will never be published among the Greeks
that when it came down to me and Pandion's city,[52]
then the gods' ancient law was brought to nothing.

CHORUS LEADER:
Take heart. In preserving the light of Justice,
you will avoid the many harsh words of men.

---

52. *562: Pandion's city* is Athens: Pandion was Aegeus' father (see line 7).

HERALD:
May I answer in brief what you have just said?

THESEUS:
Say whatever you wish. You aren't one to hold back.

HERALD:
You will never take the sons of Argos from our land.

THESEUS:
Hear now what I have to say in answer to you.

HERALD:
I'll hear you out, only because it is your turn.

THESEUS:
I shall go to Asopian land and bury the bodies.

HERALD:
First you will have to run the risk of armed combat.

THESEUS:
Before this I have risked undergoing many other labors.

HERALD:
Did your father bring you up to take on all comers?

THESEUS:
Yes, all the insolent. We do not side against the good.

HERALD:
You and your city make a habit of meddling.[53]

THESEUS:
Yes, by being active we achieve many blessings.

---

53. *576:* The Herald says the Athenians are in the habit of "doing a lot" (*prassein polla*): for this the Greeks had the word *polypragmosyne* ("meddlesomeness") which was used to characterize the Athenian foreign policy of intervention (see, for example, Thucydides, *History of the Peloponnesian War* 1.70).

HERALD:
Bring it on. Our spear will catch you at your work.[54]

THESEUS:
What raging army could come from a serpent's teeth?

HERALD:
You will know when you suffer it. You are still young.

THESEUS:
For all your boasts you do not move my heart
to seethe with rage. But depart now from my land,
and take with you the empty words you brought.
We have reached an impasse.

(Herald exits stage left.)

We must muster
every man in arms and men mounted on chariots
and horsemen to drive their steeds, their mouths
dripping with foam, against the land of Cadmus.
I will go right up to the Cadmeians' seven gates
myself, wielding the whetted steel in my hands.
I will act as my own herald. Adrastus, you are
to remain here and not let your fortune get mixed up
with mine. I will lead my army under my own
guiding spirit, fresh with my own fresh spear.[55]
I need one thing only: the gods on my side, all
those who respect what's right. If they are with me,
victory is assured. Manly valor means nothing
to mankind, if they do not have the gods' goodwill.

(Theseus exits stage left.)

---

54. *578:* Literally, "the Sown Men's spear," that is, the army sown from the dragon's teeth (see Euripides, *Phoenician Women* 657–75, 931–35). The manuscript has "will catch you in our city." Another suggestion for the end of the line is "will throw you in the dust."

55. *593:* Or "glorious with my glorious spear" which is the ms. reading, but which sounds too boastful for Theseus who is most proud of his moderation and is corrected in the manuscript by the scribe who penned it.

Second Stasimon[56]

Chorus: *(alternating in two half choruses)*

[Strophe 1]

—Unhappy mothers of unhappy warriors,
I feel green fear rush into my heart!
—What is this new cry of alarm you utter?
—How will the army of Pallas face the crisis?
—Do you mean the sword or exchange of words?
—That would be good. But what if casualties
of war and battles and the noises of breast-beating
will be heard through the city? What words
will be said of me,
the unhappy cause of it all?

[Antistrophe 1]

—A change of luck may turn again on the victor proud
in his success. This brave thought comforts me.
—You speak as if the gods are just.
—Who else deals out our destinies?
—I see many different fates dealt by the gods.
—You are unnerved by the old fears.
Right calls for right, death for death,
and the gods give surcease of sorrows
to all humankind,
holding the end of all that is.

[Strophe 2]

—I wish I could reach the plains with their lofty towers
and leave Callichorus, waters of the goddess.
—If only a god would give you wings.
—I would go to the city between the two rivers.
—You would quickly know the fortunes of our friends.
—What fate, what destiny
is in store for the valiant
king of this land?

---

56. *598–633:* Morwood (2007: 191) suggests that one half of the chorus "expresses fearful mistrust of the gods, while the other . . . is more confident of success."

[Antistrophe 2]

—Again we invoke the gods invoked before.
—In our fear they are our foremost trust.
—Oh Zeus, father of Inachus,
born from the heifer, our ancient mother.
—Be a gracious ally to this city.
—Your prize,
bulwark of the city, outraged bodies,
bring them to the pyre.

Third Episode

(Messenger enters stage left.)

MESSENGER:
Women, I have come here with good news to tell.
I have myself been rescued; for I was taken
captive in the battle that the seven dead leaders
waged beside the waters of the river Dirce.
I bring news of Theseus' victory. I will save you
the trouble of asking: I was lieutenant to Capaneus
who was burnt to ashes by Zeus' fiery lightning.

CHORUS LEADER:
Dear, dear man. The news of your homecoming
is welcome and your words about Theseus. If the army
of Athens is out of harm's way, all your news is good.

MESSENGER:
Yes, it is unharmed and has succeeded as Adrastus
should have done when he led the expedition
of the Argives from the river Inachus to Cadmus' city.

CHORUS LEADER:
How then did Aegeus' son and those who wielded
the spear with him set up the trophy to Zeus? Tell us.
You were there; we were not. You can lift our spirits.

MESSENGER:
The sun's bright rays, morning's clear sign
fell on the land. I stood by the Electra gate
to watch from a tower with a panoramic view.
What I saw was three divisions of the army;[57]
the infantry in full battle gear stretching up
to the hill called the Ismenion after the river god,
and the king himself, Aegeus' renowned son,
and those with him, deployed on the right flank,
men native to the ancient land of Cecrops;[58]
the contingent from the coast,[59] armed with the spear
right by the spring of Ares; and the cavalry
deployed on both the edges of the army;
equal in number, the chariots were stationed
in the shadow of Amphion's sacred monument.
The people of Cadmus stood in front of their walls,
behind them the bodies they were fighting over.
Horsemen were arrayed in arms against horsemen,
chariots with their teams deployed against chariots.
Theseus' herald proclaimed to all assembled:
"Be silent, people, armies of Cadmus, in silence
hear me. We have come for the bodies; our purpose is
to give them burial, protecting the law of all Greeks.
It is not our wish to prolong the bloodshed."[60]
In answer to this Creon heralded not a word,
but stood silent in arms.
The masters of chariots,
all with four-horse teams, then began the battle,
driving the chariots up past the opposing line
so their spearmen were in striking position.
They battled with javelins while the drivers turned

---

57. *653:* That is, three divisions of the Athenian army.

58. *658:* Cecrops is a mythical Athenian king.

59. *659:* The word in Greek translated "contingent from the coast" is *Paralos* ("by the sea"). Does it refer to the Paraloi, the coastal population of Attica or to Paralos, the eponymous Athenian hero, for whom they were said to be named?

60. *669–72:* I do not see this as a last-minute bid for peace, but a pro forma offer that is really a declaration of war. Theseus had said (590) he would be his own herald, that is, he arrives with his troops heralding war.

the horses around in defense of the fighters.
Phorbas,[61] who was commander of the Athenian
cavalry, sighting the confused mass of chariots
and those who marshaled the Theban horsemen
joined in the fray, advancing, then falling back.
I saw this for myself and did not just hear it later.
I was there when the chariots and riders struggled.
I saw the many casualties as they happened;
I don't know what to describe first—the dust
that rose up to the sky, how it engulfed everything,
or the men tangled in the reins being dragged
up and down, and the streams of blood and gore
of men tumbling down and chariots being shattered;
the men were tossed head over heels to the ground
and lost their lives in the wreckage of the chariots.
When Creon surmised our side had the upper hand
with cavalry and chariots, he took up his shield and tore
into the fray before desperation could overcome his men.
Nor was Theseus' side broken through any hesitation,
but snatching up his shining armor he attacked at once.
In the midst of the whole army, weapons clashing,
they killed, they were killed; and with a great shout
they passed along rallying commands through the ranks:
"Strike!" "Hold your spear firm against the Athenians!"
Their army, of men reared up from the serpent's teeth,
was a fierce opponent. Our left flank was collapsing,
but theirs was being beaten back by our right wing
and was trying to retreat. The contest was well-matched.
In this, too, our commander-in-chief deserved praise:
for he was not content with achieving this success,
but he went wherever the army was struggling
and let out a cry that caused the earth to resound:
"My men, if your cannot hold back the strong spear
of these Sown men, the Athenian cause is lost."
Courage filled the spirits of the Athenian army.[62]

---

61. *680:* Phorbas was a tutor of Theseus who taught him how to drive a chariot.

62. *713:* The Athenian army is called *Cranaid* in the Greek after a mythical ancient king Cranaus ("Rocky" or "Cliff").

Theseus himself, taking up his Epidaurian weapon,[63]
a monstrous club—he swung it back and forth,
like a sling, hitting necks and heads at once,
mowing off helmets, snapping them with its bulk.
They couldn't take to their heels and retreat fast enough.
As for me, I cried out for joy and danced a victory jig
and clapped my hands. They struggled for their gates.
Weeping and wailing was heard through the city
of young, of old as they crowded the temples
in their terror. Though he could have breached
their walls, Theseus held back: "I have not come
to destroy your city," he called, "but to reclaim the dead."
This is the kind of man who should be chosen
as commander: one courageous in a crisis with a strong
aversion to arrogant people who, when they do well,
are so eager to reach the topmost rung of the ladder
that they lose the success they could have enjoyed.[64]

Chorus Leader:
Today, seeing this unexpected outcome, I trust
again in the gods' existence, and I feel my troubles
are diminished, now that they have paid the price.

Adrastus:
Oh Zeus! Why do people claim that wretched
mortals use reason? We are dependent on you,
and how we fare is whatever you want to happen.
In our minds Argos was invincible: we had strength
of numbers and our arms were young and strong.
When Eteocles was trying to negotiate a truce,[65]

---

63. *714:* Periphetes of Epidaurus was one of a series of bandits Theseus killed on his way to Athens. Periphetes used a huge bronze club which Theseus took for his own use.

64. *726–30:* This part of the messenger's speech is addressed to Adrastus (see deJong 1991: 191–92, and Morwood 2007: 200, note to line 726–27), who has been on stage throughout, visible to the audience but perhaps forgotten by readers.

65. *739:* Eteocles' effort at conciliation may be a Euripidean invention for this particular context.

offering moderate terms, we turned him down,
and so we were defeated. Their side in turn was lucky,
and like a poor man suddenly coming into wealth
grew arrogant. Their arrogance in turn ruined them,
those malicious people of Cadmus. Foolish men,
you stretched the bow beyond the mark and suffered,
as you deserved, one disaster after another.
You cities, do not listen to friends, but yield to
circumstances. When you are able to deflect disaster
through diplomacy you choose death over reason.
But what is the point?

(To Messenger)

I want you to tell me this:[66]
how did you escape? Then I'll have more to ask.

MESSENGER:
When the confusion of war entered the city
I walked out the gate by which the army came in.

ADRASTUS:
The cause they fought for—have you got the bodies?

MESSENGER:
Yes, all those who commanded the seven contingents.

ADRASTUS:
How so? And what of the remaining masses of dead?

MESSENGER:
They have been buried beside the glens of Cithairon.

ADRASTUS:
On this side or the other? Who was it that buried them?

---

66. *750–71:* Messengers usually leave immediately after delivering their news. It is unusual for a messenger's speech to continue with a passage of stichomythia (alternating lines by two speakers).

MESSENGER:
Theseus did, this side, on the shady cliff of Eleutherae.[67]

ADRASTUS:
The bodies he has not buried, where did you leave them?

MESSENGER:
Nearby. What we won with ardent effort is here at hand.[68]

ADRASTUS:
Were servants disgusted to carry them from the massacre?

MESSENGER:
No one who was a slave was assigned this task.

ADRASTUS:
. . . .[69]

MESSENGER:
You'd say so if you had been there when he tended the bodies.

ADRASTUS:
He washed the wounds of the poor wretches himself?

MESSENGER:
Yes, and he laid them out on the biers and covered them.

ADRASTUS:
It was a terrible burden, and one that brings shame.

---

67. *759: Eleutherae* is a Boeotian village near the Boeotian border that defected to Attica. It is associated with Dionysus Eleuthereus (Dionysus Liberator) whose priest had the seat of honor at the theater of Dionysus.

68. *761:* Morwood (2007: 99) translates, "the object of all your efforts is near completion."

69. *763:* A line is missing. Perhaps something like "Really? Theseus showed them that much respect?" (see Collard 1975: 303, note to line 763; and Morwood 2007: 203).

MESSENGER:
There is no shame in sharing one another's troubles.

ADRASTUS:
Ah me! I wish to god I had met my death with them!

MESSENGER:
Your lament is useless, and you are making the women cry.

ADRASTUS:
Yes, you're right. They are the ones who are my teachers.
I will go and raise my hands in greeting to the dead
and pour forth tearful dirges of death, addressing
friends of whom I am left bereft in my grief,
I weep for their loss. Lost wealth can be won back,
but this loss alone for mortals, once it is spent,
can never be recovered, the breath that gives us life.

(Messenger exits stage right; Adrastus exits stage left.)

Third Stasimon

CHORUS:

[Strophe 1]

Some good news, some sad—
glorious victory for this city
and honor for the men at arms
are shared by both city and soldiers.
And for me, to see the limbs of my child
stings my heart, and yet is a longed-for sight, if I will see it,
looking upon a day I never wished for,
the greatest grief of all.

[Antistrophe 1]

I wish ancient father time
had left me forever unwed
up to this day.
Why did I have to have children?
I expect I would have suffered

so terribly if I had been uncoupled from marriage.[70]
And now I see the most naked evil of all
the loss of my dear, dear sons.

Fourth Episode

(Adrastus enters stage left with an entourage bearing the bodies.)

First Kommos[71]

—Ah, now I see the bodies brought here
of my lost sons. Oh sorrow!
I wish I could die with my children,
going down in a common death.

[Strophe 1]

ADRASTUS:
Mothers, sound the lament
for the dead going into the ground
keening in response,
hearing my lamentation.

CHORUS:
—My children, how bitter this farewell
from loving mothers,
I speak to you, dead and gone.

ADRASTUS:
Woe, woe.

---

70. *790–91:* Difficult lines. Collard (1975: 26) renders "I would have expected that to be the extreme suffering, if I had lost my husband. . . ." Morwood (2007: 101) translates, "For what extreme suffering would I have been expecting to endure if I had abstained from marriage?" A director might choose, "if I had lost my husband," or "if I'd never married," or perhaps one half of the chorus saying each in turn.

71. *794:* A *kommos* is a lament sung by the chorus and one or more actors.

CHORUS:
Woe for my sorrows.

ADRASTUS:
Woe, woe!

CHORUS:
. . . .

ADRASTUS:
We have suffered. Oh!

CHORUS:
Most shameful, groveling grief.

ADRASTUS:
Oh city of Argos, do you not look upon my fate?

CHORUS:
—They see us, the sorrowful
childless mothers of dead children.

[Antistrophe 1]

ADRASTUS:
Bring forward the bloody
bodies of the ill-fated dead,
slaughtered unworthily by an unworthy foe
among whom the contest was fought.

CHORUS:
—Let me hold my children
close in my embrace.
Let me put my arms around them.

ADRASTUS:
Here they are for you.

CHORUS:
A heavy burden of grief.

ADRASTUS:
Ah me!

CHORUS:
Have you nothing to say for the parents' grief?

ADRASTUS:
You hear me.

CHORUS:
You keen for us both.

ADRASTUS:
I wish the ranks of the Cadmeians had laid me low in the dust.

CHORUS:
—I wish I had never been coupled
to a man in wedlock.

[Epode]

ADRASTUS:
Look on the ocean of sorrows,
unhappy mothers of children.

CHORUS:
—We have furrowed our flesh with our nails
and poured ashes on our heads.

ADRASTUS:
Ah me, ah me!
I wish the earth would swallow me up.
I wish a whirlwind would tear me to pieces.
I wish the flame of Zeus would crash through my head.

CHORUS:
—Bitter the marriages you have seen.
Bitter the oracle of Phoebus.
The Fury full of grief
has left the house of Oedipus deserted,
has come now to haunt you.

(Theseus enters, stage left.)

THESEUS: *(To Adrastus)*
I had it in mind to question you as you poured out
your grief before the army, but held off. Since I let
the tale pass then, now I look to Adrastus for answers.
How did it happen that these men were so outstanding
in courage? Since you knew them better, speak
to the young citizens here. You have the knowledge.
For I saw their acts of courage by which they expected
to capture the city were greater than words can tell.
One thing I will not ask you, so you will not laugh at me:
which opponent each of them faced in battle,
or whose was the spear that brought him down.
These are worthless words both for the listeners
and the speaker. When a man is in the heat of battle,
when spears are flying thick and fast before his eyes,
how could he report which of the warriors was brave?
I could neither ask such a question and, if anybody
had the gall to tell such things, I would not believe him.
It's hard enough for anyone to see what he has to
when he is standing to face an enemy in battle.

ADRASTUS:
Hear me now. I welcome the opportunity
you offer me to give the dead their due and say
what is true and genuine in eulogy of my friends.[72]

---

72. *857–917:* Pindar (*Olympian* 6.12–17) tells of Adrastus eulogizing Amphiareus, whom he calls "the eye of my army" (16) at the funeral for the Seven. The meaning of Adrastus' Funeral Oration has been much discussed. In view of these men's reputations for violence and excess and the failure of the ill-considered expedition, is the speech ironic? Or is it a positive part of the education of the young citizens, which is a theme in the play? Or perhaps it is more neutral, a traditional part of the funeral rite and a recognition of the warriors' martial valor. Most of what Adrastus says is similar to the clichés mouthed by the "friends and neighbors" of fallen soldiers that we hear today. For that reason I think all three views may apply: the speech is Euripidean and it is tragic. For a brief and useful summary of opinions see Morwood's comments on lines 857–917 (2007: 209–10).

You see the man struck by the fiery lightning bolt?
This is Capaneus. He had a prosperous life,
but was never uppity about his wealth; in fact he had
no more self-importance than a man of slight means,
avoiding anyone at the sumptuous table who was
overbearing or disrespected moderation. Good, he said,
lay not in gluttony, but moderation was enough.
To his friends he was a true friend whether they were
by his side or far away. Not many people are like that.
He didn't know how to tell a lie, though in conversation
he was good-natured. He made good his obligations
to his household and fellow citizens.[73] My second subject
is Eteoclus, who was practiced in another kind of virtue:
he was a young man of very limited means,
but he had held many honors in the land of Argos.
Though his friends often tried to enhance his wealth,
he did not accept it into his home, to avoid
becoming its slave by taking on the burden of riches.
Those who misruled incurred his hatred, but not the city
itself, since he felt the city was not to blame if it came
into disrepute because of a failed leader.
The third is Hippomedon. His character was like this:
from childhood he had no heart for indulging
in the pleasures of the Muses and the easy life,
but living in the country, he was eager to strengthen
his physique to manly hardness, going to the hunt,
exercising his horses, stretching the bow in his hands,
because he wanted to make his body useful to the state.
Next is Parthenopaeus, the son of the huntress
Atalanta; the handsomest man of his generation,
he was an Arcadian, but he came to Inachus' streams
and was brought up in Argos. When he came of age,
first, as becomes outsiders who are guests in a country,
he was not prickly or offensive to the citizens,
nor was he given to divisive speech, which makes
a citizen or an alien especially annoying.

---

73. *870–71:* Here I follow the manuscript reading. Some editors choose to emend to "he was in no way excessive." It is important to say this, since Capaneus vowed to scale the city walls with or without the gods' will, but it has already been said at 862–66.

He entered the ranks as if he were a native son
and defended the country. Whenever the city did well
he was happy, but took it hard when we suffered a loss.
[He had many lovers and was popular with women too,
but was careful never to cause any hard feelings.[74]]
My great esteem for Tydeus I shall put in few words:
he was not flashy in speech, but a skilled craftsman
in the practice of war, lethal to men of lesser skill.
[Though he was no match intellectually for his brother
Meleager, he attained equal fame by his skill in battle.
He made an exact science of the military arts.
His nature was ambitious for honor, and his intelligence
was rich in deeds but not equally so in words.][75]
From these words, then, do not be surprised,
Theseus, that these men dared to die before the towers.
Noble upbringing carries a lifelong sense of respect,
and any man who is practiced in goodness
is ashamed to be a coward. Valor can indeed be taught
if it is true that even an infant is taught to speak
and to hear words that he cannot yet understand.
What a person learns he is likely to keep until he is old.
For that reason, take care in bringing up your children.

CHORUS:
Oh, my child, I reared you
to die young; I carried you under my heart
enduring the pangs of childbirth.
And now Hades has taken
the fruit of my ill-fated labor.
I do not have you to tend my old age:
to my sorrow I once had a son.

THESEUS:
The noble son of Oecles—the gods snatched him
still alive into the depths of the earth with his chariot

---

74. *899–900:* Many editors believe these lines are an interpolation on grounds of propriety, appropriateness, and usage.

75. *901–8:* Some lines (904–6) may have been inserted from another play of Euripides; others (907–8) may be an actor's inflation or the work of a lesser poet (see Collard 1975: 45 and his notes to the text at 907–8).

and team of four, a blessing clear for all to see.
The son of Oedipus, I'm talking about Polynices:
we wouldn't be false in lauding him to the skies.
He was my guest-friend after he left Cadmus' city
in exile, before he chose to settle in Argos. Now,
do you know what I would like you to do with them?

ADRASTUS:
All I know is I must assent to your request.

THESEUS:
Capaneus, the one struck by Zeus' thunderbolt . . .

ADRASTUS:
Do you want to bury him apart as a sacred corpse?

THESEUS:
Yes, but all the rest are to lie on the same pyre.

ADRASTUS:
Where will you place the monument set apart for him?

THESEUS:
Here, I will build up a tomb beside this temple.

ADRASTUS:
This is a task that slaves can take care of.

THESEUS:
And these will be my care. Let the bodies come forward.

ADRASTUS:
Come, grieving mothers, approach your sons.

THESEUS:
Oh no, no. What you have just said is not right.

ADRASTUS:
What? Shouldn't mothers touch their sons' bodies?

THESEUS:
They would die if they saw their sons so mutilated.[76]

ADRASTUS:
Yes, it's painful to see gore and disfigurement of the dead.

THESEUS:
So, then, why do you suggest adding to their grief?

ADRASTUS:
You're right. You must endure to stay there. Theseus
has the right idea. After we put the remains on the pyre
you will take away their bones. Oh wretched mortals,
why do you take up spears and inflict bloodshed
on each other? Give it up, I tell you. Cease your toils
and keep your cities at peace with peaceful neighbors.
Life's necessities are small. We should pass through
them as simply as possible, without taking on added labors.

(Theseus and Adrastus exit with the Chorus of Children stage right.)

Fourth Stasimon

CHORUS:

[Strophe]

—A happy mother, no more,
no more a mother at all. I have no share
in the happiness of Argive mothers, mothers of sons.
Artemis, helper of birthing,
has no words for the childless.
Life is not worth living.
Like a cloud I flutter,
tossed by wintry winds.

76. *944:* Worry about a mother's distress over her son's mutilated flesh is central to Kevin Powers' *The Yellow Birds: A Novel* (2012, Chapter 10); see Translator's Note.

[Antistrophe]

—Seven unhappy mothers
we gave birth to seven
sons, noblest among the Argives.
And now without a child, without a son,
I grow old in ceaseless misery,
counted not among the dead,
not among the living—
my fate is apart from theirs.

[Epode]

—Tears are left to me.
In my home lie
sad memories of my son,
hair cut in mourning, crowns for festivals,[77]
<libations for the dear departed dead,>[78]
and songs, though not the kind golden-haired
Apollo is glad to hear.
Waking to sounds of grief,
I wet the folds of my robes,
on my breast, drenched with tears.

Fifth Episode

(Evadne appears on the rooftop,
wearing her wedding dress.)

CHORUS:
—Here I see the covered chamber
of Capaneus and his sacred tomb
outside the temple,
Theseus' offerings to the dead,

---

77. *973:* Since crowns or garlands are not used for funerals, some editors prefer a change to "ungarlanded hair."

78. Between lines 974 and 975 an earlier editor inserted a line from Plutarch, who quotes Euripides' *Suppliants* lines 975–76 with this line included. It seems to have been skipped by the scribe. When written in capitals the first words of both lines are very similar.

and, look up there, near the man killed by the lightning bolt,
his noble wife Evadne,
daughter of Iphis the king.
Why is she standing on the towering rock
that looms over the temple,
moving along the path?

[Strophe]

EVADNE:
What light, what brilliance
the sun conveyed
and the moon bright in the sky,
where swift stars
shoot through the dark,[79]
when at my wedding
the town of Argos
towered up songs
and blessings and praised the bridegroom,
Capaneus, armed in bronze.
To you I have come rushing
like a Bacchant from my home,
seeking the pyre's flame
and the same tomb,
in death to end my painful life
and the sadness of living.
Sweetest is this death,
to die with my dead lover,
if destiny will allow it.

CHORUS:
And truly near where you are standing you can
see his pyre, Zeus' reliquary, where your husband
lies, struck down by the thundering flames.

---

79. *993–94:* Collard (1975: 363–64) calls these lines a *locus desperatus* (a hopeless passage). The manuscript has "where swift Nymphs ride the light through darkness." Others suggest a reference to the wedding torches and the bridal carriage (that brought the bride to her new home).

[Antistrophe]

EVADNE:
I see my journey end
here where I stand. Fortune
joins her footsteps with mine.
For glory's sake I hurried here to leap
from this cliff
onto the pyre
to meld my body
into the bright flame
with my husband's, my loving
flesh lying with his flesh,
I will go down to Persephone's chamber,
beneath the earth. Never by prolonging my life
will I betray your death.
Life, marriage, farewell!
Let births of children bring brightness to
other loving unions, sung of in Argos.[80]
Here a wedded husband
is fused by guileless winds of love
to his generous wife.

(Iphis enters stage left.)

CHORUS LEADER:
Look, your own father is coming here, the aged Iphis,
into this strange exchange of words, which will add
to his grief when he hears things he never imagined.

IPHIS:
Unhappy women, I have come, a sad old man,
nursing in my heart a double grief for my children,
to convey my dead son home, Eteoclus, slain by

80. *1026–27:* The text is corrupt. Since Evadne is recalling her wedding, it has been suggested that the verses recall words that might be sung in the wedding songs (see Collard 1975: 372–73). Toher (2001: 339) explains the passage by saying, "There will be other child-producing marriages in Argos; she however will remain loyal to her husband." Evadne is thus rejecting a second marriage and "her duty" to the community.

the Theban spear, into the land of his fathers,
and hoping to find my daughter who is gone
in a frenzy from her home, the wife of Capaneus.
She is struck by a longing to lie dead with her husband.
Earlier we kept her closely watched in the house.
But when I let down my guard in the present troubles
and left her unattended, she bolted. I think it very
likely she is here. Tell me if you have seen her.

EVADNE:
Why question them? Here I am on this cliff
like a bird hovering above Capaneus' pyre, Father.
In my despair I feel weightless on this height.[81]

IPHIS:
My child, what ill breeze, what wanderlust, oh why
did you steal away from your home and come here?

EVADNE:
You would become angry with me if you heard
my reasons. I don't want to tell you, Father.

IPHIS:
What's this? Doesn't your father have a right to know?

EVADNE:
No, you would not be a wise judge of my thinking.

IPHIS:
Why have you dressed yourself in this costume?[82]

EVADNE:
My dress means to bring me my share of glory, Father.

---

81. *1045–47:* Iphis did not look up at first. We might be reminded of Jason's final entrance in Euripides' *Medea*, looking for Medea and his children. Medea upstages his final entrance with her own, from the machine, from which she addresses him (1317).

82. *1054:* It is likely that Evadne is wearing her wedding dress.

IPHIS:
You do not look as if you are in mourning for your husband.

EVADNE:
I am dressed for something wonderful and new.

IPHIS:
And yet you are appearing beside his pyre and tomb.

EVADNE:
I have come here for my own glorious victory.

IPHIS:
What victory will you win? You must tell me this.

EVADNE:
I will surpass all women under the eye of the sun.

IPHIS:
In the crafts of Athena or in the mind's good sense?

EVADNE:
In my heart's courage. I will lie in death with my husband.

IPHIS:
What are you saying? What do you mean by this crazy riddle?

EVADNE:
I will leap onto my dead Capaneus' pyre.

IPHIS:
My dear daughter, do not tell this story in public.[83]

EVADNE:
That is just what I want, for all the Argives to know.

---

83. *1066–67:* Respectable women are not to be talked about outside the home: see Pericles' Funeral Oration in Thucydides, *History of the Peloponnesian War* (2.45.2) and many proverbial sayings. Evadne, however, like Antigone, wants her glorious deed to be known (Sophocles, *Antigone* 84–87).

IPHIS:
No, I will never allow you to do this drastic deed.

EVADNE:
It doesn't matter. You will never catch me in your arms.
And now I let my body plummet—not to your liking,
but to mine and my dead husband's who will burn with me.

(Evadne leaps onto the pyre behind the stage building.)

CHORUS LEADER:
Ah! Woman, you have done something awful.

IPHIS:
Oh, my grief. I am ruined. Oh, women of Argos.

CHORUS LEADER:
Ah, ah. You have suffered cruelly.
To your grief you see the awful daring of this deed.

IPHIS:
You could not find an unhappier man in all the world.

CHORUS LEADER:
Yes, your life is tragic.
You have had your share of Oedipus' luck,
you, along with my unhappy city.

IPHIS:
Oh god. Why can't humans have a second chance,
to be young twice and in time to be old again?
If something doesn't turn out well in our homes,
we can make it right by understanding we gain after.
But this is not possible in life. If we were young
twice and then old, if a person made a mistake,
we could fix it with our gift of second life.
Look at me. I saw other men who had children
and I wanted to be a father. Desire was ruining my life.
If I had been there; if I had had the experience of
what it is like for a father to lose his children,
I would never have come into the grief I feel now.

I, who fathered a son and was parent to the best,
most wonderful young man, have lost him now.
There it is. What should I do, a devastated man like me?
Go home? And then I would look at the empty rooms
of my house, so many of them, and nowhere to go?
Or should I go to the house of Capaneus here?
I loved to go there when my daughter was alive.
She is gone now, too. She used to kiss my cheek,
take my head in her hands every time I came over.
There's nothing that gives a father greater pleasure,
when he is old, than a daughter. Our sons' natures
are high-spirited, not as sweet or affectionate as theirs.
Will you not take me with all haste to my home?
Hide me in the darkness where my aged body can
waste away in starvation until I finally shuffle off.
What comfort will it be to touch my child's ashes?
Old age, you have gotten the best of me. Now I have you
how I hate you. I despise those who desire to prolong
their lives with foods and drinks and magic spells,
trying to reverse nature's course and avoid death.
Since they are a burden to the earth, they should
pass away in death and make room for the young.

(Iphis exits stage left.)

Second Kommos

(Children enter stage right carrying the urns.)

CHORUS:
Woe, woe! Here are the bones,
bones of our dead boys. Hold me up, servants,
hold up this weak old woman—my grief
leaves no strength in me—
I have lived too many lengths of time,
shed my tears in too many sorrows.
What greater sorrow could you find
among mortals than this
than to live to see your children in the grave?

[Strophe 1]

CHILDREN:
I'm bringing them, I'm bringing them,
unhappy mother, my father's bones from the pyre,
a weight made heavier from grief;
all I have is squeezed into this tiny space.

CHORUS:
Woe, woe!
Why do you bring tears to the loving
mother of the dead?
A tiny bit of dust instead of their bodies
once glorious in Mycenae?[84]

[Antistrophe 1]

CHILDREN:
Childless, you are childless.
But to my sorrow I have lost my unlucky father,
and I will live in a house empty and fatherless,
not held in my father's arms.

CHORUS:
Woe, woe! Where is the toil for my children,
where the loving return for childbirth?
Mother's worries and the cares of sleepless eyes,
loving kisses on their faces?

[Strophe 2]

CHILDREN:
They are gone, no more alive. Ah me, Father.
They are gone.

CHORUS:
The sky holds them now,
burnt to dust on the pyre,
they have flitted off to Hades.

84. *1131:* Mycenae and Argos are used interchangeably in tragedy.

CHILDREN:
Father, do you hear your children's keening?
Will I one day take up a shield to avenge
your death, Father? I pray it will happen.

[Antistrophe 2]

CHILDREN:
If god wills it, vengeance will
come for my father.

CHORUS:
The sorrow does not yet sleep.
Woe, woe, in lamentation. Enough destiny,
enough grief is mine today.

CHILDREN:
The bright water of Asopus will welcome me
in bronze armor at the head of an army of Danaans,
righteous avenger of my father.

[Strophe 3]

CHILDREN:
I think I see you still before my eyes, Father.

CHORUS:
Planting a loving kiss on your cheek.

CHILDREN:
Your consoling words
are blown away in the winds.

CHORUS:
For us both he has left pain, for his mother,
and grief for your father will never leave you.

[Antistrophe 3]

CHILDREN:
I bear so heavy a burden that it is killing me.

CHORUS:
Come, let me take the ashes to my breast.

CHILDREN:
These words of yours bring tears to my eyes.
It's so sad, it breaks my heart.

CHORUS:
My son, you are gone. Now I will never see you
any more, precious darling boy of your loving mother.

Exodos

THESEUS:
Adrastus and you women, natives of Argos,
you see these children bearing in their arms
the bodies of their heroic fathers that I recovered.
I bestow them as a gift upon you, I and the city.
You must be ever mindful of this and keep
gratitude in your hearts, seeing how I acted for you,
and repeat these same words to your children
to honor this city, and to their children's children,
passing down the tradition of how you were treated.
Zeus be our witness along with the heavenly gods
of what you received from us as you go on your way.

ADRASTUS:
Theseus, we are aware of all the good you have done
to benefit the land of Argos in our need, and we will have
eternal gratitude toward you. We have experienced
your noble generosity and owe you a like return.

THESEUS:
Is there any other way I can be of service to you?

ADRASTUS:
Farewell, for you and your city are worthy.

THESEUS:
So it will be. And may you have the same good fortune.

(Athena appears above on the rooftop.)

ATHENA:
Hear, Theseus, these words spoken by Athena,
which you must heed, and if you do you will prosper.
Do not give the bones to these children to carry
into the land of Argos, letting them go so easily,
but in return for your hardships and those of the city,
first take an oath. This oath Adrastus must swear;
he holds sway, and as master of all the territory
of the Danaans, it is up to him to take the oath.
This is to be the oath: "Never will the Argives bring
hostile troops in armor into this land; if others
attack they will deploy their army to oppose them.
If, abandoning their oath, they come against our city,
the land of the Argives will perish utterly in return."
In what vessel you must slay the victims, I will tell you:
there is within the halls a tripod with bronze feet,
which, after he had overthrown the foundations of Troy,
and before starting out on another adventure, Heracles
commanded you to set up at the Pythian hearth.
On this, first cut the three throats of three sheep,
and then inscribe the oath in the hollow belly
of the tripod and give it to the god who oversees Delphi
as a memorial of the oath and a witness to Greece.
The sharp-bladed knife with which you carry out
the sacrifices and draw their blood, bury it in the depths
of the earth beside the pyres where the seven bodies are burnt.
The sight of it will strike fear in them if ever they come
against the city and cause them a tragic homecoming.
Once this is done the urns may be carried out of our land.
Where the bodies were purified by fire, keep that place
as a sacred precinct, just by the turn-off to the Isthmus.
That is all I have to say to you, but to the sons of Argos:
when you reach manhood you will sack the city
of Ismenus, avenging the deaths of your slain fathers;
you, Aigialeus,[85] as a young man, in your father's place,

85. *1216:* Aigialeus was the son of Adrastus (and so, not strictly one of the sons of the seven slain warriors). He did lead the Epigonoi and was the only one to die at Thebes.

will be commander of the army, and the son of Tydeus,
called Diomedes by his father, will come from Aetolia.
But you must not delay, once the beard shadows your jaw,
to deploy the bronze-armed forces of Danaans
against the seven-gated battlements of Thebes.
To their regret you will come upon them, reared up
as the cubs of these lions, for the overthrow of their city.
There is no other way. "Avenging Sons"[86] you will be
called through Greece in songs for future generations.
So great an army you will bring, with god on your side.

THESEUS:

Queen Athena, I will obey your words.
You keep me in the right so I do not miss the mark.
I will bind him with oaths. Only guide me right,
for if you are propitious to our city,
our future is assured for all time to come.

(Theseus exits stage right.)

CHORUS:

Let us go, Adrastus, let us swear the oath
to this man and city. It is only right that
we honor those who have toiled for us.

(The Chorus, Adrastus, and Chorus of Children exit stage right.)[87]

---

86. *1224: Epigonoi*, "the Afterborn," "the Next Generation."

87. *1234:* Possibly they all exit following Theseus to take the oath. Or Adrastus (with or without the Chorus of Children) follows Theseus and the Chorus(es) go home stage left.

EURIPIDES

Phoenician Women[1]

1. *Title*: The Greek name of *Phoenician Women* is *Phoenissae* (traditional Latin spelling) or *Phoinissai* (transliterated Greek): it is named after the chorus of captive women from Tyre, who happened to be caught behind enemy lines inside Thebes when it came under siege by the Argives and their allies.

Cast of Characters

Jocasta	wife and mother of Oedipus
Paidagogos	servant, attendant to Antigone
Antigone	daughter of Jocasta and Oedipus
Chorus	young Phoenician Women
Polynices	exiled son of Jocasta and Oedipus
Eteocles	king of Thebes, son of Jocasta and Oedipus
Creon	brother of Jocasta
Tiresias	famous Theban seer (with his daughter, a non-speaking role)
Menoeceus	son of Creon
Messenger 1	Eteocles' lieutenant
Messenger 2	
Oedipus	former king of Thebes, son and husband of Jocasta

The play was first performed at the Greater Dionysia around 410 BCE.

Phoenician Women

SCENE: *The setting is the palace of Cadmus at Thebes. The city is under siege. It is morning of the day of the battle of the Argives against the Thebans (known as the War of the Seven against Thebes). Stage right leads to the town and stage left to the battlefield.*

Prologue[2]

Scene 1 (Jocasta's monologue)

(Enter Jocasta from the palace. She is dressed in black and her white hair is cut in mourning.)

JOCASTA:
Morning sun, on swift steeds pulling out the daylight,[3]
it was a tragic day for Thebes when you sent down

---

2. The prologue is the part of the play before the entrance of the chorus. Euripides usually begins his plays with a monologue by one of the characters (as in *Medea* and *Electra*) or by a god (as in *Alcestis* and *Hippolytus*). A character usually enters from the *skēnē* (stage-building) and identifies it, here as the house of Cadmus. What slice of the epic banquet is being offered here? In most plays this monologue is followed by a dialogue, as here. This kind of monologue, which gives the back story and situates us (the audience/reader) in the legend, has been called "the Playbill prologue." Through selection, juxtaposition, choice of words, and parallel actions it also alerts us to the themes in the particular showing and telling of the story being staged. Although the tragedians used traditional material, each reworking of a myth or legend is a unique combination of innovation and convention.

3. *3:* The translation begins at line 3 because the first two lines in the manuscript are deleted by most editors as too pretentious:
Cutting a roadway through the sky among the stars, mounted aboard your gold embellished chariot . . . (1–2) Her address to the rising sun indicates the time of day, confirmed in the next scene in which Antigone and her slave discuss what they see in the early dawn light.

your rays, the day that Cadmus[4] reached this land
crossing from Phoenicia's island in the sea.[5]
Cadmus married Harmonia, Cypris' daughter,[6]
and fathered Polydorus.[7] From him they say
Labdacus was born, and from him came Laios;
this is where I come in. I am Menoeceus' daughter[8]
—and Creon is my brother, my own mother's son—
they call me Jocasta, a name my father
gave me. Laios became my husband. But when
he was childless after years of marriage to me,
he went to question Phoebus' oracle[9]
and ask for male children to carry on his line.
The god intoned,[10] "King of Thebes, keeper of fine horses,
do not try to plant a crop[11] of children against gods' will,
for if you father a child, he that is born will kill you
and your whole house will wade in its own blood."

---

4. *5: Cadmus*, descendant of Zeus and Io, brother of Europa, was the legendary founder and first king of Thebes, and patriarch of the line from Polydorus through the sons of Oedipus. The long history of Thebes is the *chronos* (time as a block) in which the *kairos* (the critical time) takes place. For Jocasta it is compressed into a series of special days of passage for the members of the ruling family: Cadmus' literal passage to Thebes, marriages, births, comings of age, and deaths. These are the historical events that are enumerated to mark special days off from every span between sunrise and sunset.

5. *6:* Literally, *sea-girt Phoenicia*: Cadmus came from Tyre, an island city of Phoenicia (joined to the mainland by Alexander; now Soúr in Lebanon). Through Jocasta, Euripides makes the Phoenician connection stronger than in other Theban tragedies.

6. *7: Cypris*: a name for Aphrodite, the *Cyprian*, so called because she came forth from the sea foam on Cyprus. Ares was the father of Harmonia.

7. *8–9:* The succession of kings of Thebes, after Cadmus.

8. *10:* It was a common practice to name a son after his grandfather. Creon's son, who has a part in this play, is named Menoeceus.

9. *15:* Phoebus, a name for Apollo; Laios went to the famous oracle in Delphi.

10. *17:* See the Introduction for a comparison of the oracles given to Laios in the Theban plays.

11. *18:* In Greek, one speaks of "sowing" a woman's body.

But he gave in to pleasure: under the influence of Bacchus,[12]
he planted in me a son and—when the baby was born—
the god's words came back to him and he knew his mistake.
He gave the infant to herdsmen to expose[13]
in Hera's sacred meadow on craggy Cithairon,[14]
but first he pierced its ankles through with iron pins,
which is why Greece has named him Oedipus.[15]
But instead, Polybus'[16] horse herders took him,
brought him home, put him into their queen's arms.
The object of my birth pangs she put to her own breast
and convinced her husband the child was hers.
When he came to puberty, the hair reddening on his chin,[17]
either my son intuited it[18] or heard somebody talking
and wanted to find out who his real parents were.
Off he went to Phoebus' temple; my husband Laios set out
for Delphi too; he had to find out about the exposed child,
hoping that it was no longer alive. They fell into step together
the two of them, where the road to Phocis splits off.[19]
Laios' driver shouted out the command:
"Stranger, make way for the king's men."
But he, in pride, continued along, without a word.

---

12. *21:* Either he was intoxicated or in a Dionysiac frenzy.

13. *24:* Exposure of unwanted children was a practice in the ancient world.

14. *25: Cithairon*: a mountain near Thebes.

15. *27: Oedipus*: here interpreted as "Swollen Foot." On the theme of naming, see lines 12 and 57–58.

16. *28:* Polybus was king of Corinth.

17. *32:* The Greeks perceived the first growth of beard (peach fuzz) as reddish.

18. *33:* An important theme introduced in Jocasta's speech is knowledge. Sophocles' *Oedipus the King* is universally recognized as a play about knowledge. Jocasta brings up over and over how knowledge is reached. Knowledge is reached by chance, and its value is negative: knowledge leads to destructive actions.

19. *38:* In the various versions of this legend, Laios and Oedipus meet at a crossroads; here both men are heading for Delphi and neither reaches it. Laios had disobeyed the earlier oracle; Oedipus never even gets to question the oracle. He has no reason to suppose that he has killed his father nor that he is destined to marry his mother, as he has been told in Sophocles' *Oedipus the King*.

The horses' hooves bloodied the tendons of his feet.
At that—why go through the details of our tragedy?—
son killed father and took the chariot home as a gift
for his stepfather. The Sphinx[20] then came to torment us,
ravaging the city. And with my husband dead
my brother Creon offered my bed as prize:
if anyone could solve the monster's cunning riddle
he would win me as his wife. It happened somehow
that my son Oedipus figured out the Sphinx's song
[and for this he became king of Thebes][21]
and won the scepter of this kingdom as his prize.
In ignorance the poor wretch married his own mother;
in ignorance, I, his mother, went to bed with my son.
To my son I bore two male children,
Eteocles and Polynices,[22] known for his strength,.
and two girls, Ismene,[23] named by her father,
and the older of the two, Antigone—I chose her name.
When he learned he was bedding his mother
on top of all the sufferings he endured, Oedipus
inflicted bloody butchery on his own eyes[24]
and gored his eyeballs with my golden brooches.
And when our sons' cheeks began to darken,

---

20. *45: Sphinx*, a winged female creature, part maiden, part dog; a symbol of death who posed a riddle to young men and devoured those who could not answer it. In brief, the best known version of the riddle asks, "what goes on four feet at dawn, two at midday, and three in the evening?"

21. *51:* Considered by most editors to be an interpolation, because the next line makes it redundant.

22. *56:* Literally, "the famous force of Polynices": instead of naming him outright, Jocasta uses a periphrasis, putting a characteristic in place of his name. This is a common usage in Homer for strong men: "the might of Heracles" is "mighty Heracles." In a further twist, the characteristic is more suited etymologically, to Eteocles, whose name means "true glory." Polynices means "full of strife."

23. *57–58:* Ismene has a part in *Seven against Thebes*, *Antigone*, and *Oedipus at Colonus*. Euripides adds the information that Antigone is the older.

24. *61:* See Sophocles' *Oedipus Tyrannus* (*Oedipus the King*) 1268–80 for a full narrative of Oedipus' self-blinding. In Sophocles, Oedipus removes the brooches from the corpse of his dead mother.

they hid their father under lock and key, hoping the story
of his unfathomable fate would pass out of memory.
Oedipus is alive still in the house. Sick from his tragic fate,
he brings down the most heinous curses on his sons
willing them to split their estate with sharpened steel.[25]
The two of them became terrified that the gods
would fulfill his curses if they lived together.
They agreed then that first the younger, Polynices,
would leave the country in voluntary exile,
and Eteocles would stay and hold the scepter.
At year's end they would change places. But when he sat
in the yoke of power, he refused to leave the throne,
and sent Polynices away a refugee from his country.
And so he went to Argos[26] and married into Adrastus'[27] family.
He recruited a massive force of Argives which now he leads
against the walls of our seven-gated city
to demand his father's scepter and a share in his country.
Trying to end their strife, I persuaded my son Polynices
to come under truce to my son Eteocles, before taking up arms.
He has sent a messenger to say he will come.

(Jocasta looks to the sky and assumes
a posture of prayer.)

You who dwell in the shining recesses of the sky,
Zeus, preserve us and reconcile my sons.
You must not, if you are really wise, permit
the same unhappy man to always have bad luck.[28]

(Jocasta exits into the palace.)

---

25. *67–68:* See Aeschylus, *Seven against Thebes* 785–89 for Oedipus' curse on his sons to divide the estate by the sword.

26. *77:* Argos refers to both a city and an area (the Argolid) in the Peloponnese. In the play it is indistinguishable from Mycenae. The people are variously called Argives, Mycenaeans, Pelasgians, Danaids, and Danaans (from King Danaus).

27. *77:* Adrastus: the Argive king, son of Talaos; best known for the expeditions against Thebes. He was not killed and lived to lead the expedition of the children (*Epigonoi*) of the Seven.

28. *86–87:* Scenes in Greek tragedy often end with a general reflection.

Scene 2 (Dialogue between Antigone and her Minder, the *Paidagogos*)

(From the rooftop, the voice of the Paidagogos is heard. He appears on the roof first, and then helps Antigone up onto the roof.)[29]

PAIDAGOGOS:
Antigone, flower of your father's house,
your mother has heard your pleas and let you
leave your maiden's chamber[30] to come up here
to the top story of the house to see the Argive army,
but wait there while I look up and down the street
to see if any of the townspeople are on the path
and a nasty slur fall on me, a slave, or on you,
a royal princess. I asked around and can tell
everything I saw and heard from the Argives
when I went to bring your brother the terms of the truce
from here to there and back here again from him.
Well, I don't see anyone coming this way from town.
Come, put your foot onto this old wooden ladder.
Look over the expanse of land and out by Ismenus' waters
and Dirce's stream.[31] See how vast the enemy's army is.

ANTIGONE: *(singing)*
Hold out your old hand to my young one, hold it out
to help me lift myself up and steady my step
on the stair.

---

29. *88:* This is a distinct scene, a set piece, but it is also innovative. It is reminiscent of the *teichoscopia* (or view from the walls) in Homer, *Iliad* 3, beginning at line 161, in which Helen identifies the Greek warriors to the old men watching from the wall of Troy; its subject might also remind us of Andromache in *Iliad* 6, 433–37 when she expresses her concern about defenses. Like Hector in the *Iliad*, the old man is certain that the besiegers have justice on their side. The rooftop is more commonly used for the appearance of gods (as in Euripides' *Electra*, *Heracles*, and *Hippolytus*), but Aeschylus' *Agamemnon* opens with a watchman on the roof.

30. *90:* Women had separate quarters in a Greek house, and unmarried girls were carefully guarded to preserve their virginity.

31. *101–2:* Ismenus (Hismenos) and Dirce are the two rivers of Thebes.

PAIDAGOGOS:
Here, hold tight, my girl. We are just in time.
At this very moment the Pelasgian[32] army is on the move,
dividing up into their separate companies.

ANTIGONE:
Goddess Hecate, daughter of Leto,[33]
the whole plain
is flashing with bronze.

PAIDAGOGOS:
Yes, it's no puny force Polynices has led against our country,
but a thundering host of horsemen and ten thousand men in arms.

ANTIGONE:
Are the city gates shut tight with bars,
and the bronze bolts, are they fitted into the stoneworks
of Amphion's wall?[34]

PAIDAGOGOS:
No need to worry. We are safe inside the city.
Look there if you want to learn about the first company.

ANTIGONE:
Who is that with the white plume?
out in front, leading an army,
lifting a solid bronze shield lightly on his arm?

PAIDAGOGOS:
The leader of a company, my lady.

---

32. *107: Pelasgian* is another name for either Peloponnesians or Thessalians, after a supposed founder, Pelasgus. (The word could be omitted in performance, or "Argive" or "enemy" substituted.)

33. *109–10:* Leto was also the mother of Artemis and Apollo. Hecate is closely connected with Artemis; she is goddess of the crossroads, and is associated with magic and the moon.

34. *114–15:* Amphion with his twin brother Zethus ruled Thebes and built the walls around the city to the accompaniment of Amphion's lyre. Amphion married Niobe.

ANTIGONE:
But who? Where is he from?
Tell me, old man, what is his name?

PAIDAGOGOS:
He claims Mycenaean origin and lives
by the waters of Lerna. He is King Hippomedon.[35]

ANTIGONE:
Ooh, how haughty he is and scary-looking,
a giant sprung from the earth, just the way they look
in paintings, glowing bright as a star, like an alien creature.

PAIDAGOGOS:
See that man crossing Dirce's water?

ANTIGONE:
He looks different. The style of his armor is strange.
Who is he?

PAIDAGOGOS:
He is Oeneus' son,
Tydeus.[36] In his heart he carries the war-lust of Aetolia.

ANTIGONE:
Is he the one who married
the sister of Polynices' bride?
How alien he is in his armor, so outlandish.

PAIDAGOGOS:
All the Aetolians carry light shields, my child,
and are good shots with the javelin.

ANTIGONE:
Tell me, old man, how can you see everything so clearly?

---

35. *125–26:* Hippomedon was an enormous man from Lerna.

36. *134–40:* Tydeus, an Aetolian, son of Oeneus, committed murder and had to go into exile. His son Diomedes is well known from the *Iliad* and the *Aeneid*.

PAIDAGOGOS:
I got to know the insignia on their shields
when I went to bring your brother the terms of truce,
and now I can recognize the men in their armor.

ANTIGONE:
Who is this passing by the monument of Zethus?[37]
He has curly hair and eyes like a Gorgon,[38]
a young man by the look of him,
leader of a company, since a crowd fully armed
follows at his heels?

PAIDAGOGOS:
That is Parthenopaeus, Atalanta's son.[39]

ANTIGONE:
Well, I hope Artemis who roams the mountains
with his mother shoots him down with her arrows
and kills him—the man who came to destroy my city.

PAIDAGOGOS:
I hope so too, my child. But they have justice on their side.
I'm afraid the gods may favor them, and rightly so.

ANTIGONE:
Where is the man born of the same mother as I,
doomed to misery,
dear, dear old man, tell me, where is Polynices?

---

37. *145:* Zethus, twin brother of Amphion (115), was the strong, violent type; Amphion was the artistic and musical brother.

38. *146:* In Greek, *gorgos*, the adjective meaning "grim, fierce," from which *Gorgo*, the *Gorgon*, is derived. The best known Gorgon was Medusa, whose severed head turned to stone anyone who looked at her. Her head was ultimately fixed to Athena's shield or in the middle of her aegis.

39. *150:* Parthenopaeus ("maiden-faced") son of Atalanta, the famous huntress who was raised by a bear.

PAIDAGOGOS:
There he is, near the tomb of Niobe's seven daughters.[40]
He is standing next to Adrastus.
Can you see him?

ANTIGONE:
Yes, I see him, but not clearly.
I can just make out a faint outline, the shape of his body.
I wish I could race through the air
with feet like a cloud blown in the wind
to my own dear brother and at long last
throw my arms around his dear, dear neck,
poor refugee.
How splendid he is in his gold armor, old man,
glinting like the sun's rays at dawn.

PAIDAGOGOS:
He is coming home under truce to fill your heart
with joy.[41]

ANTIGONE:
That one, old man, who is he,
the one mounted in the chariot guiding a team of white horses?

PAIDAGOGOS:
He is the seer Amphiaraus,[42] mistress. The fresh sacrifices
he holds are streaming blood onto the thirsty ground.

---

40. *159–60:* Niobe was the daughter of Tantalus, wife of Amphion, and the mother of seven sons and seven daughters, of whom she boasted to Leto who had only one of each. Leto, being a goddess, got her son and daughter, Artemis and Apollo, to kill all of Niobe's children. According to Pausanias (9.5.9) they died of a plague.

41. *170–71:* For a comparison of Polynices' mission with the embassy of Menelaus and Odysseus to Troy to try to avert the Trojan War (*Iliad* 3.206), see Papadapoulou (2008: 44–45) and Scholia *ad* 170.

42. *171–74:* Amphiaraus is a seer who was tricked by his wife into joining the expedition. In Aeschylus he is the one just and modest member of the Argive forces.

ANTIGONE:
Selene,[43] daughter of bright-banded Helios,
circle of golden moonlight,
how calmly and modestly he guides his course straight,
by applying the goad to the horses in turn.
But where is the man who insults our city so savagely,
Capaneus?[44]

PAIDAGOGOS:
He is over there meticulously marking out
the approaches to the towers, gauging the walls up and down.

ANTIGONE:
Oh no!
Nemesis[45] and loud-roaring thunder of Zeus
and fiery bolt of lightning, beat down
his overbearing arrogance.
He is the one who claims he will enslave us,
hand over the women of Thebes, captives of the spear,
to Mycenae and Poseidon's streams
and the waters of Lerna.[46]
Never, goddess Artemis,
golden-haired daughter of Zeus,
never let me suffer such bondage.

PAIDAGOGOS:
My child, it's time to go back inside the house
and stay in your maiden's chambers,
now that you have seen what you longed to see.

---

43. *175:* Selene is the Moon, daughter of the Sun (Helios), a lunar deity like Artemis and Hecate.

44. *180:* Capaneus ("Smokey"), son of Hipponous. In Euripides' *Suppliants*, his wife Evadne throws herself upon his burning funeral pyre.

45. *182:* Nemesis, daughter of Night (Nyx), personification of divine vengeance, whose duty was to curb excess. On the connection of the four goddesses Antigone invokes, see Craik's note on line 109.

46. *186–88:* Literally "to Lerna's Trident [Triaina] and Poseidon's Amymonian waters." The story is that Poseidon created the stream for Amymone (a daughter of the Argive king Danaus), whom he desired as a lover, by striking the ground with his trident.

As havoc advances on the city, I see a mob of women
making its way to the royal palace.
Females are a breed of faultfinders:
if they find the slightest grounds for criticism,
they pile it up out of all proportion. Women take a perverse
pleasure in having nothing good to say about each other.[47]

(They exit down the ladder from the roof.)

Parados[48]

*(The Chorus enters singing along the
two side entrances [parodoi].)*

CHORUS:

[Strophe 1][49]

Tyre's swollen seas left far behind, I came here
as living war-spoils for Loxias[50]
from Phoenicia's island-city
to be a slave in Phoebus' house,

---

47. *198–201:* The old man ends with an unwarranted sneer about women—a bow perhaps to the Eteocles of *Seven against Thebes* who reproaches and harangues the chorus of Theban women through the first half of the earlier play.

48. The *parodos* is the entrance song of the chorus, made up of fifteen men, who enter along the two *parodoi* or side entrances. In other Theban plays (*Seven against Thebes*, *Antigone*, *Oedipus the King*), the chorus is native to Thebes; in *Seven*, women of citizen families; and in *Antigone* and *Oedipus*, Theban elders. The chorus here represents Phoenician captive women who are on their way to Delphi to serve in Apollo's temple, but they have been caught in the hostilities and are now trapped in Thebes. They would be dressed in exotic costumes as is suggested by Polynices' addressing them as foreigners (278–79).

49. STROPHE ("turning") and ANTISTROPHE ("opposite turning") are metrically matched stanzas, during which the chorus performs equal dance movements and gestures but in opposite directions. Sometimes there is an unmatched stanza in between two sets (as here, the MESODE) or at the end of an ode (EPODE).

50. *204:* Loxias is another of Apollo's cult titles.

where under the snow-struck ridges
of Parnassus[51] he came to dwell.
Over the Ionian sea with
circling oar I was sailing
on the sea's unplanted surface
past Sicily, with Zephyr's[52] breezes
riding in the sky,
so lovely a sound.

[Antistrophe 1]

Hand-picked throughout the city
most beautiful offerings to Loxias,
I have come to Cadmus' country,
to the land of Agenor's[53] noble sons
sent here to Laios' towers,
the towers of our kin.
Like votive statues worked in gold,
we are singled out as slaves of Phoebus.
But still the water of Kastalia[54]
waits for us to wet
our hair's maiden glory
for Phoebus' service.

Mesode

Oh, rock gleaming with the fire's[55]
twin-peaked flash above Dionysus'
frenzied crags,
and you, vine, that every day
lets drop the ripened clusters

51. *207:* Parnassus: a mountain near Delphi, sacred to Apollo.

52. *211:* Zephyr: the west wind.

53. *217:* Agenor: descendant of Io, ruler of Tyre, father of Europa, Cadmus, Phoenix, and Cilix. When Europa was carried off, the sons were sent to search for her and founded other settlements when they realized their quest was futile.

54. *222:* Kastalia: a spring near Delphi, used for ritual washing.

55. *226–30:* Dionysus is worshiped on Parnassus with torch dances. There was a legendary vine that produced fresh fruit every day. Both Dionysus and Ares are associated with Thebes.

of the grape's flower;
holy dens of the serpent,[56]
lofty lookouts of the gods,
sacred snow-struck mountain.
If only we could be whirling
in the chorus of the undying goddess,[57]
fearless, by the glens of Phoebus
at Earth's navel,[58] leaving Dirce far behind.

[Strophe 2]

But now for us before the walls,
the onset of impetuous Ares
fires up the blood of enemies
against this city—heaven help us.
For the troubles of kin are shared in common.
In common too, if this seven-towered
land should suffer anything
it is shared with the Phoenician people.
Common is the blood, common the children
of Io the horned.[59]
In their troubles, we too have a share.

[Antistrophe 2]

And around the city a cloud
thick with shields outlines in fire

---

56. *232:* This serpent or dragon is the Pytho, the guardian of the oracle originally belonging to Themis, which Apollo killed when he took over the oracle at Delphi.

57. *236:* The undying goddess is probably Earth (Ge, Gaia).

58. *238:* Delphi was considered the center of the earth and Earth's birthplace. Sculptural representations of navels ("outies" in this case) can be seen at the archaeological site both inside the museum and outside.

59. *248:* Io, descendant of Inachus, is the common ancestor of the Phoenicians and the Thebans. She was loved by Zeus and turned into a cow by Hera, who tormented her with a gadfly and sent her wandering. She gave birth to Epaphus, ancestor of the Egyptian Danaus, who founded Argos and Cadmus the Phoenician founder of Thebes (see line 676).

the choreography of bloody war
which Ares soon will know,
when he brings the agony of the Furies
to the sons of Oedipus.
O Pelasgic Argos,
we fear your valor.
What comes from the gods we fear. For with justice truly
into this struggle rushes under arms the son
who comes to seek his birthright.

First Episode[60]

(Polynices enters along the stage left parodos.)[61]

POLYNICES:
The gatekeepers have unlocked the bolts
and let me pass freely inside the walls.
But now I'm afraid they will catch me in their traps
and not let me out again unbloodied.
That is why I turn my eyes in every direction,

60. *261:* An *episode* is the part spoken by actors, with songs sometimes mixed in (as in Jocasta's monody in this episode), that comes between the odes. Episodes may use two or three actors. This is a three-actor scene: Polynices, Jocasta, Eteocles. This episode is unusually long and complex and can be divided into several parts.

1. 261–90 Enter Polynices carrying a sword, perhaps fully armed, alone.
2. 291–354 Enter Jocasta from the palace: reunion of mother and son.
3. 355–442 Dialogue of Polynices and his mother
4. 443–587 Enter Eteocles, perhaps along the opposite parodos (probably with one or two attendants). This is the central *agōn* (debate scene).
5. 558–637 The dialogue deteriorates into a balanced match of insults.

61. *261:* Polynices' costume: we have a description of Polynices' golden armor (168–69), but we do not know if (in the original performance) he entered fully armed or in his tunic. He is carrying a sword and wearing a scabbard (268, 276). Various considerations would go into determining his attire in a contemporary performance.

that way and this, to look out for a trick.[62]
The sword in my hand gives me confidence.
Whoa—who is that? Or am I startled by a sound?
To the brave everything is alarming,
if they happen to set foot into enemy territory.
I trust my mother who convinced me to come here
under truce; at the same time I do not trust her.
Well, help is at hand—the altar fires
are here and the palace is not deserted.[63]
I'll slip my sword back inside its sheath
and ask these women who they are
and why they are standing in front of the palace.
Women, strangers to our land, tell me,
where have you come from to these Greek dwellings?[64]

CHORUS:[65]
Phoenicia is the homeland that nurtured me,
the sons of Agenor's sons sent us here
as offerings to Phoebus, chosen from the spoils of war.
Oedipus' illustrious son was prepared to send us
to the sacred oracle and altars of Loxias
just when the Argives made war on the city.
But tell me who are you to have come
into the seven-gated citadel of Thebes?

POLYNICES:
My father is Oedipus, son of Laios;
Jocasta, daughter of Menoeceus gave me birth.
The people of Thebes call me Polynices.

---

62. *266:* Like the chorus of the *Seven against Thebes*, Polynices fears every sound.

63. *275:* At this point Polynices would notice the women of the chorus as he makes his way to the front of the palace.

64. *278–79:* Polynices is a native, returning to his homeland after something more than a year's absence but he is made by the staging—the foreign chorus being there to meet him—to be a stranger among strangers. It is likely that the chorus is recognized as foreign by their costuming.

65. *280:* When the chorus speaks in an episode, the lines are spoken by one person, the chorus leader.

CHORUS:
Kinsman of Agenor's children,
my rulers, who brought me here,
I fall before you on bended knee, Oh king, [*singing*]
as is the custom in my home.
You have come at last to your homeland.
Oh, oh, mistress come out, hurry.
Throw open the gates.
Do you hear, Mother of Polynices?
Why do you delay to cross through the high halls
and take your son in your arms?

JOCASTA: *(entering from the palace, singing or chanting; later dancing around her son)*[66]
Your Phoenician cry
I heard, young women, and drag
my elderly foot on quivering step. My son,
at last after days and endless days I see your face.
Throw your arms around
your mother's breast,
hold out your cheek and let your dark curls
hang down to cover my neck.
Ah, ah, appearing beyond hope,
at last in your mother's arms past expectation.
What can I say to you? How can I relive the pleasure
in every way with my hands and words
dancing happily
that way and this,
spinning around you as in the old days
full of joy? Ah my child,
you left your father's home desolate,
a refugee driven off by your brother's wrong,
sorely missed by your family,
sorely missed by Thebes.
This is why I cut my gray hair in grief[67]
giving way to my tears in sorrow,

66. *314:* Jocasta dances around her son to protect him and to keep him close.

67. *322:* Cutting the hair is a sign of mourning.

took off my white dress, my son,
and wear instead
these dark and gloomy rags.
But inside the house your old father, eyeless,
forever in tears of longing
for his two sons,
unyoked now from the family,
rushed for the sword
and suicidal slaughter,
or a noose hanging from the ceiling beams;
moaning curses on his sons
with tears streaming all day long,
he is hidden in darkness.
And you my son, I hear,
are yoked in the joy of matrimony
and have a foreign family,
are busy with foreign kin,
anathema to your mother
and to Laios of days long gone—
doom of marriage far from home.
And I did not light the torch for you
a custom at our weddings[68]
for the happy mother.
No wedding hymn, to yoke Ismenus in marriage,
no ceremonial bath for the bridegroom.
All through Thebes there was silence for your bride's entrance.
My curse upon it: Is it the sword
or discord? Is your father to blame
or has god made sport of
the house of Oedipus?
Deep in my heart has come the pain of these miseries.

CHORUS:
Giving birth holds a strange power over women,
and all womankind is child-obsessed.

---

68. *344–49:* At a Greek wedding the bride was escorted from her chamber in a procession of the wedding party (family and friends), carrying torches and singing the wedding song, and led to the door of her new husband's home. A child who was a close relative of the bridegroom's carried water for his wedding bath.

POLYNICES:

Mother, I have both good and bad feelings about
coming here into enemy territory. Still, all men are destined
to love their homelands. If anyone says otherwise
he is playing with words, but home is where his heart is.
So troubled was I and so fearful that some trick
on my brother's part would kill me that with sword drawn
I walked through the city casting my eyes every which way.
One thing gives me the confidence to go on:
the truce and my trust in you, which led me
inside the walls of my homeland. I have come here in tears,
my eyes at long last gazing on the gods' shrines and altars,
the gymnasia where I spent my youth, and Dirce's stream,
from which I was unfairly driven away to live
in a foreign city with tears gushing from my eyes.
From one pain flows another as I see you again
your head shorn, your body draped in black.
Ah me, I cry in anguish for my troubles.
How terrible a thing is hatred inside the family, Mother,
and reconciliation is so hard to achieve.
How is my elderly father getting by in the house,
his eyes in darkness? How are my two sisters?
Do the poor girls cry over my exile?

JOCASTA:

A sadistic god is crushing the family of Oedipus,
starting when I first gave birth breaking the taboo,
then married your father and gave birth to you.
Why speak of this? We must endure what gods give us.
How to ask what I want to know, for I'm afraid
I will hurt your feelings. Still, there are things I long to know.

POLYNICES:

Don't hold back. Please, ask anything you want to know.
Whatever you desire, Mother, is what I want most.

JOCASTA:

Then I'll ask first what I most want to know.
Losing your homeland—is it a terrible misery?

POLYNICES:
The very worst, even worse living it than telling it.

JOCASTA:
What is it like? What is so hard for refugees?

POLYNICES:
One thing is worst: not to be able to say what you think.

JOCASTA:
That is the role for a slave, not to speak freely.

POLYNICES:
A refugee must put up with any fool in power.

JOCASTA:
That is a problem: to be a fool among the fools.

POLYNICES:
It goes against the grain, but you act the slave to get by.

JOCASTA:
Exiles are nourished by hope, so the saying goes.

POLYNICES
It leads us on with bright eyes, but takes its time.

JOCASTA:
Didn't time show your hope to be empty?

POLYNICES
It has an allure that sweetens my troubles.

JOCASTA:
How did you support yourself before your marriage?

POLYNICES:
One day I had enough, the next, nothing.

JOCASTA:
Your father has friends and allies, didn't they help?

Polynices:
Better be rich. Lose your fortune, lose your friends.

Jocasta:
Didn't your high birth improve your status?

Polynices
It's bad to be poor. High birth does not put food on the table.

Jocasta:
Homeland, it seems, is a man's dearest possession.

Polynices:
No words can express how dear it is.

Jocasta:
How is it you went to Argos? What goal did you have in mind?

Polynices:
Loxias had given a certain oracle to Adrastus.

Jocasta:
What was it? What do you mean? I don't understand.

Polynices:
To join his daughters in marriage to a boar and a lion.

Jocasta:
What do you have to do with these animal names, my son?

Polynices:
I don't know, but destiny called me to this opportunity.

Jocasta:
Yes, the god is wise. How did you attain this marriage?

Polynices:
It was night when I arrived on Adrastus' doorstep.

Jocasta:
A homeless wanderer looking for a place to stay?

Polynices:
That was it. And then another refugee arrived there too.

Jocasta:
Who was he, this second unfortunate soul?

Polynices:
Tydeus. They say he is the son of Oeneus.

Jocasta:
Why then did Adrastus compare you to wild animals?

Polynices:
We came to blows over a place to sleep.

Jocasta:
Is that how Talaus' son figured out the oracle?

Polynices:
Yes, and he gave his two daughters to the two of us.

Jocasta:
Are you happy in your marriage or not?

Polynices:
To this day I find no fault in my marriage.

Jocasta:
How did you convince an army to follow you here?

Polynices:
Adrastus made a vow to his two sons-in-law:
[Tydeus and me—he's my brother-in-law]:
to restore us both to our homelands, starting with me.
Many leaders of the Danaans and Mycenaeans
are with us, providing a bitter service to me,
but needed. For I am leading an army against my own
home city. I swear to the gods that against my will

I take up arms on those I love. They want it, not I.
Well, the resolution of these troubles depends on you,
Mother, reconcile us, kin of one blood.
Put an end to our troubles, mine, yours, the city's.
The old chant goes—and I will repeat it—
"Money is most precious to men
and holds great sway among them."
I have come to get what is mine and am leading
a vast army. A poor man has no respect.

CHORUS:
Look, here comes Eteocles to take part in the truce.
Jocasta, it's up to you, as their mother
to say the right words to reconcile your sons.

(Enter Eteocles along the stage right parodos.)

ETEOCLES:
Here I am, Mother. I have come as a favor to you.
What has to be done? Let the debate begin.
I have postponed posting the citizens around the walls
and matching up my divisions, to hear from you
the mutual arbitration to which I gave my consent,
to admit *him* inside the walls under truce.

JOCASTA:
Not so fast. Haste, you know, does not lead to justice,
but slow deliberation sets the wisest course.
Give up your glaring looks and angry snorting.
You are not looking at the Gorgon's severed head[69]
but at your brother who has come to meet you.
And you, turn your face toward your brother,
Polynices.[70] If you look each other in the eyes
you will speak more to the point and pay closer attention.
And I want to give you both some sound advice.

---

69. *455:* The head of Medusa turned to stone those who looked at it.

70. *454–58:* Jocasta gives an order, but do the brothers actually look at each other? Jocasta's request cannot simply be ignored: whether Eteocles and Polynices do as she asks or pointedly ignore her, it is a significant action that affects the way we react to the scene (see Altena 2000: 313–14).

When a friend is angry with a friend
and they come together and meet face to face,
they should think only of the reasons why they have come
and keep no memory of past wrongs.
Yours is the first turn to speak,[71] Polynices, my son,
since you have come at the head of an army of Danaids,
deprived of your right, as you allege. May one of the gods
be judge and conciliator of these troubles.

POLYNICES:[72]

To speak the plain truth is a simple matter:
justice needs no elaborate disputation.
It has its own authority. But the unjust argument
because it is sick requires intricate medicine.
My only concern is with my father's estate,
both my share and *his*. In my desire to evade
the curses which Oedipus uttered against us,
I left the country on my own in voluntary exile.
I gave *him* the right to rule for one year's span
so that I would rule the next, taking my turn,
not coming out of hatred and envy of him
to cause the damage that is happening now.
And he agreed and swore an oath to the gods,
but now he breaks his promise and keeps for himself
both royal power and my share of the estate.
Even now I am ready to take what is mine,
dismiss the army to withdraw from this country,
and live in my own house enjoying my share;
then in turn yield an equal share for an equal time

---

71. *465:* As is common in a theatrical debate scene (*agōn*), reference is made here to contemporary courtroom procedure in which the accuser speaks first.

72. *469–585:* This is the central *agōn* (or debate scene). Usually an *agōn* consists of two matched speeches by the antagonists, neither of which prevails or affects the outcome. Nearly every tragedy has a debate scene, which attests to their popularity with the Athenians, known for their litigious spirit. Euripides here adds a third speech that should win rhetorically and logically, but is also without effect and is ignored by the two contenders. On the debate as a conflict between "traditional beliefs and sophistic relativism" see Meltzer (2006: 1–27).

to him and not to lay waste my homeland
and not bring ladders to scale the battlements,
which I will do if justice is denied me.
I call the gods to witness these words
that though all my deeds are just, without justice
I am most indecently deprived of my homeland.
These separate points I have spoken, not piling up
deceptive arguments, but only what is right,
to wise men and, I think, to common folk, as well.

CHORUS:
I think so too. Even though I am not native
to Greece, still you seem to speak to the point.

ETEOCLES:
If the same things seemed good and wise to everybody,
we would not have debates or strife,
but as it is nothing is the same or equal to people
except in name. And that is not the real thing.
I will speak, Mother, and hide nothing.
I would go to the risings of the stars in the sky
and down under the earth[73] to attain this one thing:
to grasp in my hand the greatest god of all, Power.[74]
This advantage, Mother, I am not willing to hand over
to anyone else, but I shall keep it for myself.
It would be cowardice to let go the greater share
and accept the lesser. And besides this I am ashamed
that *he* could come under arms to destroy our homeland
and achieve his desires. This would be a disgrace
to Thebes if in terror of the Mycenaean spear
I were to yield my scepter for him to wield.
He ought not to be making the truce with arms,
Mother; for words can achieve everything
that the arms of an enemy can conquer.
If he wishes to live in this country under other terms
he may do so. I will never step down of my own free will:

73. *505:* A typical polarity of which Greek though is very fond.

74. *506:* Eteocles is an immoralist modeled on the likes of Euripides' well-known contemporaries, Alcibiades and Thrasymachus.

as long as I am able to rule, I will not be a slave to *him*.
Knowing this, come fire, come sword;
yoke the horses, fill the plain with chariots,
since I will not yield my power to him.
If one must do wrong, best do wrong
for Power,[75] otherwise you might as well be good.

CHORUS:
It is not right to use fine words to support ugly deeds.
This is not good, but galling to the eyes of justice.

JOCASTA:
My son, not everything turns out worse
in old age, Eteocles, but experience of life
has some things to say more soundly than youth.
Why do you go after Ambition, my son, of all gods
the most wicked? Don't do it. She is an unjust god.
She comes into homes and prosperous cities
and leaves those who welcome her in ruins.
Yet you are crazy for her. This is better, my son:
to honor Equality,[76] who always binds kin to kin,
city to city, allies to allies. Equality is a constant
in human life. Less and more are always at war
and this is the beginning of the day of hatred.
Measures and divisions of weights were established
for mankind by Equality, and she has defined the numbers.
Night's lightless eye and the fire of the sun
take equal steps through the year's orbit.
Neither of them by overreaching incurs the other's envy.
The sun and nighttime serve the needs of mortal men,
but you will not put up with an equal division of the estate
and share with him? What justice is in that?
Why do you pay homage to Power, so easy an injustice,
with such excess, and think it so important?
Is it honorable to have fame? If so it's an empty honor.
Do you want to have a surplus in your house at such a cost?

---

75. *525:* Power: in Greek *tyrannis*, also in line 506.

76. *536:* Jocasta's talk about equality (*isotes*) adds a new, political cast to the old theme of the equality of the brothers.

What is the advantage in that? It is only a name.
To reasonable people having enough is sufficient.
We humans do not possess property to keep as our own;
we are but stewards of what belongs to the gods.
When it strikes their fancy they take it back again.
Wealth is not forever; it lasts a day and is gone.
Listen, let me pose to you two questions:
Do you want to be king or to save the city?
Will you say, "To be king"? And if he beats you
and the Argive army defeats the Cadmeians
you will see our city of Thebes overwhelmed;
you will see many young girls taken prisoner
and raped by the violence of enemy soldiers.[77]
The wealth you seek will come at a cost to Thebes.
You are power-mad. That is all I have to say to you.
And now, Polynices, I have something to say to you.
Adrastus' favor to you was wrong-headed
and you come like a fool to lay waste your city.
Listen, if—god forbid—you conquer this country,
for gods' sake how will you set up trophies to Zeus?
After seizing your homeland, how will you make sacrifice
and put your name on the spoils beside Inachus?[78]
"After burning Thebes to the ground, Polynices dedicated
these shields to the gods." I hope you will never
have this kind of fame among the Greeks.
And if you are beaten and his side triumphs how will you return
to Argos leaving behind untold numbers of dead?
And someone will say, "Adrastus you have crushed us
with your daughters' marriages. Because of one bride
we are ruined." My son, you are headed for disaster
both ways: to lose what you have there and to fail here.
Give up your excess, do give it up. When two men
confront each other in madness the result is tragedy.

77. *565:* When a city was captured the men were killed and the women and children were enslaved, becoming the property of their masters. Rape and sexual slavery were common acts of war. Even the wise Nestor tells the soldiers not to go home until each has bedded the wife of a Trojan in revenge for Helen's adultery (Homer, *Iliad* 2.354–56).

78. *574:* Inachus was a river and a river-god of Argos.

CHORUS:
Oh Gods, turn aside these catastrophes,
and somehow reconcile the sons of Oedipus.

ETEOCLES:[79]
Mother, the contest of words is now over, but meanwhile time
is being wasted for nothing. Your good intentions come to naught.
For we cannot come together except on the terms I have stated,
that I will wield the scepter as king of this country.
Give up your long-winded admonishments and let me go.
But, you, get outside of the city walls or you will die.

POLYNICES:
At whose hand? Who is so invulnerable that he could
cast a murderous spear at me and not suffer the same doom?

ETEOCLES:
He is right here and has not moved. Take a look at my hands.[80]

POLYNICES:
I see them. But wealth is a coward and runs for its life.

ETEOCLES:
Yet you have come with a vast army to do battle with a nonentity?

POLYNICES:
A careful general is better than an impetuous one.

ETEOCLES:
You are a braggart, trusting in a truce that protects you from death.

---

79. *588–637:* The meter changes from iambic trimeter to iambic tetrameter, which is used to indicate agitation, haste, and heightened emotions.

80. *596–625:* This is a long passage of *stichomythia*, a convention in tragedy in which speakers each speak a single line of verse, or sometimes two: sometimes the line is divided between the two speakers: this shows more heated emotion and is called *antilabē*.

Polynices:
You are too. Again I demand the scepter and my share of my country.

Eteocles:
I take no orders from you. I will live in my own house.

Polynices:
And have more than your share.

Eteocles:
I tell you, get out of the country.

Polynices:
Altars of my fathers' gods,

Eteocles:
which you have come to destroy.

Polynices:
Hear me.

Eteocles:
Who hears you, coming to wage war on your homeland?

Polynices:
Temples of the gods of white horses,[81]

Eteocles:
who hate you.

Polynices:
I am driven from my homeland.

Eteocles:
Yes, because you have come to destroy it.

Polynices:
Unjustly, oh gods.

---

81. *606:* Amphion and Zethus, the Theban version of the Dioscuri.

ETEOCLES:
Call on the gods in Mycenae, not here.

POLYNICES:
You are godless,

ETEOCLES:
but not like you, an enemy to my country.

POLYNICES:
You drive me out without my share.

ETEOCLES:
Yes, and besides that I will kill you.

POLYNICES:
Father, do you hear what I suffer?

ETEOCLES:
Yes, and he hears what you are doing.

POLYNICES:
And you, Mother?

ETEOCLES:
It is wrong for you even to speak of your mother.

POLYNICES:
Oh city!

ETEOCLES:
Go to Argos and call on the waters of Lerna.

POLYNICES:
I will go, do not trouble yourself. Thank you, Mother.

ETEOCLES:
Get out of the country.

POLYNICES:
I am going. Let me see my father.

ETEOCLES:
No, you cannot.

POLYNICES:
My sisters then.

ETEOCLES:
You will never set eyes on them.

POLYNICES:
Sisters . . .

ETEOCLES:
Why do you call on them when you are their enemy.

POLYNICES:
Mother, I'll say good-bye then.

JOCASTA:
I suffer very much, my dear son.

POLYNICES:
I am gone, no more your son.

JOCASTA:
I am very very unhappy.

POLYNICES:
Yes, he abuses us.

ETEOCLES:
And I am abused in return.

POLYNICES:
Where will you be posted in front of the towers?

ETEOCLES:
Why do you want to know?

POLYNICES:
I will station myself opposite to kill you.

ETEOCLES:

I desire exactly the same.

JOCASTA:

Oh no! What are you doing, children?

POLYNICES:

The deed itself will show.

JOCASTA:

Will you not avoid your father's blood-curse?

ETEOCLES:

The whole house can go to hell!

(Exit Jocasta into the palace.)

POLYNICES

Soon my sword will set to work and drip with blood.
I call the gods to witness and the land that nurtured me
that I am driven in bitter anguish without honor from my
country
like a slave, not like the son of the same father Oedipus.
And if you, my city, suffer harm, blame him, not me.
I'm here against my will, driven against my will from my home,
and you, Lord Phoebus, protector of our doors, and palace,
farewell,
and my companions, images of the gods where sacrifice is made,
I do not know if I will ever address you again.
Hope is not yet asleep, and I have confidence with gods' help
that I will kill this man and take control of the land of Thebes.

(Exit Polynices stage left.)

ETEOCLES:

Get out! Father gave you the name Polynices
with inspired foresight, a name full of strife.

(Exit Eteocles into the palace.)[82]

82. *637:* The staging is not clear here. Eteocles may remain in front of the scene-building through the choral ode.

First Stasimon

CHORUS:

[Strophe]

Cadmus came to this land
from Tyre; for him the four-footed
heifer, not forced to its knees,
lay down, fulfilling
the oracle that told him where to settle[83]
on the wheat-bearing plains of his new home.
The divine voice proclaimed:
"where the beautiful stream of water
comes over the land,
the green-bearing, deep-sown
fields of Dirce."
And there by union with Zeus
his mother gave birth to Bromius.[84]
While he was still an infant,
coiling ivy, twining
its green shady tendrils
cradled him in luxury,
adored in Bacchic dance by Theban maidens
and women in ecstasy.

[Antistrophe]

There it was, the blood-thirsty dragon[85]
of Ares, cruel-minded guard,
watching over the running streams
and green runnels with its
eyes darting everywhere.
And this creature, when Cadmus the monster-killer

---

83. *642:* While he was searching for his sister Europa, Cadmus received an oracle at Delphi that told him to follow a cow until it collapsed and to found a city on the site. Thebes is in Boiotia (Boeotia) from *bous*, "cow."

84. *650:* Bromius (Roarer), another name for Dionysus (Bacchus), son of Cadmus' daughter Semele and Zeus.

85. *657:* A dragon, descendant of Ares, guarded the spring of Ares. Cadmus, needing water to sacrifice the heifer (line 640) to Athena, killed the dragon with Athena's help.

came for ritual water,
he killed it with a rock, crushing
its murderous head
with weapons hurled from his hands
and by command of the motherless goddess,[86]
Pallas, he cast the teeth fallen to the earth
into the deep-sown fields.
Then Earth sent up
an array in full armor above the
surface of the ground; iron-minded
murder joined them again with their own land
and with their blood soaked the earth that had revealed
them to the sun-drenched air of heaven.

Epode

And you, Epaphus,[87]
offspring long ago of Io our foremother
and child of Zeus
I call, with foreign cry.
Io, with foreign prayers I call.
Come to this land, come.
Your descendants built it and occupied it.
Goddesses named together,
Persephone and dear
goddess Demeter
queen of all, Earth, nurse of all.
Send torch-bearing[88]
goddesses; shield our land.
Everything is easy for gods.

(Enter Eteocles with a servant.)

---

86. *667:* The motherless goddess is Pallas Athena, who sprang in full armor from the head of her father Zeus. Athena advised Cadmus to sow the teeth of the slain dragon in the earth. When he obeyed grown men fully armed sprang from the earth. These are the Spartoi (Sown Men). They fought each other and all but five were killed.

87. *676:* See 248 and note on Epaphus.

88. *683–88:* Demeter and her daughter Persephone are torch-bearers at the Eleusinian mysteries.

Second Episode

ETEOCLES: *(to a servant)*[89]
Go get Creon, the son of Menoeceus,
brother of my mother Jocasta.
Tell him this—I want to communicate
my plans both strategic and domestic to him
before going into battle to face the line of spears.
But wait, here he comes just now to save you the trouble.
I can see him coming toward my house.[90]

(Enter Creon along the stage right parodos.)

CREON:
I have been all over trying to find you,
Eteocles, around the gates of the Cadmeians
and the guard posts searching for you.

ETEOCLES:
Good, I am eager to see you too, Creon.
I found the truce utterly useless
when I entered into discussion with Polynices.

CREON:
I hear that he shows contempt toward Thebes,
secure in his ties with Adrastus' family and in the army.
These things we must leave in the hands of the gods,
I have come to report what is of most immediate concern.

ETEOCLES:
And what is it? I have not heard any news.

---

89. *690:* Eteocles either enters from the palace or simply begins talking from where he remained in front of the *skēnē*, calling to a servant. By line 695 Creon, entering along the stage right parodos, becomes visible to Eteocles.

90. *696:* Allusions to earlier Theban tragedies bring out Eteocles' lack of control over affairs in *Phoenician Women*. In *Oedipus the King* Oedipus had sent Creon to the oracle; and in *Seven against Thebes* the Aeschylean Eteocles had sent a spy across enemy lines and announces his arrival. Here Eteocles tries to send for Creon and is forestalled by Creon's coming along on his own.

Creon:
A captive[91] from the Argive army has fallen into our hands.

Eteocles:
What news does he have to tell us about them?

Creon:
That all around the towers the army of the Argives
is getting ready to encircle the city of the Cadmeians with arms.

Eteocles:
Then the city of Cadmus must march out in arms.

Creon:
Where? You are too young to see what you should see.[92]

Eteocles:
Here outside the trenches, since soon we will fight.

Creon:
Our army is small, far outnumbered by theirs.

Eteocles:
I know they are bold in words.

Creon:
Argos has a reputation among the Greeks.

Eteocles:
Take courage. I will soon fill the plain with their massacre.

---

91. *708:* In Aeschylus' *Seven against Thebes* this information comes from a spy Eteocles has sent out.

92. *713:* The fact that Creon is a better strategist than Eteocles takes away the one thing his namesake had in his favor in the *Seven*: that he was an active and able commander, intelligent and swift in his decisions. In the earlier play there had been no older man to dampen his fire. But here, each of his suggestions is shown to be thoughtless, whereas in the *Seven*, each of his choices was militarily and morally brilliant. Even his exit line "I will go" (748) is ruined by his appending a long speech (some of which has been suspected by editors) in which he ties up loose ends.

CREON:
I hope so. But I see that this is a dangerous course.

ETEOCLES:
Well, I will not keep my army inside the walls.

CREON:
And yet, strategy is everything if you plan to win.

ETEOCLES:
Do you want me to turn to a different course?

CREON:
Yes every possible course, before rushing into danger.

ETEOCLES:
What if we ambush them at night?

CREON:
Yes, if you fail you will be safe back here.

ETEOCLES:
Darkness levels the field and is an advantage to the bold.

CREON:
Night's darkness is frightening in case of disaster.

ETEOCLES:
Well, should I attack them at their dinner?

CREON:
It would be a surprise, but beating them is crucial.

ETEOCLES:
Yes, Dirce's ford is deep if we have to retreat.

CREON:
Every course is inferior to keeping up one's defenses.

ETEOCLES:
But what if we charge the Argive army on horseback?

CREON:
Their army too is encircled with chariots.

ETEOCLES:
What should I do then? Hand the city over to the enemy?

CREON:
Not at all. But make plans since you are a good strategist.

ETEOCLES:
What strategy do you think will work better then?

CREON:
It is said they have seven men, that's what I heard.

ETEOCLES:
Posted for what? It is a small force.

CREON:
To be posted at the seven gates as leaders of companies.

ETEOCLES:
What do we do? I will not wait for an impasse.

CREON:
You also choose seven men to face them at the seven gates.

ETEOCLES:
To command companies or for single combat with the spear?

CREON:
Companies. Choose those who are the best warriors.

ETEOCLES:
I get it, to keep them from scaling the walls.

CREON:
Yes, and as fellow officers. One man cannot see everything.

ETEOCLES:
Should I choose them for bravery or tactical skill?

CREON:
Both. One is nothing without the other.

ETEOCLES:
I will do it. I will go around to the seven towers
and station officers at the gates as you suggest,
matching equals against equals on the other side.
It would take too long to give all the names,
with the enemy encamped outside our walls.[93]
I will go and not delay the action of my hand.
I pray that it turns out that I face my brother
and take him in battle with my spear and kill him,
the man who has come to destroy my homeland.
As for the marriage of my sister Antigone and your son
Haemon,[94] if I should fall short of victory,
you must take care of it. Now at my departure
I reconfirm the betrothal already made.
You are my mother's brother. Why go on at length?
Take care of her, as is your duty for your sake and mine.
But as for Father, for blinding himself, he deserves
the charge of weak-mindedness. I have lost all respect
for him. He will kill us with his curses, if he gets the chance.
There is one thing left for us to do: if there is
any oracle that the soothsayer Tiresias has to tell
find it out from him. Your son, Menoeceus,
your father's namesake, I will send him
to get Tiresias and bring him back here, Creon.
The seer will agree to speak with you,
but I found fault with his prophetic skill
in the past and now he has cause to resent me.
This charge I lay upon you and the city, Creon,
if my side prevails, the body of Polynices,
—never inter it in Theban soil and put to death anyone

---

93. *752:* A criticism of Aeschylus' *Seven*, in which the central scene is the naming of the attackers and defenders.

94. *758:* In Sophocles' *Antigone*, the marriage of Haemon and Antigone is forestalled by Antigone's death. Haemon, by then the last of Creon's sons, commits suicide.

who tries to bury it, even a member of the family.[95]
That is all I have to say to you. Now, attendants,
bring my armor,[96] defense against enemy blows
so that I may set out into the struggle that lies
before us with justice, bringer of victory.
I send my prayer to that most expedient of goddesses,
Caution,[97] protect and preserve our city.

(Exit Eteocles with attendants carrying the armor. Creon remains to wait for Tiresias.)

Second Stasimon

CHORUS:

[Strophe 784–800][98]

Ares full of struggle, why, why are you possessed
of blood and death out of tune with the festivals of
  Bromius,
and at the graceful dances of garland-crowned young
  women
do not let loose your hair and sing to the blowing of the
  flute
a song to which the graces set the dance,
but with men in arms inspiring the legions of Argives
with bloodshed for Thebes
you choreograph a revel with no sound of flutes?
Not under the thyrsus-craze[99] of fawnskins,

---

95. *777:* Eteocles reduces Creon's responsibility (his defining trait in the Sophoclean *Antigone*) for refusing to bury Polynices by making it his own last request. It is, of course, the duty of family members to tend their dead.

96. *779:* This line recalls Eteocles' last lines in *Seven against Thebes* (675ff.), in which he calls for his armor and perhaps arms himself on stage.

97. *782:* It is typical of the Euripidean Eteocles to pray to an abstraction rather than the traditional gods.

98. *784–800:* The strophe is an invocation to Ares that refers to the present. Ares is invoked in language appropriate to Dionysus: the potential violence of the revel-band is transferred to the war god. The image of the dance applied to the movements of war is compelling and terrible.

99. *792:* The thyrsus is a staff decorated with ivy carried by Dionysus and his worshippers in their ecstatic rites.

but with chariots and bits, you swirl the horses' hooves
advancing upon Ismenus' stream
on horseback you charge, inspiring against the Argives
the race of Sown Men,
a shield-bearing revel-band
of enemies, against the stone walls,
decked out with bronze.
Strife is a direful goddess—
she has plotted troubles for the kings of the land
for the children of Labdacus full of struggle.

[Antistrophe 801–17][100]

Sacred thickets, full of beasts
snow-filled valley, eye of Artemis, Cithairon,
you never should have nurtured the fruit of Jocasta's labor,
exposed for death, Oedipus, infant cast out of the house,
marred with gold-set pins.
The winged virgin, mountain-bred monster, never should have come
—sorrows for the land—
with its museless Sphinx-songs
that once with bird-claws on all its four feet
coming to the walls bore into the pathless light of the air
the children of Cadmus,—Hades from below the ground
sent it against the Cadmeians. God-forsaken strife
thrives all the more among the children
of Oedipus in the halls and in the city.
What is not good never breeds the good,
illicit children,
their mother's birth pangs, pollution of their father,
and the man who went to bed with his mother.

---

100. *801–17:* The antistrophe refers to the recent past. It is full of life and breeding of a hostile, sinister, or monstrous kind, first the natural beasts (801) of the mountain; then the brood of Jocasta (803), the nurturing (804) of Oedipus, a monster marred by prophecy and abuse; next comes the "mountain-bred" portent (806), the Sphinx who carried off those born of Cadmus (808) and was sent from Hades against the Cadmeians. Artemis' presence turns the animals into beasts for the hunt and kill. Oedipus' exposure suggests that the beasts should have preyed on him or the elements worked for his death by exposure.

Epode 818–32[101]

You bore, Oh Earth, once you bore
as I learned—I learned the foreign tale at home—
from a beast-bred bloody-plumed dragon
the race grown from its teeth, for Thebes a most glorious shame.
And once to the wedding of Harmonia
gods came from heaven and to the sound of Amphion's lyre
the walls of Thebes rose and the towers rose to his lyre
at the crossing between the twin rivers
where Dirce waters the green-growing plain
opposite Ismenus.
And Io the horned foremother of our race
bore kings for the Cadmeians,
an endless succession of good giving way to
more good, this city stands on the top
of Ares' circling crowns.[102]

---

101. *818–32:* In the epode there is yet more breeding (818, 820, 821, 826, 828, 829). Here the result is mixed: even the savagery of the dragon and the teeth-bred generation is oxymoronically a glorious shame to Thebes. On the positive side, the gods came to the wedding of Harmonia; the walls of Thebes rose to Amphion's lyre; the plain between the rivers is fertile; and Io the horned foremother produced a royal line. The plain between Dirce and Ismenus is now full of armed men hostile to Thebes. The very walls are under attack. One clear theme is change (831), the *sine qua non* of tragedy.

102. *832:* The crowns of the strophe (786) that decorated the heads of young girls in the choral dance have become at the very end of the epode (832) crowns or circlings of Ares, the exact meaning of which is unclear, with the outcome still unknown. Ares' dance is the image that carries through the ode from beginning to end along with the breeding of strife and the ambiguity of good fortune, success, and victory. The god who is "full of struggle" (or suffering, 784) does not suffer himself, but brings suffering to the human beings who are also called "full of struggle" (or suffering, 800). It is difficult to tell whether the ode is finally optimistic or despairing, or as may be more likely, ambiguous. The crown reappears as a sign of victory on Tiresias' head.

Third Episode

TIRESIAS: *(enters with his daughter*[103] *and Menoeceus along the stage right parodos. He is wearing a crown of victory.)*
Lead me on, daughter, since you are the eyes
to my blind feet, like a star to sailors.
Guide my step here to level ground and walk
in front so we don't trip. Your father is feeble.
Hold tightly in your young hands the oracles[104]
which I took by reading the bird signs
at my sacred place of prophecy.
Menoeceus, my boy, son of Creon, tell me
how much longer is it to town and to your father?
My knees are weary and it's difficult
for me to make such a long journey.

CREON:
Don't worry, Tiresias, you have almost reached
your friends. Take him in hand, my boy.
An old man's foot is like a wagon's wheel
in need of support from another's hand.

TIRESIAS:
Good. We are here. Why did you call me in haste, Creon?

CREON:
I haven't forgotten. But gather your strength
and catch your breath, to recover from the hard trek.

---

103. Tiresias' daughter would have been a surprise. Usually he is accompanied by a boy, his servant or apprentice.

104. *838:* The word here is *klērous*, "lots"; perhaps the seer has drawn several from a collection of lots and has his daughter carry them as evidence. The daughter would be clutching tablets or scraps of papyrus (see Mastronarde 1986: *ad loc.*). The blind seer, removed from direct vision of bird flight patterns or the entrails read at sacrifices and even from reading the written lots that might record such things, boggles the mind.

TIRESIAS:
Yes I am worn out. Just yesterday I was
brought back here from the Erecthids;[105]
there was a war there too, waged by Eumolpus.
I gave glorious victory to the sons of Kekrops
and wear this golden crown as you see
which I was granted as the first fruits of the war spoils.

CREON:
I take your crown of victory as a good omen.
We are at sea as you know yourself:
Thebes is engaged in a great struggle with the Danaid army.
Our king Eteocles has gone armed for battle
to face the might of the Mycenaeans.
He asked me to find out from you if there is
anything in particular we can do to save the city.

TIRESIAS:
As far as Eteocles is concerned, my lips are sealed
and I would keep the oracles to myself. But to you I will speak,
since you desire to learn. This country has long been sick,
Creon,
ever since Laios fathered a son against the gods' will
and bred a husband for his mother, unhappy Oedipus.
Then came the gory tearing out of his eyes,
gods' devising, an exhibit to all of Greece,
which the sons of Oedipus desired to conceal
with the passage of time, trying to outrun the gods;
but they made a terrible mistake. In giving their father
no respect, no way out, they turned the poor man
savage. And he breathed on them deadly curses,
being in torment and deprived of his rights.
I tried everything in word and deed and reaped
for my troubles the hatred of Oedipus' sons.

---

105. *853:* Erechtheus was king of Athens. Erechthids (Erechthidae) are the children of Erechtheus, that is, Athenians. He was fighting a war with the Eleusinians, who had as an ally the Thracian Eumolpus. Tiresias (or in other versions, the Delphic oracle) told him that he should sacrifice one of his daughters to ensure victory. When he did so his other daughters committed suicide.

Creon, suicidal death is upon them
and many dead will fall on top of the dead,
Argive and Cadmeian limbs commingled,
will visit bitter lamentation on the land of Thebes.
And you, unhappy city, will go down with them
unless someone heeds my words.
This is best: that not any of Oedipus' descendants
be a citizen or ruler of the country
—they are god-maddened and will bring down the city.
Since evil is more powerful than good
there is one other means of preservation
but it is unsafe for me to speak of it,
and bitter to those whom fortune has chosen
to provide a remedy to preserve the city.
I must go now. Goodbye. With all the others
I will suffer the future, if need be. What else can I do?

CREON:
Stay here old man.

TIRESIAS:
Do not lay hands on me.

CREON:
Wait. Why are you rushing off?

TIRESIAS:
Not I, but your fortune is running from you.

CREON:
Say what it is that will save the city and its people.

TIRESIAS:
Now you want to know, but soon you will not.

CREON:
How could I not want to save my homeland?

TIRESIAS:
Then you want to hear? You insist upon it?

CREON:
What else could I feel more strongly about?

TIRESIAS:
Well then, you can hear my oracles now.
First I want you to give a clear answer to this:
Where is Menoeceus who brought me here?

CREON:
He hasn't gone anywhere. He is right next to you.

TIRESIAS:
Send him away, far from my prophecies.

CREON:
He is my own son and will keep secret what he must.

TIRESIAS:
Do you want me to speak in his presence?

CREON:
Yes, he will be glad to hear how to save the city.

TIRESIAS:
Hear then the course of my oracles:
what you must do to save the city of Cadmeians.
Since you insist on hearing—you must sacrifice
your son Menoeceus on behalf of your homeland.

CREON:
What are you saying? What story is this, old man?

TIRESIAS:
Just what has been revealed. You must do this.

CREON:
In a single breath your tongue has done much harm.

TIRESIAS:
To you, yes, but to our homeland great deliverance.

CREON:
No, no I did not hear. Let the city go.

TIRESIAS:
He is not the same man now, but he changes his tune.

CREON:
Goodbye. I have no use for your oracles.

TIRESIAS:
Is the truth to be lost because your luck has changed?

CREON:
By your knees and grey hair, please . . .

TIRESIAS:
Why supplicate me? You ask what's impossible.

CREON:
Be silent. Do not tell these things to the city.

TIRESIAS:
You command me to do wrong. I cannot be silent.

CREON:
What will you do to me? Will you kill my son?

TIRESIAS:
Others will do that, but I will tell my story.

CREON:
Why has this curse fallen upon my son?

TIRESIAS:
You have every right to question my words now.
You must sacrifice him in the chamber
where the watcher of Dirce's waters, earth-born dragon,
arose, and offer his blood as a libation to earth.
Because of Ares' ancient anger with Cadmus,
he demands death to atone for the serpent born of earth.
If you do this you will have Ares as your ally.

And if earth receives fruit for fruit and for blood
human blood, the land will favor your side
which once sent up the golden-helmeted crop
of Sown Men. Out of that race one must die
who is a child born from the dragon's jaw.
You are the last of us left here of the Sown Men,
unmixed both on your mother's and your father's side,
you and your children. The coming marriage of Haemon
precludes his sacrifice, for his status is not unwed.
He has not yet touched her, but still he has a bride.
This young colt, roaming free, may die for the city
and preserve the land of his fathers.
A bitter homecoming he will cause for Adrastus
and the Argives, casting dusky death over their eyes
and he will make Thebes glorious. Of two destinies
you must choose one: save your son or save your city.
You have heard all that I had to say. Daughter,
take me home. Anyone who practices the art of prophecy
is a fool. If he reveals offensive things
he will reap resentment from all who hear his omens
but if, out of pity for those who come to him, he lies
he wrongs the gods. Only Phoebus should
tell the gods' will to men, for he has no one to fear.

(Tiresias and his daughter begin their slow departure,
leaving by the same parodos as they entered.)

CHORUS:

Why are you speechless, Creon, gaping in silence?
I too am just as dumbfounded as you.

CREON:

What could anyone say? It is obvious what my words
must be. I will never reach such a point of misery
that I would offer my son as a sacrifice for the city.
For all mankind love of children is a way of life
and no one would offer his child for slaughter.
Let no one try to flatter me into killing my son,
but I am more than willing to die—I have reached
a ripe age—to keep my homeland safe.
Come, my boy, before the whole city learns of it,

reject the crazy ramblings of that oracle monger
and go into exile—leave the country as quick as you can.
He will tell this to the leading citizens and officers,
going around to the seven gates and company commanders.
If we act quickly you can be saved
but if you are slow we are lost and you will die.

MENOECEUS:
Where should I go then? What city? What foreign friends?

CREON:
Wherever you will be farthest from this country.

MENOECEUS:
Yours to command me and mine to carry it out.

CREON:
After you go past Delphi . . .

MENOECEUS
Where must I go next, father?

CREON:
To the Aetolian country.

MENOECEUS:
And from there, where next?

CREON:
To Thesprotian territory.

MENOECEUS:
The sacred site of Dodona?[106]

CREON:
Yes, you understand.

---

106. *982:* Dodona in Epirus (northwest Greece) was the most important oracle of Zeus, the site of his speaking oak. Zeus was a protector of suppliants.

MENOECEUS:
What protection will I get there?

CREON:
The god will be your guide.

MENOECEUS:
What will I do for money?

CREON:
I will provide you with money.

MENOECEUS:
Thank you, Father.
But you go now. I will go see your sister,
Jocasta, at whose breast I was first nursed
when I lost my mother and was an orphan.[107]
I will go speak to her and then look to my safety.
But go now. Don't hinder me on your side.

(Exit Creon by stage right parodos.)

Women, do you see how well I calmed my father's fear
cheating him with words, to achieve my aim?
He is trying to send me away, deprive the city of its destiny,
and make a coward of me. It is forgiveable
in an old man. But for my part there is no excuse
if I become a traitor to my homeland, which gave me life.
Just so you know—I will go and save the city
and give my life to die for this country.
It is shameful—when some men, who are free of oracles
and do not come under divinely imposed obligation,
stand by their shields and are not reluctant to die
fighting before the towers for their homeland—
but will I betray my father and my brother,
betray my city too and like a coward flee the country?
Wouldn't I be seen as a deserter wherever I live?

---

107. *987–89:* Another relationship for Jocasta, foster mother of Menoeceus. In Sophocles' *Antigone*, Creon's wife is alive and kills herself when she hears of the death of Haemon, the last of her sons.

I will not, by Zeus in the heavens and bloody Ares
who once established the Sown Men who rose up
from the earth to be kings of this country.
I will go now to stand upon the highest tower
and immolate myself into the deep dark den
of the dragon where the prophet directed
and I will preserve the homeland. My word is final.
I go now to offer my death to the city, no paltry gift,
and I shall deliver the land from its sickness.
If everyone, would take advantage of whatever
opportunity offers to benefit the common welfare
of his country, future cities would experience
less dissension and people's lives would be better.

(Exit Menoeceus by stage left parodos.)

Third Stasimon[108]

CHORUS:

[Strophe]

You came you came
oh winged brood of earth,
brood of the underground monster Echidna,[109]
snatcher of Cadmeians
full of death, full of sorrow
half girl
deadly freak
with whipping wings
flesh-eating claws
who snatched the young
from Dirce's lands
to music without the lyre

---

108. *1019–66:* The third stasimon is a lamentation for the men who were victims of the Sphinx, the Dragon, and the family blood-lust. It describes the lament and repeats it and becomes at the same time a dirge for the latest victim.

109. *1020:* An echidna is a viper and symbol of treachery; as a supernatural monster, she is half nymph and half snake, an eater of raw flesh. See Hesiod, *Theogony* 295–305.

avenging Fury[110]
sorrows and more sorrows you kept bringing to our land
with your murders. A killer sent by the gods
did this.
Keenings of mothers,
keenings of girls
they sobbed in the houses.
A cry of woe
a strain of woe[111]
another and then another cried out
in succession up and down the city
the moaning roared like thunder
and there was the same sound of sorrow
when the swooping monster Sphinx
caused one more of the men to vanish from the city.

[Antistrophe]

In time he came
sent by Delphi
Oedipus unhappy man
here to the land of Thebes.
They welcomed him then for heartache later,
for he joined his mother
in marriage, no marriage there,
the wretch, after his glorious victory
in riddles,
and he poisoned the city.
Through blood he wades;
into unclean struggle—
he has sent his children there by his curses,
unhappy man. Amazed, we are amazed
at the one who is gone to death
for his native land
leaving behind the same songs of sorrow for Creon

110. *1029:* Erinys, a fury or spirit of vengeance or family justice, an avenger.

111. *1036–37:* The wailing sounds of the mothers and maidens (*ieieion boan, ieieion melos*, an untranslatable sad sound) are made in the present by the maidens of the chorus, mourning for the orphan boy.

but he has gone to make the seven-towered gates of the land
glorious in victory.
I pray, adored
Pallas, we will be mothers like that
and be blessed in our children—
you caused the blood of the dragon
to flow down—struck with a stone—
you stirred Cadmus' mind to his work
and there fell on this land, by god-sent rapture,
A DOOM.

Fourth Episode

MESSENGER: *(enters along the stage left parodos)*
Halloo! Is there anyone at the palace gates?
Open up. Send Jocasta out of the house.
Halloo, I call again. Though it is a long way, still
come out and hear me, noble wife of Oedipus,
cease from your laments and tears of grief.

JOCASTA:
My dear, it is you who stand beside Eteocles in battle[112]
and shield him from hostile missiles,
you have not come to announce his death—?
Have you? What news do you have to report?
Is my son dead or alive? Please, tell me.

MESSENGER:
He is alive. Of that terror I can relieve you.

JOCASTA:
What is it then? Are our seven circling towers still standing?

MESSENGER:
They stand unscaled. The city is not taken.

---

112. *1072:* Compare with Electra, who does not recognize the messenger even though he is one of her brother's slaves and had just left her house (*Electra* 765).

JOCASTA:
Have they faced the peril of battle with the Argives?

MESSENGER:
Yes, peril in the extreme, but Theban Ares
prevailed over the Mycenaean spear.

JOCASTA:
In the name of the gods, tell me one thing, if you know—
about Polynices. I care about him—is he alive?

MESSENGER:
Both your sons are alive up to this moment.

JOCASTA:
Bless you. But how did you, from your post on the towers,
drive away the Argive army from our gates?
Tell me so that I may go and bring pleasure
to the old blind man inside with the news that the city is safe.

MESSENGER:
Creon's son stood on the highest tower to die
for his country, staining his sword dark with blood
as he thrust it through his throat, our land's salvation![113]
Your son, then, divided the companies into seven
and assigned commanders to the seven gates, guards
against the enemy, and he stationed horsemen
in reserve for horsemen, infantry for fellow shield-bearers
so that there would be a quick defense
for trouble spots along the walls. High on the battlements
we spot the white shields of the Argive army
pouring down from Teumessus[114] and near the trench
they are charging the city of the Cadmeians at a run.
From their side and from our walls, at the same time
exactly, bugles trumpet a paean call to war.

---

113. *1090–92:* Menoeceus dies before the battle, but his death has no obvious effect on the battle, which has its own natural back-and-forth rhythm. At this point there is no way of knowing whether the city is saved.

114. *1100:* A hill about five miles from Thebes, where the Argives had probably camped overnight.

First to the Neitan gate a company bristling
with close-packed shields marched forth
under command of the huntress' son, Parthenopaeus.
On his shield he carried his family crest:
Atalanta taking down the Aetolian boar with arrows
shot from far away. Then to the Proetid gate advanced
the prophet Amphiaraus with fresh-slaughtered victims
on his chariot, displaying no violent insignia
on his shield, but calmly carrying arms without sign.
To the Ogygian gate strode King Hippomedon:
in the middle of his shield the insignia showed
all-seeing Panoptes[115] spotted all over with eyes.
Some of the eyes opened with the risings of stars
others were shuttered with their settings—
we were able to see this later, after he had died.
Up to the Homoloid gate Tydeus led his company;
on his shield he carried a lionskin with bristling mane.
And on the right the figure of Prometheus the Titan
was carrying a torch to set ablaze the city of Thebes.
At the Krenaian gate your son Polynices led his force.
On his shield he bore the sign of Potnian horses[116]
running wild. They were rearing in alarm.
Inside the rim, right under the handle there were pivots
cleverly circling to make the horses appear mad.
And no less heart-set on war and battle
Capaneus led a company to the Electran gate.
On the iron-backed circle of his shield there was fixed
an earth-born giant bearing on his shoulders an entire city,
which he had pried up from its foundations with levers—
he wanted to show us what our city was going to suffer.
Adrastus was poised to breach the Seventh gate.
His shield was covered with a hundred snakes
in silhouette and he wore hydras on his left arm
an Argive boast—the serpents held in their jaws

115. *1115:* Panoptes is Argus who guarded Io. He had eyes all over his body so that while some slept others were open.

116. *1125:* The Potnian horses were from the town of Potniae near Thebes where there was a well, the water of which drove animals mad if they drank from it. The most famous were Glaucus' maddened horses, who killed and devoured their master.

Theban children they were seizing from the walls.
I was able to look at their shields when I brought
a message to the shepherds of the contingents.[117]
We fought first with bows and arrows and javelins
and far-shooting slings and pounded them
with stones. We were beating them in battle
when a sudden cry went up from Tydeus and your son:
"Sons of Danaans, before you are crushed with missiles,
why do you hold back from rushing the gates, all together,
infantry, cavalry, and drivers of chariots?"
When they heard the shout, no one was a laggard.
Many fell, blood gushing from their heads.
On our side you could see men tumbling from the walls
thick and fast like divers, the breath knocked out of them
watering the parched earth with streams of their blood.
And then the son of Atalanta, an Arcadian, no Argive,
like a hurricane falling upon the gates, is shouting
for fire and pick-axes to dig down the city.
But Periclymenus,[118] son of the sea-god, stopped him
as he raged in his fury, hitting him on the head with a rock
the size of a wagon, a cornice from the battlements.
It shattered his blond head, smashed the sutures
of his bones and bloodied his just-reddening cheek.[119]
He will not come back alive to his mother,
the beautiful huntress, daughter of Mainalos.
When he saw that we were successful at this gate,
your son went on to the next and I followed him.
I saw Tydeus and a thick phalanx of men armed
with Aetolian spears flinging at the topmost lip
of the towers so that men in flight were leaving
the steep sides of the battlements. Again, like a hunter
with his hounds your son rounded them up
and posted them back on the towers. On to the other gates
we hurried after we had settled this disorder.

---

117. *1140:* In Homer the commanders are called "shepherds of the people."

118. *1156:* Besides Eteocles, Periclymenus is the only Theban defender named.

119. *1160:* "Reddening cheek" refers to the first growth of his beard, indicating how young he was (see note on line 32).

Capaneus—how can I put into words how wild he was?
Holding a long-reaching ladder to scale the wall,
as he approached he was making the boast,
that not even Zeus' sacred fire could prevent him
from leveling the city from its highest turrets.
As he was saying this, though pelted by rocks,
he kept crawling up, crouched under his shield,
setting his feet on the ladder's rungs one by one.
Now he was passing the coping-stone of the walls
when Zeus struck him with lightning. The earth bellowed.
All our hearts were struck with terror. And from the ladder
he swung round in a circle; his limbs went separate ways;
his hair flew up to the sky; his blood spurted to the ground;
his hands and legs were spinning like Ixion's wheel.[120]
He fell to the earth, his body a ball of fire.
When Adrastus saw that Zeus was his army's enemy,
he restrained his Argives on the other side of the trench,
but our side, seeing the happy omen from Zeus
kept up our assault—drivers of chariots, cavalry,
infantry—and into the midst of Argive arms
we closed on them with spears. It was total chaos.
They were dying, falling over the sides of their chariots;
wheels popped off; axles piled up on axles
and dead bodies were piled on top of bodies.
And so we have kept safe the towers of our homeland
up to the present day. Whether our country will stay lucky
in the days and years to come depends on the gods.
But for now, one of the gods has kept us safe.

Chorus:

Oh glorious victory. If the gods have in mind
something better, I pray our good fortune will last.

Jocasta:

What concerns the gods and fortune is going well.
My sons are alive and our country has survived.
Poor Creon has reaped the bitter harvest

---

120. *1185:* Ixion's *wheel*: in punishment for an attempt to rape Hera, Ixion was bound for eternity to a burning (or flying) wheel.

of my marriage and Oedipus' tragedy,
losing his son for the common good, but grief
to him. But, please, take up your story again,
What are my sons planning to do next?

MESSENGER:
Let the rest be. Up to now things are still going well.

JOCASTA:
What you just said makes me suspicious. I can't let it go.

MESSENGER:
Your sons are safe. What more do you need to know?

JOCASTA:
To hear if the future still brings good news.

MESSENGER:
Let me go. Your son will be missing his aide.

JOCASTA:
You are hiding some trouble, trying to keep me in the dark.

MESSENGER:
I would prefer not to spoil the good news by telling the bad.

JOCASTA:
You will tell it, unless you can fly up to the sky.

MESSENGER:
Very well then. Why couldn't you just let me go
after the good news and not make me tell the bad?
Your two sons are getting ready—it's a deplorable
act of daring—to fight apart in single combat.
Speaking to the Argives and Cadmeians
in public, a speech that should never have been made,
Eteocles went first. Standing on a steep tower
he ordered silence to be heralded to the army
and spoke: "Commanders of the Greek land,
chief men of the Danaans who came here
and people of Cadmus, do not for Polynices' sake

nor for mine, squander your lives.
To free you from this peril, I will myself
alone stand to face my brother in battle.
And if I kill him I will live alone in my house,
but if I am defeated I will hand it over to him alone.
You, Argives, give up the struggle and return
to your country, do not leave your lives here;
the people of the Sown Men lying dead are enough."
That is what he said, and then your son Polynices
jumped up from the ranks and applauded his speech
and all the Argives shouted their approval and so did
the people of Cadmus, since they thought it was right.
At this the generals made a truce and in no man's land
between the armies they swore oaths to abide by it.
Then they covered their bodies in their bronze armor,
gray-headed Oedipus' two sons in their youthful prime.
They were outfitted by their friends, our commander,
by the Sown Men, the other by the chiefs of the Danaids.
They stood there gleaming in arms and did not blanch
with fear, furiously eager to hurl the spear at each other.
One after another their friends came up to them
with words of encouragement saying this sort of thing:
"Polynices, it is in your power to raise an image of Zeus
as a trophy and to bestow a glorious reputation on Argos."
But to Eteocles in turn: "Now you are fighting for the city.
If you win glorious victory the scepter is yours to wield."
With words like these they exhorted them to battle.
The prophets made sacrifice of sheep and observed
the burning tips and fissures; in the moisture of the flesh
opposite the top of the flame they found two meanings:
one a sign of victory, the other of defeated men.[121]
If you have any means to stop them, words of wisdom
or magical charms, go, restrain your sons
from this terrible battle. The danger is great
and the prize will be tragic tears for you
if you are to lose both your sons on this day.

121. *1255–58:* For interpretations of this difficult passage see Mastronarde *ad loc.*

JOCASTA:
Antigone, daughter, come out of the house,
not to dance at the maidens' festivals[122]
but now god-ordained fate propels you
and you must come along with your mother
to stop two good men, your brothers, veering
toward death from dying at each other's hands.

ANTIGONE:
What, Mother? What new alarm for our family
are you calling out in front of the house?

JOCASTA:
My daughter, your brothers' lives are over.

ANTIGONE:
What is it?

JOCASTA:
They are set on fighting a duel.

ANTIGONE:
Oh no, what are you saying, Mother?

JOCASTA:
Not words of comfort. You must come with me.

ANTIGONE:
Leave my maidens' chamber? Where are we going?

JOCASTA:
Through the army.

ANTIGONE:
I feel awkward in front of a crowd of men.

JOCASTA:
Shyness does not suit your situation.

---

122. *1265:* The various coming-of-age celebratory rituals that girls participated in.

ANTIGONE:
What will I do?

JOCASTA:
You must settle your brothers' quarrel.

ANTIGONE:
How, Mother?

JOCASTA:
Fall down on your knees at my side.
Lead us to where they plan to fight. There must be no delay.
Hurry, daughter, hurry, because if I get there before
my sons' spear-fight my life will go on,[123]
but if they die I will lie down with them in death.

(Exit Messenger stage left, followed by Jocasta and Antigone.)

Fourth Stasimon

CHORUS:

[Strophe]

Aiai, aiai
trembling, trembling with dread I hold my heart.
Through my flesh
pity flows, pity for the unhappy mother.
Two children—who will shed whose blood?
Ah me for the troubles, oh Zeus, oh earth,
brother's neck, brother's life
with weapons, in bloodshed
sorrow, more sorrow,
which dead man murdered will I keen?

123. *1282:* A line (1281) has been omitted because the manuscript line, which reads "but if you are slow we are lost and you will die," is a repetition of line 976, where it is more appropriate.

[Antistrophe]

Feu da, feu da[124]
paired beasts, murderous souls,
brandishing spears,
they fall, savage falls; both will soon shed blood.
Unhappy ones, why in the world did they come
to the thought of single combat,
with alien call the keening cry
of tears for the dead we shall shrill.
The fate of death is almost here.
This day's light will decide the future.
Hapless death, hapless death from the Furies.

Exodos[125]

*(Enter Creon along right parodos,
carrying his son's body.)*[126]

CHORUS:
I see Creon in a cloud of sorrow coming here
to the house and so will end my present lamentations.

CREON:
Ah. What to do? Shed tears in pity
for myself or for the city, which is under a cloud

---

124. *1284, 1296: aiai,* and *feu da* are untranslatable tragic noises

125. *Exodos*: everything that comes after the last choral ode. This one falls into three parts:

1. 1308–1479 Another long messenger's speech, delivered to Creon.
2. 1480–1581 The messenger leaves and three corpses are brought back by Antigone and attendants; Oedipus comes out into the light.
3. 1582–1766 The family of Oedipus comes to an end.

The exodos is a four-character scene: Creon, Messenger, Antigone, Oedipus, but the actor playing the messenger would leave after his speech and return as Oedipus.

126. *1308:* Creon's entrance with Menoeceus' body is reminiscent of the scene at the end of *Antigone,* when he comes in carrying the body of Haemon, the last of his sons.

of gloom like the journey across Acheron?[127]
My son is gone, by dying for his country
he won a glorious reputation, but bitterest gall to me.
Mournfully I lifted him from the dragon's den
I carried him in my arms, victim of suicide.
My whole house is wailing. But here I am,
an old man, looking for my aged sister, Jocasta,
to wash and lay out my dead son.[128]
Those not yet dead must give honors
to the dead and pay respect to the gods of death.

CHORUS:
Your sister is gone, Creon. She left the house
and her daughter, Antigone, has gone with her.

CREON:
Where? On what errand? Tell me.

CHORUS:
She heard that her sons were going to face each other
in single combat of spears for the royal house.

CREON:
What are you saying? I was tending to the body
of my son and heard nothing about this.

CHORUS:
Your sister left some time ago, Creon.
I expect the life and death struggle
has already been fought by the sons of Oedipus.

CREON:
Ah me. I see evidence of this,
the tragic face and bearing of a messenger
coming here; he will report the awful news.

(Messenger enters along the parodos stage left.)

---

127. *1312:* Acheron is the river of sorrow in Hades.

128. *1319:* Women were associated with transitional events in human life, like birth and death, and with the physical body.

MESSENGER:
Oh horrors! What story or what words shall I speak?

CREON:
We are ruined. Your words promise disaster.

MESSENGER:
Horrors! No other word will do. I bring great sorrows.

CREON:
On top of the troubles we have already suffered.
What more do you have to tell?

MESSENGER:
Your sister's sons are dead, Creon.

CREON:
Oh no. You tell of a great tragedy for me, for the city.
House of Oedipus, did you hear this,
the sons dead, meeting the same doom?

CHORUS:
So awful, the house itself would weep if it were able.

CREON:
Ah me, this is the heaviest, most tragic fate.
[Ah me, unhappy in my sufferings, wretched as I am.][129]

MESSENGER:
If you knew the bad news on top of this . . .

CREON:
How could there be more misery than this?

MESSENGER:
Your sister is dead with her two sons.

---

129. *1346:* Several of the manuscripts omit this bathetic line.

CHORUS:
Raise a wail, raise a wail of women
beating their hands over the head.[130]

CREON:
Poor Jocasta. What an end to your life and marriage
you have suffered all because of the Sphinx's riddle.
How did it happen, the death of her two sons,
a struggle caused by Oedipus' curse? Tell me.

MESSENGER:
The success of our homeland before the towers
you already know. The surrounding walls are not so far
that you could fail to know all that happened there.
When aged Oedipus' two young sons
had arrayed themselves in their armor of bronze
they stepped into no man's land and took their stands,
two commanders, two leaders of their men,
for single combat and a test of valor with the spear.
Looking toward Argos, Polynices sent out his curse:
"Goddess Hera,[131] I belong to you since I joined
in marriage the daughter of Adrastus and dwell in his land.
Grant to me that I kill my brother and in victory
soak my right hand with his hated blood,"
and prayed for this most sordid crown, to kill his own kin.
Tears of pity for their doom welled up in many eyes.
They looked into each other's eyes, exchanging glances.
And then Eteocles, looking toward the temple of Pallas
Athena of the golden shield prayed, "Daughter of Zeus,
grant to my hand to hurl a victorious spear
from my arm striking my brother's heart
and to kill the man who came to lay waste my homeland."
And when the torch was let go like the blast
of an Etruscan trumpet,[132] signal of murderous battle,

---

130. *1350–51:* Literally, "white-armed beating of hands over the head": lightness was a sign of beauty and delicateness, and it was traditional to depict women's flesh as white, whether because they spent most of their time indoors or because they used white lead as a cosmetic.

131. *1365:* Hera was the chief god at Argos.

132. *1378:* The battlefield trumpet was considered an Etruscan invention.

they rushed at terrifying speed upon each other
like boars whetting their savage jaws
they came together, chins dripping with foam,
they raced on with spears. They crouched behind their shields
so the steel would glance off without success.
If one spotted the other's eye rising above the rim
he directed the spear at his face, hoping for the first kill,
but cleverly they turned the eye to the shields'
eyelets, so that the spear had no effect.
In shock for their friends, more sweat was dripping
from the onlookers than from those actually engaged.
Then Eteocles' foot brushed aside a rock
that was rolling under his step and he let his leg slip
outside the shield. Polynices rushed to meet him with the spear,
catching sight of the opportunity for his weapon to strike
and pierced through the leg with his Argive spear
and the entire Danaid army raised a cry of triumph.
During this struggle, seeing the shoulder exposed,
Eteocles, though first wounded, threw his spear powerfully
through Polynices' chest and drew a cheer
from the citizens of Cadmus. But he broke the tip of his spear.
Faced with the loss of his spear, Eteocles backs up a step
and lifts up a slab of marble and heaves it,
breaking Polynices' javelin in two. The battle was tied,
the hands of both were deprived of their shafts.
Then grasping the hilts of their swords
the two came together setting shield to shield
standing firm on each side they made a great din of battle.
Somehow Eteocles from his familiarity with the country
thought of the Thessalian stratagem[133] and brought it into play.
Backing away from the present standoff,
he sets his left foot behind him
and protecting his abdomen, he advances
on his right foot and straight through the navel
he thrusts his sword and fixes it into his brother's backbone.
Poor Polynices, cramping up his sides and stomach,
stumbles in the pools of his own blood.
And his brother, thinking he had won the contest,

---

133. *1408:* The Thessalian stratagem may have been a wrestling technique; see Mastronarde's note on 1409–13 (1994).

throwing his sword onto the ground, began stripping the body
not keeping his mind on himself, but on his object
and that is what tripped him up. Still breathing a little,
and holding onto his weapon even after his mortal fall
with one last effort Polynices who had fallen first
stuck his sword into his brother's liver.
Their mouths full of dust the two lie fallen side by side.
They have left behind the royal power undivided.

CHORUS:
It is a tragedy. Oedipus, I grieve for your sorrows.
A god, it seems, has fulfilled your curses.

MESSENGER:
Listen now to this—there was worse to follow.
While her two fallen sons are giving up their lives
their unhappy mother throws herself onto the scene
on scurrying feet with her young daughter in tow.
Seeing them wounded with mortal blows,
she cried out, "My sons I am here too late
to help." Throwing herself on each in turn
she sobbed, she howled in grief for her lost labor
of nursing them, and their sister stood alongside her,
"Keepers of Mother's old age, you betray my marriage,
my dear, dear brothers." And then a dying gasp
whistling from his chest, King Eteocles
heard his mother, and placing on her a clammy hand,
let out no further sound, but from his eyes
he spoke with his tears to show her a sign of love.
But the other, Polynices, was still breathing and, looking
toward his sister and his gray-haired mother, spoke to them:
"We are done for, Mother. I feel sorry for you
and my sister and my dead brother.
He was loved, lost my love, but still I loved him.
Bury me, Mother, you too, my sister, here
in my homeland, and though the city is angry
persuade them with soothing words so that I may have
that much of my country, though I have lost my father's house.
Shut my eyelids with your own hand,
Mother," and he placed it on his eyes himself,
"and farewell. Already darkness closes in on me."

Both sons together breathed out their pitiful lives.
And when their mother had witnessed this tragedy,
overwrought with grief, she snatched the sword[134]
from between the bodies and performed a horrific act.
She thrust the iron straight through her neck. She lies there dead
between her beloved sons, her arms embracing both.
Then the army rose up in strife of words.
We argued that my master was victor,
and they that theirs was. The leaders were quarreling,
one side that Polynices had struck the first blow,
the other that both were dead so there was no victory.
In the midst of this Antigone slipped off unseen.
But they—the men—rushed to arms. By lucky forethought,
the people of Cadmus were sitting under arms
so that we got the jump on them, still unarmed,
when, without warning, we fell upon the Argive army.
No one could withstand. The plains were filled with men
in flight and blood was streaming from untold numbers
fallen to the spear. And as we were victorious in battle
some were setting up a victory statue to Zeus,
others stripping shields from the Argive dead
and bringing the spoils inside the walls.[135]
Others with Antigone are carrying the bodies
of the dead here for their loved ones to mourn.

(Antigone and a procession of extras carrying the bodies enter along the parodos from the battlefield, stage left.)

Of the city's struggles some have turned out
most happily, others most tragically.

(Exit Messenger stage right.)

---

134. *1456:* This would be the sword Eteocles threw down at line 1417. The sword is the usual masculine suicide weapon. Women are more likely to choose hanging, but here Jocasta uses what opportunity has presented. Stabbing herself in the neck, however, is feminine; men aim for the heart or liver (see Loraux 1987: 7–17).

135. *1466–75:* Thebes is saved. Not necessarily by the heroism of Menoeceus, nor by the seven defenders, nor even by the single combat of the enemy brothers, but because the Theban fighting men had the good sense to keep their arms at the ready. The citizen army prevails.

Chorus:

No longer is the tragedy of this house
just a report, for all can see now
the fallen bodies of these three
here before the palace—in a shared death,
they have drawn fate's dark lot.

Antigone: *(singing)*

Not veiling the soft skin of my cheek,
covered with ringlets or like a bashful girl
hiding the red blush of my face under my eyes
I carry myself along, a bacchante of the dead[136]
throwing the cloth from my head
casting off my soft saffron robe
leading a procession of mourning for the dead.
Alas, ah, Polynices, you were well-named. Ah, Thebes,
your strife, not strife, but death on death
overthrew the house of Oedipus
with blood of horror, blood of gloom.
What musical lament
what song in tune
with my tears, my tears—house, my house
I call upon you
bearing three bodies, kindred blood,
mother and sons, the Fury's delight
that destroyed all the house of Oedipus
when he read the riddle clear to him
of the savage singing Sphinx,
hard to fathom, and he killed her.
Ah me, ah me
what Greek, what foreign speaker
or who else of well-born men
from ages past endured so many evils
of human blood
such sufferings brought to light
in misery? How can I mourn?

---

136. *1489:* Bacchante: Intense emotion is common to both Bacchic ritual and funeral lamentation, both practiced by women in groups (see Segal 1997: 363).

What bird then in the high-leaved branches
of oak or pine
in laments of a solitary mother
sings along with my pains?
Woe with woeful sounds
I weep, soon to pass
a lonely lifetime
in tears always,
tears streaming from my eyes.
On which of them should I cast
the first offering of locks torn from my hair?
Here by my mother's two
breasts once full of milk
or on the fatal wounds
of my brothers' bodies?
Ototototoi![137] Leave your
home, coming with blind eyes,
aged father, show yourself,
Oedipus, reveal your wretched life,
you who in the house have cast over your eyes
dark gloom and drag out a slow-footed life.
Do you hear? Wandering
in the halls, unhappy man
resting your aged feet on the bed?

OEDIPUS:

(Enters from the palace.)

Why, daughter, do you bring me
with a staff for my blind feet out into the light
from my bed of pain, from my dark chamber
with most piteous tears,
a gray unseen image of air
a ghost from below
a dream in flight?

137. *1530: Ototototoi*: an untranslatable wail of grief.

ANTIGONE:
You will bear the unhappy telling of news,
Father. Your sons no longer look upon
the light nor your wife who always helped you
with kind support for your blind step,
Father, it's so sad.

OEDIPUS:
Ah me for my sufferings. I am left to grieve
and cry out. Three lives, by what doom,
how did they die? Tell me, child.

ANTIGONE:
Not in reproach or mocking
but with sorrow I speak. Your spirit of vengeance
weighted down with swords
and fire and brutal battles has come over your sons.
Ah Father, ah me.

OEDIPUS:
Woe . . .

ANTIGONE:
Why do you mourn?

OEDIPUS:
My children.

ANTIGONE:
You have waded into misery.
But what if you could still see the sun's passage through the sky[138]
and look on these bodies of the dead
with the sight of your own eyes?

OEDIPUS:
The evil fate of my children is clear
but my poor wife, daughter, how did she die?

---

138. *1562:* See line 3 where Jocasta invokes the Sun starting his course through the sky as the day and play begin.

Antigone:

Letting fall tears of grief
clear to all,
she offered her breast, yes, offered to her children,
a suppliant, holding it out in entreaty.
She had found her sons at the Electra gate
beside the meadow where lotus grows,
amid spears in fraternal slaughter,
their mother found them like lions in their den
battling, already wounded,
the cold deadly spilling of blood,
Hades' portion, gift of Ares.
From between the corpses she seized a bronze sword
and dyed it red inside her flesh, in grief for her sons she fell between them.
On this day, Father, upon our house
the god who brings these things to pass
has brought together all the heartbreak.

Chorus:

This day has been the beginning of many evils
for the house of Oedipus. I pray for a happier life.

Creon:

Desist now from your wailing since it is time
to be mindful of the funerals. Oedipus, listen
to my commands. Your son Eteocles handed over to me
the leadership of the country, entrusting to me the dowry
for Haemon and the marriage of your daughter Antigone.
You, I will not allow you to live any longer in this country.
Tiresias in fact told me clearly that Thebes will never
be prosperous while you are living inside its walls.
Go then. I say this not in a spirit of insult or hostility
toward you, but because of your vengeful spirit
I am afraid that the land will suffer more disaster.

Oedipus:

My destiny! From the start you brought me forth
to sorrow and suffering, if any man ever was.
Even before I came into the light from my mother's womb,
Apollo had declared to Laios that still unborn

I would become my father's murderer. Oh the misery—
and when I was born, the father who gave me life
tried at once to kill me, believing I was his enemy
because he was destined to die at my hand. He disposed of me,
still crying for my mother's milk, to be devoured by wild beasts.
I was saved from that fate, and how I wish Cithairon
had gone to the bottomless pit of Tartarus[139]
because it did not destroy me, but my destiny gave me
to Polybus as my master to be his slave.
Then I killed my father and to my misery
I entered the bed of my doomed mother and fathered sons,
my own brothers, and now I have destroyed them.
I inherited Laios' curses and passed them on to my children
for I was not naturally so devoid of intellect
that I devised these horrors against my own eyes
and the lives of my children without the hand of the gods.
And now in my misery what am I to do?
Who will guide my blind step? The dead woman here?
If she were still alive I know she would.
Or my pair of noble sons? They too are lost to me.
Am I still young enough to find a livelihood?
How can I? Why do you cause my death, Creon?
Yes, you will kill me if you drive me out of my country.
I will not wrap my arms around your knees[140]
to beg and appear a coward. I will not betray
my own nobility, not even in my broken condition.

CREON:

Thank you for not pleading at my knees
I still would not allow you to remain in this country.
Of these dead—this one is to be laid out in the house,
but this one who came here to lay waste his homeland
with a foreign army, Polynices' corpse,
cast it out unburied beyond the borders of the territory.
This proclamation will go out to all the Cadmeians:
If anyone is caught tending this body

---

139. *1605:* Tartarus was the lowest region of the world, beneath Hades where the gods imprisoned their enemies.

140. *1622:* That is, in an act of supplication.

or covering it with earth, he will be put to death.
[But leave him unwept, unburied, for birds to scavenge.]
And you, Antigone, leave now the lamentation
for these three dead and go inside the house.
Conduct yourself as befits a young woman preparing
for tomorrow and marriage to Haemon that awaits you.[141]

ANTIGONE:
Father, how we are sunk in troubles and misery.
I pity you more than the dead.
For to you one thing is not heavy and another less so,
but you were born unlucky in everything, Father.
But tell me, newly named king, why do you abuse
my father by driving him from his homeland?
Why do you make decrees over a pitiful corpse?

CREON:
It is Eteocles' decision, not mine.

ANTIGONE:
It is senseless, and you are a fool to go along with it.

CREON:
How so? Am I wrong to carry out his last wish?

ANTIGONE:
Yes, if it is a wicked and wrong decision.

CREON:
What is this? Is it wrong to throw him to the dogs?

ANTIGONE:
The penalty you exact is not lawful.[142]

CREON:
It is. He was not born an enemy to the city, but became one.

---

141. *1637–38:* Antigone combines associations of the wedding with the funeral procession she is enacting (see Seaford 1994: 350–52).

142. *1651:* Basic Panhellenic values forbade withholding burial from a fallen enemy (see Euripides *Suppliants*, 526)

ANTIGONE:
Then he gave up his life to his doom.

CREON:
And now let him pay the penalty to the grave.

ANTIGONE:
What wrong did he do, if he came for his share of his homeland?

CREON:
Just so you know, this man will not be buried.

ANTIGONE:
I will bury him even if the city forbids it.

CREON:
Then you will bury yourself along with his corpse.

ANTIGONE:
Well, it is glorious for two kin to lie side by side.

CREON:
Take hold of her and drag her inside the house.

ANTIGONE:
No, you don't. Since I will not let go of his dead body.

CREON:
Fate has decided this, young woman, not what you choose.

ANTIGONE:
This too is decided—not to abuse the dead.

CREON:
No one will put dust on this body, nor pour ablutions on him.

ANTIGONE:
I will. In the name of my mother Jocasta, I beg you, Creon.

CREON:
You are wasting your efforts. You will not have your way.

Antigone:
Let me pour water over the body.

Creon:
That would be one of the things forbidden by the city.

Antigone:
But let me put bandages around his raw wounds.

Creon:
There is no way you will honor this corpse.

Antigone:
Oh my dear, dear one. At least I will kiss your mouth.

Creon:
Do not ruin your marriage with your grieving.

Antigone:
I will never—as long as I live—marry your son.

Creon:
But you must. How will you escape the marriage?

Antigone:
That night I will be one of Danaus' daughters and kill him.[143]

Creon:
Look at the audacity with which she taunts me.

Antigone:
Let this weapon know it, the sword of my oath.[144]

Creon:
Why are you so eager to avoid your marriage?

---

143. *1675:* Literally: "That night will turn me into one of Danaus' daughters," that is, a killer of her husband: all but one of the fifty daughters of Danaus (the Danaids) killed their husbands, the fifty sons of Aegyptus, on their wedding night.

144. *1677:* She touches the sword with which Jocasta killed herself.

ANTIGONE:
I will go into exile with my unhappy father.

CREON:
You show nobility of spirit, along with your lunacy.

ANTIGONE:
And I will die with him too, so you know the rest.

CREON:
Go then. You will not murder my son. Leave the country.

(Exit Creon into the palace.)

OEDIPUS:
My daughter, I admire your spirit, but . . .

ANTIGONE:
If I marry, you will have to go into exile alone.

OEDIPUS:
Stay and be happy. I will endure my troubles.

ANTIGONE:
You are blind. Who will take care of you?

OEDIPUS:
I will fall wherever fate takes me and lie on the ground.

ANTIGONE:
Where is Oedipus of the famous riddle?

OEDIPUS:
He is gone. One day blessed me. One day ruined me.[145]

ANTIGONE:
May I not have my share of your miseries then?

145. *1689:* See Sophocles, *Oedipus the King* 438: "This day will give you birth and destroy you."

Oedipus:
Exile is disgraceful for a daughter with her blind father.

Antigone
Not for a sensible one, Father, but noble.

Oedipus:
Help me so I can touch your mother.

Antigone:
Here, reach out your hand and touch the dear, dear old woman.

Oedipus:
Mother, most unhappy partner.

Antigone:
She lies there pathetically, all her troubles around her.

Oedipus:
And the bodies of Eteocles and Polynices, where are they?

Antigone:
The two lie stretched out next to each other.

Oedipus:
Lay my sightless hand on their unhappy faces.

Antigone:
Here. Put your hand on your dead sons.

Oedipus:
Dear, unhappy dead of an unhappy father.

Antigone:
Dear name, dear to me, Polynices.

Oedipus:
Now, daughter, Loxias' oracle is coming to pass.

Antigone:
What oracle? Are you telling more troubles on top of these?

OEDIPUS:
That I will die a refugee in Athens.

ANTIGONE:
Where? What rampart of Attica will welcome you?

OEDIPUS:
Sacred Colonus,[146] home of the horse god.
But come, tend to your blind father,
since you are set upon sharing my exile.

ANTIGONE:
Go into gloomy exile. Stretch out your dear hand,
aged father, with me
as guide, like a breeze escorting a ship.

OEDIPUS:
Here, here, I set out,
my poor child, you be a guide to my feet.

ANTIGONE
I am, yes, I am full of woe,
saddest of all the Theban girls.

OEDIPUS:
Where do I put my aged step?
Where set my cane, child?

ANTIGONE:
This way, this way, come to me.
This way, this way, put down your foot
like a potent dream.

OEDIPUS:
Ah, ah! To drive me, an old man,
from my homeland into most gloomy exile.
Ah me, ah me! I have suffered terrible, terrible things.

---

146. *1707:* Colonus was the region of Athens, sacred to Poseidon, where Oedipus died; see Sophocles, *Oedipus at Colonus*.

ANTIGONE:
Why "suffered"? Why say "suffered? Justice does not see the wicked.
And does not punish men's perverse deeds.

OEDIPUS:
I am he who reached the song
of glorious victory towering to the sky,
solving the impenetrable riddle
of the half-human girl.

ANTIGONE:
You bring up the Sphinx's disgrace;
do not speak of past good fortune.
This sad tragedy has awaited you
to become a refugee from your homeland,
Father, to die somewhere else.
And I am going far away from my home
leaving tears of longing to the friends of my youth,
a refugee, a girl no more.
Alas. The goodness of my feelings
towards my father's sufferings
will bring me glory.
Unhappy for your misery and my brother's
who is gone from our home, an unburied corpse,
to be pitied. Even if I must die, Father,
I will bury him in the darkness.

OEDIPUS:
Go to your companions.

ANTIGONE:
Enough of my sufferings.

OEDIPUS:
You—pray at the altars.

ANTIGONE:
Enough of my troubles.

OEDIPUS:

Go to the enclosure of Bromius,
sacred untrodden space in the mountain of the maenads.

ANTIGONE:

For whom once I put on
the Theban fawn skin when I danced
on the sacred ground of Semele in the mountains,
offering the gods a favor with no return?

OEDIPUS:

Citizens of a glorious land, this is Oedipus
who understood the famous riddles and was a great man,
who alone restrained the power of the murdering Sphinx,
now myself without honor, pitiful, I am driven out of the land.
But why do I sing these sad songs and mourn in vain?
As mortals we must bear the gods' compulsions.[147]

(Exit Antigone and Oedipus by the stage right parodos.)

CHORUS:

Victory much revered sustain
my life
and never cease to crown it.[148]

(Exit the Chorus by the two parodoi.)

---

147. *1700–63:* The lament breaks down in non-sequiturs. Creon disposes of the remaining members of the house of Oedipus. Oedipus laments his fate, once more reciting the crucial events of his life. What about Antigone? Her future is in doubt.

148. *1764–66:* The Chorus files out with the usual meaningless tag line.

Appendix A: Division of Roles

In dividing the characters among the two or three available actors, *Seven against Thebes* and *Suppliants* present few problems.

Seven is a two-actor play.[1]

Protagonist: Eteocles, Antigone
Deuteragonist: Messenger(s), Ismene

Suppliants: the division of roles is not as clear-cut. One quite reasonable possibility (see Storey 2008: 106–7) is:

Protagonist: Theseus, Messenger
Deuteragonist: Adrastus, Iphis
Tritagonist: Aethra, Herald, Evadne, Athena

Phoenician Women, with its eleven characters, is much more complicated. *Phoenician Women* has an unusually large cast of characters distributed through the scenes as follows:

Jocasta (prologue, first episode, fourth episode)
Paidagogos (slave attending Antigone: prologue)
Antigone (prologue, fourth episode, exodos)
Polynices (first episode)
Eteocles (first episode, second episode)
Creon (second episode, third episode, exodos)
Tiresias (third episode)
Menoeceus (third episode)

---

1. With many other readers, I believe that *Seven against Thebes* ends at line 1010 before the arrival of the Herald, who would add a third actor to a two-actor play. The Herald was very likely added by a later producer to make the plot conform with those of *Antigone* and especially *Phoenician Women*, which had become very popular in revivals. It is also possible that the parts assigned to the two sisters were actually sung by the chorus.

First Messenger (fourth episode)
Second Messenger (exodos)
Oedipus (exodos)

Several mutes (non-speaking roles) are also required: attendants of Eteocles, Creon's attendants, Tiresias' daughter, and attendants carrying the bodies in the exodos.

Each of the scenes includes no more than three speaking parts at a time. There are actually four speaking roles in the exodos, but the scene is long enough for the actor playing the Second Messenger to exit, change masks, and return as Oedipus near the end of the scene. Messengers usually leave as soon as they have delivered their news, though in *Suppliants* the Messenger stays around for a short discussion with Adrastus (734–77).

Because the unity of *Phoenician Women* is not immediately obvious, it is interesting to consider how the roles might be assigned among the actors to help us see how they bear on each other and especially how Jocasta's part relates to the others, if it is she who (as I believe) provides the tragedy's unifying force. Since we cannot know all the factors that went into assigning roles, this exercise is speculative. Below are several possibilities, beginning with those of other critics:

1. Protagonist: Jocasta, Antigone (in prologue and exodos), Tiresias
   Deuteragonist: Paidagogos, Polynices, Creon, First Messenger
   Tritagonist: Eteocles, Menoeceus, Antigone (in the fourth episode: 1270–83), Second Messenger, Oedipus[2]
2. Protagonist: Jocasta, Tiresias, Second Messenger, Oedipus

2. This arrangement (Mastronarde 1994: 16) has the virtue of taking into consideration the scholiast (ancient commentator), who explains the delay of Antigone's appearance by the need for the protagonist to change masks from that of Jocasta to Antigone (*ad* 93). It gives the same actor the two singing roles (Jocasta and Antigone) and a third character, Tiresias, who might use recitative in his predictions. It is clear that the Second Messenger and Oedipus must be played by the same actor. Not much else is absolute. It does, however, uneconomically, in my opinion, divide the role of Antigone between two actors.

Deuteragonist: Paidagogos, Polynices, Creon, First Messenger
Tritagonist: Antigone, Eteocles, Menoeceus[3]

3. Protagonist: Jocasta, Antigone (in prologue and exodos), Menoeceus
Deuteragonist: Eteocles, Tiresias, Messengers, Oedipus
Tritagonist: Paidagogos, Polynices, Creon, Antigone (1270–82)[4]

These distributions of roles imply that voice, singing skill, and physical build were the primary criteria for distribution. On the other hand, singing ability must have been rather common. Other criteria may have been used. I would suggest:

4. Protagonist: Jocasta and Creon
Deuteragonist: Paidagogos, Eteocles, Tiresias, Messengers, Oedipus
Tritagonist: Antigone, Polynices, Menoeceus

This scheme gives the two major mature roles to the protagonist and has him on stage in every scene (except the rooftop dialogue) and playing to all the other characters (except Antigone's slave). That the same actor would play the brother and sister, both elderly, both serious practitioners of statecraft, both trying to save their city, and both parents of grown children trying to save their sons, adds to the *ethos* and the *pathos* of the tragedy. In this scheme the deuteragonist plays all the functional roles as well as Eteocles and Oedipus, an appropriately professional range for one actor. The three young people, then, are played by the tritagonist, also an accomplished actor. That Antigone and the brother she most

---

3. This distribution (Mastronarde 1994: 16 and note 1) has the virtue of using the same actor to play Antigone in all her scenes and giving the roles of three young persons to the same actor. An added asset is that it gives a fuller part to the protagonist and keeps him on stage for most of the play (excepting only the second episode).

4. This scheme (Craik 1988: 46) has the same merits as those above with minor variations. Craik is in favor of having Eteocles and Tiresias played by the same actor to explain the actions and departure of Eteocles in the second episode. She also prefers the three lighter roles (the two women and Menoeceus) to be played by the same actor.

loves would be played by the same actor adds *pathos* to the sad fact that the two never meet again. Menoeceus, who dies because of the selfishness of Polynices and Eteocles and shares the altruism of Antigone, is an appropriate third role. This division assumes a highly skilled professional troupe of actors and implies a desire by the author to show an ethical connection among the characters represented by the same actor, a notion that is by no means universally accepted but is worth considering.[5]

Does the protagonist—in the double role of Jocasta and Creon—form a unifying element even more than Jocasta alone? All the other characters play to them, argue with them, report to them. The division of roles suggested above also explains why neither set of brother-sister siblings meets on the scene. Antigone had anticipated throwing her arms around her brother, but was denied that pleasure when Polynices was ejected from Thebes by their other brother Eteocles. In *Oedipus the King*, one of the most dramatic scenes is that between Oedipus, Creon, and Jocasta in which she tries—as she does in *Phoenician Women* with her sons—to reconcile the two adult men in her life.

5. *Ēthos* is the word Aristotle uses for "character."

Appendix B: Scenic Outlines

Aeschylus' *Seven against Thebes*

Prologue: (1–77) Eteocles, Messenger

Eteocles addresses the Theban citizens. The messenger, Eteocles' spy, arrives with updates on the battle strategies of the enemy.

Parodos: (78–180)

Chorus enters in terror.

Episode 1: (181–288) Eteocles, Chorus

Eteocles upbraids the Chorus for being frightened.

Stasimon 1: (289–375)

Chorus sings of a city captured.

Episode 2: (375–719) Eteocles, Messenger with the chorus commenting

Description of the attackers and defenders chosen to face them: the battle of the shields.

Stasimon 2: (720–91)

Chorus sings of the curse on the family from Laios through Oedipus to his sons.

Episode 3: (792–820) Chorus, Messenger

The city is saved; the brothers are dead.

Stasimon 3: (821–74)

The curse and its fulfillment.

Exodos: (875–1010) Chorus, Antigone, Ismene

Kommos (lament): Chorus [and later Antigone and Ismene] grieve over the brothers. The children of Oedipus are all gathered for the last time. [The Herald enters to forbid the burial of Polynices.]

The focus at the beginning of the play is on the city, but moves to the family and finally to the last two sons and their fulfillment of the curse.

Euripides' *Suppliants*[1]

Prologue (1–41) Aethra

Aethra introduces the scene: a tableau of suppliant women and Adrastus with children in mourning. The setting is the festival for the first fruits celebrated at Eleusis.

Parodos (42–86)

Song of grief and supplication.

First Episode (87–364) Theseus, Aethra, Adrastus, Chorus

1. First *agōn*, between Theseus and Adrastus: Theseus' rejection of the suppliants.
2. Aethra persuades Theseus to take up the suppliants' cause on the grounds of pity, piety, and glory.

First Stasimon (365–80)

Invocations of Argos and Athens.

1. On the use of spectacle in *Suppliants*, see Storey (2009: 112) and Kornarou (2008: 31–38).

Second Episode (381–597) Theseus, Herald, Adrastus

Second *agōn*: Theseus and the Theban Herald debate the merits of democracy and monarchy, war and peace, and honoring the dead with burial. The Herald withdraws; the Athenians march off to war.

Second Stasimon (598–633)

Chorus worries about the war in progress.

Third Episode (634–777) Messenger, Adrastus, Chorus

The Messenger announces victory and describes the battle in vivid detail. Adrastus deplores war.

Third Stasimon (778–836)

Chorus reacts to the news with more sadness.

Fourth Episode (837–954) Theseus, Adrastus, Chorus

First *Kommos*: Adrastus laments with the Chorus. Adrastus and Theseus eulogize the dead.

Fourth Stasimon (955–89)

Chorus laments the loss of children.

Fifth Episode (990–1113) Evadne, Chorus, Iphis, Adrastus

Capaneus' wife Evadne sings of her grief and leaps onto her husband's pyre. Her father Iphis bemoans his losses and loneliness and goes home in despair.

Second Kommos (1114–64): Two Choruses

Chorus and grandsons lament their losses. Children call for revenge.

Exodos (1165–1234) Theseus, Adrastus, Athena, Chorus

Athena validates the victory and future revenge and announces an alliance between Argos and Athens.

This play, too, falls into two parts: war and the preliminary discussions leading up to it, and the funeral and grief for the fallen. From the third stasimon to the exodos the play is one long funereal lamentation.

Euripides' *Phoenician Women*

Prologue (1–201) Jocasta; Antigone, Paidagogos

1. Jocasta's monologue: history of the Theban kings, the life and career of Oedipus.
2. Antigone and her old minder: view of the armies from afar, the seven company commanders.

Parodos (202–60)

The Chorus' story and Cadmus' story.

First Episode (261–637) Jocasta, Polynices, Eteocles

1. Arrival of Polynices.
2. Lyric reunion of mother and son.
3. Rational dialogue between Jocasta and Polynices.
4. Debate among Polynices, Eteocles, and Jocasta.
5. Balanced insults between Eteocles and Polynices.

First Stasimon (638–89)

The gods in Theban history.

Second Episode (690–783) Creon, Eteocles

Discussion of strategy; Eteocles' last will: instructions for the future.

Second Stasimon (784–833)

Ares, Cithairon, Gaia.

Third Episode (834–1018) Tiresias, Creon, Menoeceus

Ancient violence in Thebes' dark heart; sacrifice of Menoeceus.

Third Stasimon (1018–66)

The Sphinx; dirge for the young victims; Menoeceus.

Fourth Episode (1067–1283) Jocasta, Messenger, Antigone

The Messenger's two speeches: the battle and the seven company commanders; departure of Jocasta and Antigone.

Fourth Stasimon (1284–1306)

A dirge for the brothers' deaths.

Exodos (1307–1766) Creon, Messenger, Antigone, Oedipus

1. Return of Creon; Messenger's speech: fratricides, suicide, more war; Theban victory.
2. Corpses brought back; Antigone's lament; Oedipus comes out.
3. Creon, Oedipus, Antigone: exile, lament, betrothal, burial.

Annular (ring) composition of *Phoenician Women*:The play begins with Jocasta telling the stories of the immigration of Cadmus to Thebes and of Oedipus' origins and ends with Oedipus' retelling of his own story and the exit of Oedipus and his daughter from Thebes. An inside circle focuses on Antigone seeing her brother from afar and at the end standing among the corpses of her brothers and mother. The next ring contains the two *agōnes* ("struggles") of Polynices and Eteocles, one of words, one of swords. The former is followed by Eteocles discussing strategy with Creon, which is matched in the first messenger's reports of the facts of the battle and Eteocles' carrying out the strategy. At the very center is Menoeceus and his self-sacrifice in the dragon's den.

Glossary of Theatrical Terms

Agōn: A formal debate in which characters deliver speeches (often of equal length). There is no *agōn* in Aeschylus' *Seven against Thebes.* In Euripides' *Suppliants* there are two: between Adrastus and Theseus (162–249) and between Theseus and the Theban Herald (409–587); in Euripides' *Phoenician Women* the *agōn* (469–637) has matched speeches by Polynices, Eteocles, and Jocasta. As usual they end in a stalemate with a shouting match.

Eccyclēma: A device rolled out of the *skēnē* to reveal what has taken place in the house. This is not used in any of these Theban plays. It may have been used in Sophocles' *Antigone* and *Oedipus the King* to reveal the bodies of Creon's wife Eurydice and Jocasta, who commit suicide inside the stage-building.

Eisodoi or **Parodoi:** Side entrances for choral entry and exit, and for actors coming from or going to offstage places.

Episode: The dialogue portion of the play, consisting of speeches and back-and-forth conversation, between the choral odes. There are usually between three and five episodes in a play.

Exodos: The part of the play after the last choral song.

Kommos: A song of mourning shared by chorus and actors.

Mēchanē: The flying machine, a crane used to fly in gods who take part in the plays. It is possible that Athena comes in on the *mēchanē*, but since there is no reference to her strange arrival or to her destination, it seems unlikely.

Messenger Speech: A narrative delivered by a character coming from offstage to describe actions that have taken place elsewhere. In the three Theban plays selected here, the messenger speeches announce and describe the outcomes of the battles. In *Phoenician Women* the messenger's speech is unusual in being divided into two quite long speeches, between which Jocasta and Antigone go off to the battlefield to try to prevent the brothers from killing each other.

Orchestra: The circular area used for choral singing, dancing, and most acting. An altar is a permanent feature of the orchestra. It may also be furnished with statues of the gods, as in *Seven against Thebes*.

Parodos: The entrance song of the chorus. This is sometimes shared between the chorus and one of the actors. The *parodos* of Euripides' *Suppliants* is unusual in that the chorus is already in place at the altar in the orchestra before they sing their first song.

Prologue: The part of a play before the entrance of the chorus. This is usually a monologue (as in Euripides' *Suppliants*) or a monologue followed by a dialogue (as in *Seven against Thebes* and *Phoenician Women*).

Skēnē: The stage-building; a flat-roofed structure with double doors, used for changes of mask and costume and many exits and entrances of actors, as in *Phoenician Women*. It may represent a palace, a temple, a house, or even a cave. In *Seven against Thebes*, the *skēnē* is not prominent—if it is there at all. In Euripides' *Suppliants*, the *skēnē* is not used for exits and entrances, though it is referred to.

Stasimon (pl. stasima): A choral song and dance. The songs are divided into *strophes* and *antistrophes*, stanzas and matching stanzas (literally, "turnings" and "opposite turnings"). An unmatched stanza is called a *mesode* if it occurs between one strophe/antistrophe pair and the next, an *epode* if it comes after the last antistrophe.

Stichomythia: Dialogue in which single lines are spoken in turn by two or more characters.

Theologeion: The top of the stage-building or "god-dais." In *Phoenician Women* it is used for the scene between Antigone and her old servant; in Euripides' *Suppliants* it is used for the suicide of Evadne and the epiphany of Athena.

Select Bibliography

Altena, Herman. "Text and Performance: On Significant Actions in Euripides' *Phoenissae*." In Cropp, Fantham, and Scully, 303–23.

Arnott, Peter D. *Public and Performance in the Greek Theatre*. London and New York: Routledge, 1989.

Arthur, Marilyn B. "The Curse of Civilization: The Choral Odes of the *Phoenissae*." *Harvard Studies in Classical Philology* 81 (1977): 163–85.

Bacon, Helen. "The Shield of Eteocles." *Arion* 3.3 (1964): 27–38

Baldry, H. C. "The Dramatization of the Theban Legend." *Greece and Rome* 3 (1956): 24–37.

Barlow, Shirley A. *The Imagery of Euripides*. Bristol: Bristol Classical Press, 1986 (1971).

Bowie, A. M. "Tragic Filters for History: Euripides' *Supplices* and Sophocles' *Philoctetes*." In Pelling, 39–62.

Burgess, Dana. "The Authenticity of the Teichoscopia of Euripides' *Phoenissae*." *Classical Journal* 83 (1978): 103–13.

Burian, Peter, and Brian Swann, trans. *Euripides: The Phoenician Women*. Oxford and New York: Oxford University Press, 1981.

Burian, Peter, ed. *Directions in Euripidean Criticism: A Collection of Essays*. Durham, NC: Duke University Press, 1985.

Collard, Christopher, ed. *Euripides: Supplices*. 2 vol. Groningen: Bouma, 1975.

———. *Tragedy, Euripides, and Euripideans: Selected Papers*. Exeter: Bristol Phoenix Press, 2007.

Conacher, D. J. "Religious and Ethical Attitudes in Euripides' *Suppliants*." *Transactions and Proceedings of the American Philological Association* 87 (1956): 8–26.

Conacher, D. J. "Themes in the *Exodus* of Euripides' *Phoenissae*." *Phoenix* 21 (1967): 92–101.

Conacher, D. J. *Aeschylus: The Earlier Plays and Related Studies*. Toronto: University of Toronto Press, 1996.

Cousland, J. R. C., James R Hume, and Martin Cropp, eds. *The Play of Texts and Fragments: Essays in Honour of Martin Cropp*. Leiden: Brill, 2009.

Craik, Elizabeth, ed., trans. *Euripides: Phoenician Women*. Warminster, UK: Aris and Phillips, 1988.

Cribiore, Raffaella. "The Grammarians's Choice: The Popularity of Euripides' *Phoenissae* in Hellenistic and Roman Education." In *Education in Greek and Roman Antiquity*, edited by Yun Lee Too, 241–60. Leiden: Brill, 2001.

Cropp, Martin, Elaine Fantham, and S. E. Scully, eds. *Greek Tragedy and Its Legacy*. Calgary: 1986.

Cropp, Martin, Kevin Lee, and David Sansone, eds. *Euripides and Tragic Theatre in the Late Fifth Century. Illinois Classical Studies* 24–25 (1999–2000). Champaign, IL: Stipes, 2000.

Daneš, Jaroslav. "The Political Thought of the *Suppliant Women*." *Graeco-Latina Brunensia* 16 (2011): 17–30. Accessed online: https://digilib.phil.muni.cz/bitstream/handle/11222.digilib/118186/1_GraecoLatinaBrunensia_16-2011-2_3.pdf?sequence=1.

Dawson, Christopher M., ed., trans. *The Seven against Thebes: Translation and Commentary*. Englewood Cliffs: PrenticeHall, 1970.

Demand, Nancy. *Thebes in the Fifth Century*. London: Routledge and Kegan Paul, 1982.

Dodds, E. R., ed. *Euripides: Bacchae*. 2nd ed. Oxford: Clarendon Press, 1960.

Faber, M. D. *Suicide and Greek Tragedy*. New York, 1970.

Foley, Helene. *Ritual Irony*. Ithaca, NY: Cornell University Press, 1985.

———. *Female Acts in Greek Tragedy*. Princeton, NJ: Princeton University Press, 2001.

Fraenkel, Eduard. "A Passage in the *Phoenissae*." *Eranos* 44 (1946): 81–89.

Gamble, R. B. "Euripides' *Suppliant Women*: Decision and Ambivalence." *Hermes* 98 (1970): 385–405.

Garner, Richard. *From Homer to Tragedy: The Art of Allusion in Greek Poetry*. London and New York: Routledge, 1990.

Garrison, Elise P. *Groaning Tears: Ethical and Dramatic Aspects of Suicide in Greek Tragedy*. Leiden: Brill, 1995.

Goff, Barbara E. "The Shields of *Phoenissae*." *Greek, Roman and Byzantine Studies* 29 (1988): 135–52.

———. "Aithra at Eleusis." *Helios* 22 (1995): 65–78.

Hartigan, Karelisa. *Greek Tragedy on the American stage: Ancient Drama in the Commercial Theater, 1882–1994*. Contributions in Drama and Theatre Studies 60. Westport, CT: Greenwood Press, 1995.

Hecht, Anthony, and Helen H. Bacon, trans. *Aeschylus: Seven against Thebes*. Oxford: Oxford University Press, 1973.

Hogan, James C. *A Commentary on the Complete Greek Tragedies: Aeschylus*. Chicago: University of Chicago Press, 1994 [[1984]].

Hutchinson, G. O., ed. *Aeschylus: Septem Contra Thebas*. Oxford: Clarendon Press, 1985.

Irwin, Eleanor. *Colour Terms in Greek Poetry*. Toronto: Hakkert, 1974.

de Jong, Irene J. F. *Narrative in Drama: The Art of the Euripidean Messenger-Speech*. Leiden: Brill, 1991.

Kaiser, Leo Max, ed. *Thoreau's Translation of* the Seven Against Thebes (1843). Hartford, CT: Transcendental Press, 1960.

Kitto, H. D. F. "The Final Scenes of the *Phoenissae*." *Classical Review* 53 (1939): 104–11.

Kornarou, Eleni. "The Display of the Dead on the Greek Tragic Stage: The Case of Euripides' *Supplices*." *Bulletin of the Institute of Classical Studies* 51 (2008): 29–38.

Lochhead, Liz. *Thebans*. Produced by Theatre Babel at the Edinburgh Festival Fringe, 2003. London: Nick Hern, 2003.

Loraux, Nicole. *The Invention of Athens: The Funeral Oration in the Ancient City*. Translated by A. Sheridan. Cambridge, MA: Harvard University Press, 1986.

———. *Tragic Ways of Killing a Woman*. Translated by Anthony Forster. Cambridge, MA: Harvard University Press, 1987.

Luschnig, C. A. E. *The Gorgon's Severed Head: Studies of* Alcestis, Electra, *and* Phoenissae. Leiden: Brill, 1995.

Luschnig, Cecelia Eaton, and Paul Woodruff, trans. *Euripides: Electra, Phoenician Women, Bacchae, Iphigenia at Aulis*. Indianapolis: Hackett, 2011.

Mastronarde, Donald J., and Jan Maarten Bremer. *The Textual Tradition of Euripides'* Phoinissai. University of California Classical Studies 27. Berkeley: University of California Press, 1982.

Mastronarde, Donald J. "Actors on High: The Skene Roof, the Crane, and the Gods in Attic Drama." *Classical Antiquity* 9.2 (1990): 247–94.

———, ed. *Euripides: Phoenissae*. Cambridge: Cambridge University Press, 1994.

———. "The Optimistic Rationalist in Euripides: Theseus, Jocasta, Teiresias." In Cropp, Fantham, and Scully, Calgary, 201–11.

Meltzer, Gary S., *Euripides and the Poetics of Nostalgia*, Cambridge: Cambridge University Press, 2006.

Mendelsohn, Daniel Adam. *Gender and the City in Euripides' Political Plays*. Oxford: Oxford University Press, 2002.

Meredith, H. O. "The End of the *Phoenissae*." *Classical Review* 51 (1937): 97–103.

Michelini, Ann Norris. *Euripides and the Tragic Tradition*. Madison: University of Wisconsin Press, 1987.

———. "Political Themes in Euripides' *Suppliants*." *American Journal of Philology* 115 (1994): 219–52.

———. "Alcibiades and Theseus in Euripides' *Suppliants*." *Colby Quarterly* 33.2 (1997): 177–84.

Mills, Sophie. *Theseus, Tragedy, and the Athenian Empire*. Oxford: Clarendon Press, 1997.

Morwood, James, ed., trans. *Euripides*: Suppliant Women, *with an Introduction, Translation and Commentary*. Oxford: Aris & Phillips, 2007.

Nicklin, T., ed. The Suppliant Women *of Euripides*. With Introduction and Explanatory Notes. Oxford University Press, 1936.

Page, Denys. *Actors' Interpolations in Greek Tragedy*. Oxford: Clarendon Press, 1934.

Papadopoulou, Thalia. *Euripides*: *Phoenician Women*. London: Duckworth, 2008.

Pearson, A. A., ed. *The Phoenissae*. Cambridge: Pitt Press Series, 1909.

Pelling, Christopher, ed. *Greek Tragedy and the Historian*. Oxford: Oxford University Press, 1997.

Podlecki, Anthony J. "Some Themes in Euripides' *Phoenissae*." *Transactions of the American Philological Association* 93 (1962): 355–73.

Rabinowitz, Nancy Sorkin. *Anxiety Veiled: Euripides and the Traffic in Women*. Ithaca, NY: Cornell University Press, 1993.

Rawson, Elizabeth. "Family and Fatherland in Euripides' *Phoenissae*." *Greek, Roman and Byzantine Studies* 11 (1970): 109–27.

Rehm, Rush. "*The Staging of Suppliant Plays*." *GRBS* 29 (1988): 263–307.

———. *Greek Tragic Theatre*. London and New York: Routledge, 1992.

———. *Marriage to Death: The Conflation of Wedding and Funeral Rituals in Greek Tragedy*. Princeton, NJ: Princeton University Press, 1994.

de Romilly, Jacqueline. "*Phoenician Women* of Euripides: Topicality in Greek Tragedy." *Bucknell Review* 15 (1967): 108–32.

Schwartz, Eduard, ed. *Scholia in Euripidem*. Berlin: Reimer, 1887. (Reprint: Berlin: Walter de Gruyter, 1966).

Seaford, Richard. *Reciprocity and Ritual: Homer and Tragedy in the Developing City-state*. Oxford: Clarendon Press, 1994.

Segal, Charles P. *Dionysiac Poetics and Euripides'* Bacchae. Princeton: Princeton University Press, 1982; expanded ed. 1997.

———. "Tragic Beginnings: Narration, Voice, and Authority in the Prologues of Greek Drama." *Yale Classical Studies* 29 (1992): 85–112.

Smith, Wesley D. "Expressive Form in Euripides' *Suppliants*." *Harvard Studies in Classical Philology* 71 (1967): 151–70.

Smyth, Herbert Weir, ed., trans. *Aeschylus*. (with an English Translation). Loeb Classical Library, vol. 1. Cambridge: Harvard University Press, 1963.

Storey, Ian C. *Euripides: Suppliant Women*. Duckworth Companions to Greek and Roman Tragedy. London: Duckworth, 2008.

———. "How Does 'Seven' Go into 'Twelve' (or 'Fifteen') in Euripides' *Suppliant Women*?" In Cousland, Hume, and Cropp: 111–25.

Taplin, Oliver. *The Stagecraft of Aeschylus: The Dramatic Use of Exits and Entrances in Greek Tragedy*. Oxford: Clarendon Press, 1977.

Thalmann, William. *Dramatic Art in Aeschylus'* Seven Against Thebes. New Haven: Yale University Press, 1978.

Thury, Eva M. "A Study of Words Relating to Youth and Old Age in the Plays of Euripides and Its Special Implications for Euripides' *Suppliant Women*." *Computers and the Humanities* 22 (1988): 293–306.

Toher, Mark. "Euripides' *Supplices* and the Social Function of Funeral Ritual." *Hermes* 129 (2001): 332–43.

Tzanetou, Angeliki. *City of Suppliants: Tragedy and the Athenian Empire*. Austin: University of Texas Press, 2012.

Verrall, A. W., ed. *The Seven against Thebes of Aeschylus: Text and Commentary*. London: Macmillan, 1887.

Walker, Henry J. *Theseus and Athens*. New York: Oxford University Press, 1995.

Walton, J. Michael. *Greek Theatre Practice*. Westport, CT: Greenwood Press, 1980.

Warren, Rosanna, and Stephen Scully, trans. *Euripides: Suppliant Women*. New York: Oxford University Press, 1995.

Winnington-Ingram, R. P. *Studies in Aeschylus*. Cambridge: Cambridge University Press, 1983.

Webster, T. B. L. "Three Plays by Euripides." In *The Classical Tradition: Literary and Historical Studies in Honor of Harry Caplan*, edited by Luitpold Wallach, 83–97. Ithaca, NY: Cornell University Press, 1966.

Winkler, John J., and Zeitlin, Froma I., eds. *Nothing to Do with Dionysos?* Princeton: Princeton University Press, 1990.

Woodruff, Paul, and Peter Meineck, trans. *Sophocles: Theban Plays.* Introduction by Paul Woodruff. Indianapolis: Hackett, 2003.

Zeitlin, Froma I. "Thebes: Theater of Self and Society in Athenian Drama." In Winkler and Zeitlin, 130–67.

Zuntz, Günther. *The Political Plays of Euripides.* Manchester: Manchester University Press, 1955.